Rationality and Reflection

Jonathan L. Kvanvig presents a conception of rationality which answers to the need arising out of the egocentric predicament concerning what to do and what to believe, and de does so in a way that avoids, on the one hand, reducing rationality to the level of beasts and elevating it so that only the most reflective among us are capable of rational beliefs. *Rationality and Reflection* sets out a theory of rationality—a theory about how to determine what to think—which defends a significant degree of optionality in the story of what is reasonable for people to think, and thereby provides a framework for explaining what kinds of rational disagreement are possible. The theory is labelled Perspectivalism and it offers a unique account of rationality, one that cuts across the usual distinctions between Foundationalism and Coherentism and between Internalism and Externalism. It also differs significantly from Evidentialism, maintaining that, to the extent that rationality is connected to the notion of evidence, it is a function both of the evidence one has and what one makes of it.

Rationality and Reflection

How to Think about What to Think

Jonathan L. Kvanvig

OXFORD
UNIVERSITY PRESS

OXFORD
UNIVERSITY PRESS

Great Clarendon Street, Oxford, OX2 6DP,
United Kingdom

Oxford University Press is a department of the University of Oxford.
It furthers the University's objective of excellence in research, scholarship,
and education by publishing worldwide. Oxford is a registered trade mark of
Oxford University Press in the UK and in certain other countries

Published in the United States of America by Oxford University Press
198 Madison Avenue, New York, NY 10016, United States of America

British Library Cataloguing in Publication Data
Data available

Library of Congress Cataloging in Publication Data
Data available

ISBN 978-0-19-871641-9 (Hbk.)
ISBN 978-0-19-879719-7 (Pbk.)

Contents

Introduction

From waking confused, wondering where one is, to theorizing about the nature of the cosmos, perplexity is a common feature of human life and the life of any organism with mental capacities. Though there are moments of experience with no apparent mysteries, nothing that baffles or befuddles, where responses are so unhesitatingly quick as to mimic instinctual behavior, the perplexity revealed by hesitance and the accompanying drive to deliberate and reflect is part of what is involved in being the kind of organism for which mental capacities help explain survival and flourishing. To be sure, there are those who don't hesitate, who don't wonder whether first reactions are right, but they are rare and nearly certain to find occasion for reflection on the wisdom of such inflated self-confidence. For perplexity is both natural and fitting, a central component of the egocentric predicament that every cognitive organism faces.

This perplexity of the egocentric predicament generates a fundamental concern about what to do and what to think. When such perplexity is resolved for a given individual, the resolution involves a decision that is best expressed in imperatival mode: get out of bed, endorse her loyalty, reject his offer of friendship, take him at his word, trust the senses, discount intuitive attitudes. The conclusions one reaches are imperatival conclusions, conclusions about what to do and what to think. We may, if we wish, put these conclusions in indicative mood, and when we do, it is natural to introduce the language of obligation and other forms of normativity: we should get out of bed, we ought to trust, reject, change our opinion, or be suspicious.

It is this perplexity and imperatival resolution that prompts the present inquiry. For out of these imperatival resolutions comes normative evaluation, and it is within the general arena of normative evaluation that the present inquiry is found: what makes a conclusion a good one about what to do and what to think?

We begin with a basic distinction between descriptive and non-descriptive cognitive features. At the descriptive level, human beings (among other things) are rational animals, not in the sense of never being irrational, but in the sense of having a capacity at least occasionally displayed in thought and behavior. When we consider displays of this capacity, we enter the non-descriptive realm. The display of this capacity can be casual or carefully controlled, but in neither case is there any guarantee that things will go well just because the capacity in question is on display. The goal of this work is to inquire into the interstices of the three dimensions just employed: the descriptive realm of what people typically do and the capacities they have, the normative realm of what they should or shouldn't do, and the evaluative realm of what is good for them to do.

These same dimensions are present not only in the arena of human behavior, but in cognition itself. Here is the natural home of the notion of epistemic appraisal. Among the things that people do are cognitive things: they think, they infer, they form beliefs, they make and reject assumptions, they hypothesize, theorize, conjecture, and judge. Whether epistemic appraisal applies outside of this domain and whether it applies only to parts of the cognitive order, I leave open at this point. All we need to notice is that there are three dimensions here as well: the descriptive realm of how people go about making sense of things, the normative realm about how they should or should not do so, and the evaluative realm of better and worse ways to do it.

The Dilemma

This distinction between the evaluative and the normative will play an important role here, but our first concern is with the notion of normativity itself, and how to identify it. Here, the notion of the normative contrasts with that of the descriptive, but since the evaluative realm contrasts with the descriptive as well, that means of identifying the normative realm is insufficient. For those familiar with work in ethics, the distinction is easy to describe: it is the distinction between the theory of value and the theory of obligation. At least at this initial stage, this characterization is sufficient for focusing our attention on the central phenomenon which this work aims to understand, that of epistemic normativity. Put in the context of the impetus for our theory, there are things that are good to do and think, and there are obligations regarding what to do or think. Both of these domains fall outside the domain of the descriptive, and we can identify each at this initial stage in terms of the evaluative and normative realms, respectively.

Regarding normativity itself, our normative interaction with the world around us involves two quite different parts. First, there is the aspect of cognition shared with the beasts, which involves cognitive responses to our environment resulting from impingement on the senses and the adaptive responses we develop as we mature. Second, there is our reflective side, displayed when we attempt to improve our success rate in responding to what we observe, and when we question the adequacy of the way in which our cognitive equipment informs us about the universe in which we find ourselves. A full understanding of rationality will involve both dimensions.

The primary difficulty in understanding the first dimension is whether rational sense can be made of it. Let me explain. It is clear that there is causal interaction between human organisms and their environment, and it is also clear that this causal interaction prompts certain patterns of response in human beings, both in terms of action and in terms of cognition. For the time being, let us think of cognitive responses in terms of belief: part of our responses to sensory input is patterns of belief formation and sustenance. How are we to understand this connection? Perhaps we can do no better than to employ the language of dispositions: upon causal interaction involving a given sensory input, the organism in question is disposed to form or sustain a belief with a given content.

Such an approach makes no rational sense of the interaction, providing no intelligible link between the inputs and outputs. On such a story, if one's sensory appearance is that of a Bengal tiger, we have no story as to why believing there is a Bengal tiger nearby is an appropriate doxastic response as opposed to believing something else, other than to say that nature has so designed us that we are disposed toward the latter on the basis of the former. Such a story provides an *explanation* of the interaction, but does not make the connection between the two *intelligible*: from the point of view of the agent forming the belief in question, the mechanisms involved are impenetrable black boxes. There is no specific story as to why believing there is a Bengal tiger nearby is an appropriate response to the sensory input in question. There may be a *general* story of why this is appropriate. For example, perhaps it is part of a divine design plan for human beings that they respond in this way, or perhaps the presence of such disposition in our ancestors is part of the explanation of why they enjoyed reproductive success enough for us to exist. But these stories are not specific stories. They do not point to some connection between the individual appearance state in question and particular resultant belief content that explains why that very belief content is appropriate to that specific appearance state, an explanation that makes it intelligible or understandable why that very belief content is a fitting, or the fitting, response to that precise appearance state.

The first motivation, then, for the present project is to explore this topic of natural rationality, but regardless of the conclusions arrived at, there is a deep dilemma facing any theory of natural rationality. If we suppose we can find a specific account that makes understandable why some beliefs are more fitting in a given circumstance than other beliefs, there is still the possibility of the organism in question reflecting on the situation in question and coming to the conclusion that a different belief is better in those circumstances. Such an organism may even engage in cognitive training, so that believing something else becomes a habit. If all we have is a theory of natural rationality, we must conclude that such an organism is believing irrationally, in spite of following the light of reason as best it can.

In schematic terms, the dilemma is this. The theory of rationality, if wholly constituted by the theory of natural rationality, yields fully general, unrestricted rules for what to believe under what circumstances. Yet, one of the distinctive features of human rationality is the ability to reflect, and among the things we reflect on are the rules that guide us. Among the things we learn about are not only the features of the universe we inhabit, but the features of our own cognitive systems and how their functioning might be improved. But if the theory of natural rationality is theory enough, it is hard to avoid attributing irrationality to a large part of our reflective pursuits, since they often lead us to view our initial response styles as inappropriate and best replaced by more sophisticated response styles.

It is my own fascination with these two aspects of human beings that leads to the present project. We are animals, and whatever cognitive functions we display fit into the natural order of things. And yet, we are reflective creatures as well, and display our rational capacities in admirable ways when we move beyond the beastly level, assessing how we behave and why, in order to improve. Two dangers arise here in an attempt to understand human rationality, both reductive. One makes the theory of natural rationality all the theory that is needed, with an accompanying burden of having to classify much of our reflective adaptations as irrational. Another makes such deliberative and reflective adaptations controlling, with the danger of over-intellectualizing the notion of rationality, denying that ordinary doxastic responses to sensory input, from early infancy on, count as rational. The present project aims to show how to avoid both forms of Procrusteanism. The goal is to find a middle way between two extremes, one in which intellectualism reigns and the other in which reflection is discounted in favor of identifying rationality with that of the beasts. I defend a perspectivalist response to this dilemma, arguing for a full honoring of the perspectival character of rationality that takes into account both the beastly and the reflective dimensions of rationality. For those who prefer labels, one might term the theory in question a version of Perspectivalism.

A word of caution is needed at this point, however, concerning the notion of rationality involved and the normativity of it. First, I use the notion as a term of art, rather than one of ordinary language. I need a term to refer to non-descriptive features of the epistemic landscape that have their source in the need for determining what to do and what to think. For that purpose, I will use the language of rationality, and its features will emerge in the course of our inquiry, not from the ordinary meaning of the term. Second, the language of obligation involved in the normativity of rationality derives from the fundamentally imperatival nature of the predicament regarding what to do and what to think. The primary implication here is that one must not begin with the assumption that is common in epistemology of describing the normativity in question in terms of obligations to believe, disbelieve, or withhold. Instead, we must think, initially, in less restrictive terms. We should think that the imperatival origins generate intellectual obligations of some sort or other, and that our theory of rationality should characterize these obligations. But we should leave open whether the obligations apply to specific beliefs, for as we shall see, there are grounds for thinking that the only obligations to be found here are less specific than that.

Value-Driven Theory and Meta-theory

The subtitle of this work shows that a full theory of rationality is not the singular goal of this work. The goal is not simply an account of what to think, but also a meta-theoretical one concerning how to go about determining a good answer to the question of what to think. Our inquiry will generate an account regarding what to think, but it is an answer derived from the more fundamental issue about how to think about what to think. Our project thus has two distinct tasks. The final goal of the project requires an articulation of schematic principles concerning the nature of epistemic rationality, principles that together constitute a theory of rationality in the sense of identifying the moving parts of the story of rational belief. The defense and explanation of this view, however, cannot be successfully undertaken without attention to meta-theoretical issues. We seek a theory that informs us about what to do and what to think, but we also seek understanding of what makes a theory appropriate for addressing this issue. In fact, I will argue, if we do not attend to the prior question of what makes a theory appropriate for addressing the issue in question, we will not be able to appreciate why the theory developed here is the right one for the job. For the reader is likely to be assuming one of the two dominant meta-theoretical stances from recent epistemology, and neither one guides this project.

The first stance is conceptual or linguistic analysis and the second is naturalized epistemology. The second requires that, in some important sense, epistemology is continuous with natural science. The first asks that we spend our time providing sets of necessary and sufficient conditions for something in the general area of the content of the central epistemological concepts or the meaning of the central terms in question.

Conceptual analysis is the natural offspring of ordinary language philosophy from the middle part of the twentieth century and the empiricist tradition deriving especially from the work of Hume. In this heritage, one finds the embarrassment of locating a home for philosophical discourse. The naturalistic movement in philosophy and epistemology shares a common origin in Hume. The mantra "philosophy of science is philosophy enough" derives from the sentiments at the heart of logical positivism and logical empiricism, sentiments that trace easily to a Humean picture of the world in which all but science and mathematics belongs in the flames.

I will not spend any time arguing against the latter approach, since I have some sympathies for the project when properly circumscribed, and when done appropriately, there will be ways to incorporate such a project under the approach I want to recommend here. But I want to distance myself from the former project, that project that recommends investigating epistemic normativity by taking ordinary language, or common intuitions, as the evidentiary basis for determining the logical features of the spaces in question. Such approaches have been taken in the past, most notably in Alston (2005) and Wedgwood (2007). What they have in common is a finding of multiplicity: when we ask about the logical space of normativity or epistemic normativity, we find multiple notions at work in ordinary language and common intuitions.

Findings of multiplicity are a cause for despair in the present context. We face a predicament regarding what to do or think, and an approach that ends with multiplicity can only say this: from this perspective, do A and believe B; from this other perspective, don't do A and don't believe B. Such a response to the predicament is rightly met with a throwing up of the hands, lamenting the uselessness of the counsel.

Here I resist multiplicity by starting elsewhere. Instead of starting with ordinary language and common intuitions, I begin by asking about the significance of normative talk and why we would want to theorize about such dimensions in the first place. As I see it, this source is of a most ancient heritage, motivating philosophical reflection in its very origins in service of the good life. In common with naturalized approaches to epistemology, I begin by looking for the source (or sources) of normativity. While it is theoretically possible that non-descriptive features of reality are free-floating, inexplicable in any way in terms of the descriptive, it is a promising idea to try to locate the source of the non-descriptive in the needs and interests, central desires and purposes, of sentient beings. In the face of plausible accounts of this sort, claims that there are normative or evaluative truths of some other sort, inexplicable in terms of any descriptive features of the world, lose their attraction, even if deeply embedded in ordinary features of thought and talk. As we will see, the theory of rationality developed here will counsel changing a significant amount of ordinary thought and talk concerning the epistemic realm, and it is a mark in favor of this more ancient source of philosophical reflection that it has the capacity of playing such an ameliorative role regarding ordinary thought and talk. For how we think and speak can both contribute to achieving the good life and leave us in the shackles of the cave as well.

So I seek a source of normativity that is value-driven, explaining where normativity comes from or that in which it is grounded, but in a way that makes obvious why such inclinations are deeply important. The guiding principle here is that the importance of the egocentric predicament is obvious, and that it provides an important and central ground of normativity. I thus intend to pursue a value-driven approach from this starting point, tracing out its implications, and issuing a challenge to those who think the results are too narrow or problematic in some way to find some other, important source for their normative judgments.

There are ways to develop a value-driven approach that differ from the way I will develop it. A natural way to do so is to think of rationality in terms of a project of doing one's best to avoid criticism, either from others or in terms of self-criticism. That path I will not follow, for the variety of criticisms that might be raised about any aspect of human behavior and thought is seemingly endless. A decision can be insensitive, unseemly, unsavory, inept, prejudiced, biased, narrow-minded, hideous, repulsive, revolting, appalling, and involve a slew of other negativities as well. A way of thinking can be unrealistic, antiquated, half-baked, quixotic, preposterous, strained, bizarre, dubious, far-fetched, even fishy. If our approach to the egocentric predicament is to find decisions and thoughts that are not criticizable in any way, the project, I suggest, will be hopeless. There are too many ways to count, and we can always invent a new way should we wish to criticize an attempt at an exhaustive list of ways to criticize: as Ernest Sosa memorably reminds us, human beings are "zestfully judgmental" (Sosa, 2007, p. 70). So we don't want to begin—indeed, we cannot begin—our inquiry by identifying the domain in question as one involving immunity from criticism either from others or ourselves, for human beings can find a basis for criticism in almost anything. Even if what we say is true, the tone can be wrong; even if we know what we are talking about, maybe nobody from Texas should be saying or thinking such a thing; etc. Humans are not only zestfully judgmental, they are eagerly creative in inventing new ways of finding fault. The arena of epistemic normativity is, to be sure, an arena in which the finding of fault is possible, but that latter landscape is of nearly infinite variety and complexity, and capable of enlargement at the slightest whiff of offense.

So, if we begin from the notion of opening oneself up to criticism, one will first have to mention that some criticisms are legitimate and important and some not. But then we've already landed ourselves in the territory of normativity, rather than helping ourselves to locate that territory in the first place. Where I begin, then, is that within the arena of zestful judgment, some criticisms connect with, arise out of, fundamental human concerns and some do not. In the arena of cognition as well as the arena of action more generally, we all face a fundamental human predicament. We often cannot tell what to do or think, what to be or become. We experience perplexity. When we begin investigating the non-descriptive aspects of reality, we can do no better than to begin with such fundamental concerns and the realities that arise either out of or in connection with these concerns. We can employ normative language to describe the phenomenon in question, should we wish to do so: we can describe a resolution of the perplexity concerning what to do or think as a "rational" one, for example. I will use such language here as well, but will remind the reader again that the use of such language is meant to be taken as a term of art, one whose meaning is fixed, if fixed at all, by the source of the investigation and the theory that results from it rather than by one's favorite lexicon, philosophical or otherwise.

There is some hope in such an approach of avoiding the disappointment that results from approaches that end with a finding of multiplicity of normative notions. Instead of ending up with the blooming, buzzing confusion that would result from an indiscriminate embracing of all dimensions and notions of normative evaluation that can be found in ordinary thought and talk, we may find a normative notion that shows what a resolution of the egocentric predicament looks like and which has the power to explain all that really needs explaining. There is, of course, no pre-theoretical guarantee of success here. It may be that our condition is simply hopeless, that nothing we can defend can satisfy the stricture of having a theory that will speak with a single voice. But that kind of theory is what is needed and what we seek.

Perhaps the best way to see what this beginning point implies is to notice what won't count as a good objection to the theory that results. Once we see the schematic character of the theory that results, it will be obvious that the theory implies that much of ordinary talk involving the concept *rationality* is mistaken. This fact is not (all-things-considered) evidence against the theory, since the theory is generated out of the fundamental human predicament concerning what to do and what to think, and not out of some concern for the concept employed in ordinary thought and talk. In this way, the resulting theory can serve as a corrective for ordinary thought and talk, to the extent that the source of the current approach is clearly as important as any other source could be. What is left open, of course, is to find some other source for defending what is involved in the parts of ordinary thought and talk rejected here, and such attempts are not ruled out by the present approach. What is ruled out, however, is the mere conservative bias in favor of ordinary thought and talk over a disciplined value-driven approach to the subject matter.

Completion of this present project will thus leave open the possibility of other normative theories that impose additional restrictions and permissions on cognition. But I do not leave this question open without a challenge. For if some other, different theory is developed, it is legitimate to ask what makes such a theory true. Why should we think that those theories are characterizing any actual feature of reality, and what descriptive features of the world could possibly be the source of such? On the latter question, my opinion, which I won't argue for here, is that there is no possible story to be told except one that adverts to features of people and other cognizers. So what we should expect, if I'm right, is that there are other fundamental concerns or features of persons that explain these other normative aspects of reality, if there are such. It is not difficult to think of possibilities here: perhaps there is a need for cooperation that gives rise to distinctively moral norms; perhaps there is some type of consistency in willing that generates the panoply of moral requirements for rational agents; or perhaps the existence of a personal creator, with expectations for that which is created, imposes such. Those projects I leave to the side in favor of the present one, noting that none of these more general ways of seeking a source for normativity look especially adept for the project of locating a source of epistemic normativity. Though I won't defend the following here, it may be that the source of epistemic normativity identified here is fundamental, and the attempt to find a source for any other kind of normativity will require an antecedent grounding of epistemic normativity itself. One route to this conclusion is to think that other notions of normativity all need to be defined in terms of epistemic normativity.[1] But whether such a position is ultimately defensible, the challenge remains: if the implications of the present approach leave one unsatisfied, the proper response is to identify some further source for epistemic normativity that can explain why the present approach is not theory enough.

This value-driven approach to the egocentric predicament in epistemology forms a central element in a larger project, and before beginning our search for a theory of normativity conceived in this fashion, it is worth noting its place in this larger project.

The More General Project

Any approach to the discipline of epistemology begins by identifying the domain of inquiry in terms of something connecting mind and world. But not just any

---

[1] For argument to this effect, see Foley (2001) and Fumerton (2004).

connection will do: we want a connection that is successful, one that matters from a certain point of view, the point of view involving our natural predilection to make sense of the world around us independently of the issue of whether or not the results we achieve connect with any other human concerns. It is natural, thus, to begin a value-driven approach to the issue of successful connections between mind and world from the starting point of true belief. In order to defend this beginning point, however, a defense is needed for the idea that true belief is a connection between mind and world, and one worth having.

An attractive starting point in this project is that suggested by James (1897), that human beings are motivated by two primary concerns, a concern for not being duped and a concern for not missing out on something important. The first concern is relevant to the issue of whether truth has anything to be said on its behalf over mere empirical adequacy. If we adopt the literary device of a narrator commenting on various scenarios, we find something of an answer to this question. If one of the scenarios is the evil demon world and the other the actual world (as we suppose it to be), with the narrator being the very same person as the individual in these scenarios, the narrative will almost certainly treat the evil demon scenario as disturbing in comparison to the actual scenario, precisely because one is being duped in the former but not in the latter. The proper explanation of this response is that we find getting to the truth valuable in virtue of our concern for not being duped. But there are causes for concern here, coming from constructive empiricists such as van Fraassen (1980) as well as from the deniers of the value of truth (e.g., Rorty (1989)). Perhaps hope can be derived from various defenses against these opponents, along the lines of Williams (2002); Blackburn (2005); Lynch (2004), and Boghossian (2006), but even if such responses are successful, the focus on true belief faces another challenge as well. The second concern, the concern for not missing out on something important, raises a further problem, the problem of whether all truth is intrinsically valuable or only the important truths (see Sosa (2003)). My own sympathies lie in the direction of full generality for the value of truth (see Kvanvig (2008)), but challenges to the value of true belief as well as to its full generality are essential to the larger project of which the present approach to rationality is but a part.

Even if defensible, however, the fully general value of truth does not exhaust that which matters from a purely intellectual or cognitive point of view. What else matters? We can get at this issue with a few examples.

You are sitting in a logic class. Your instructor informs you that not every truth in a formal system can be proved in that very system, and that this fact is one of the most important discoveries in the twentieth century. You believe your instructor and are correct in your belief. But you are lost in darkness: you cannot see that the claim is true, you have no understanding of the reasons why it is true, and you do not grasp the significance of this truth.

Another story: you are sitting on the peak of a precipice, looking at the scenery below. You marvel at the distance you can see, and in doing so, detect motion in the distance. You cannot make out what is happening, so you use your binoculars. You see animals running, some bison, some horses. Most of the horses have humans sitting on their backs, holding long sticks in one hand. You have acquired a vast array of true beliefs, but you do not understand the scene in front of you; you do not understand what is going on.

Still another story: you are sitting in your backyard when an object lands in your yard, three feet from your feet. It is silver in color, cylindrical in shape, and about four inches long. Living in an age where terrorism is a concern, you immediately conclude it is an explosive device, but the only explosive devices you've ever encountered are bullets and firecrackers. Your belief is true, it turns out, but you cannot connect the visual features of the object with what you believe.

In each of these ways, one can have true beliefs and yet miss out on something quite important, something worth having. In each case, we can easily resort to visual metaphors to describe what is missing: we can't see what is going on, even though there is nothing wrong with our visual apparatus. The visual metaphor concerns a certain type of intellection that is lacking and worth having. What, exactly, is it that we are after in such cases but do not have?

What we want in such cases cannot be explained in terms of adding more true beliefs. A trivial reason is that one can add more true beliefs by performing logical operations on present beliefs, *ad infinitum*. What we want cannot be explained in terms of adding more logically independent true beliefs about the scenario, either. There are infinitely many truths about each of the scenes described that, even if learned, would still leave us in the dark. Take the second story for example. Some of the horses have black hooves and some white. Some of the horses are galloping on a left lead, some on a right. Some horses are sorrel, some chestnut; some paints, some not. The list can go on and on, and never relieve us of the sense of being blind to what is happening.

It is this idea of having made sense of things that is important in a way independent of the importance of true belief. We should not assume, of course, that there is one thing that is missing in these examples, since the truth may be that there are a number of things missing. It is useful nonetheless to notice the ways that we describe what is missing. We do so in visual or tactile terms: what is going on is not obvious; it is not transparent; you don't see what is going on; it is not clear or evident to you what is happening; you have not yet grasped what is occurring. We also describe what's missing in more intellectual terms: one has not understood, or comprehended, or fathomed the setting. These missing elements point to the importance not only of getting to the truth, but doing so intelligibly. We legitimately want not only to find the truth and avoid error, but to see that we have done so. What we want, therefore, is account of some property or properties of beliefs that are intelligibility-rendering, not merely truth-indicating.

The present project aims to address this sense-making concern, but by itself, will not provide a full answer to it. For even if we can identify the types of cognitive attitudes that answer to the concern of the egocentric predicament regarding what to think, we may not achieve the full understanding of the situation we find ourselves in, an understanding that addresses fully this sense-making concern (for further discussion, see Kvanvig (2013)). The present project fits into this larger one in virtue of providing a necessary, but not sufficient, condition for such understanding, in much the same way that many epistemologists have defended the importance of giving a theory of justification on grounds that it is necessary, but not sufficient, for knowledge. What distinguishes the present approach to epistemology is the focus on the theory of understanding rather than on the theory of knowledge, as well as on the theory of rationality arising out of the egocentric predicament as opposed to the theory of justification and whatever motivates it (whether a functional one, in terms of its role in the theory of knowledge, or a substantive one, in terms of the required connection to truth (as argued in Cohen and Lehrer (1983)) and analogies between justified belief and justified action (as argued in Audi (1983))). It remains an interesting question what the connection is between an adequate theory of justification and the theory of rationality developed here, but that is not a question I will address, since it is not central to the current project or the larger project of which the present one is a part.

Once we connect an interest in truth with this notion of sense-making, a quite natural human concern for guarantees of truth is certain to arise. We want not only to be correct in our intellectual assessments and our attempts to make sense of ourselves and the world around us, we want to be able to do so in a way that eliminates every possibility of error. While I agree that such an achievement would be wonderful indeed, it isn't a realistic goal, and the present project is developed from a starting point that admits this point in full generality. The standpoint underlying the present theory is a fully general fallibilism, a standpoint that insists that we theorize in a way that presumes no safe refuge from the possibility of error.

The Structure

As described, this work involves both meta-theoretical and theoretical aspects. Since the theoretical task is developed in explicit recognition of the meta-theoretical constraints on a theory, we turn first to the meta-theory in chapters one and two. In chapter one, we take up the issue of the nature of the non-descriptive feature that is the object of our theory, the epistemic dimension itself. What is epistemic appraisal and where is it to be found? Chapter two then turns to the background setting for the theory to be developed beginning in chapter three. That setting is one of fully general fallibilism: the theory that we develop needs to be compatible with the idea that there is nothing, or nearly nothing, regarding which we are infallible. Making clear what this assumption involves is the topic of chapter two. Chapters three and four then sketch out an approach to the dilemma chronicled previously: an approach to rationality that is guilty neither of being overly intellectual nor overly beastly. The sketch is turned into full theory in chapter seven, but the sketch itself provides the basis for important implications about the nature of rationality that are worth noting in their own right. So in chapters five and six, the sketch is used to show how to resolve disputes about the possibility of rational disagreement as well as disputes about whether there are such things as obligations regarding what to believe. We begin the project, then, with the general idea of epistemic appraisal itself. What is it that we evaluate when we engage in the kind of evaluation that is epistemic?

Some of the material in this work was first published in other places, and I want to acknowledge these publications and thank the publishers for permission to reprint parts of these essays here. This material includes: "The Basic Notion of Justification," Christopher Menzel, co-author, *Philosophical Studies* 59 (1990), pp. 235–61; "Propositionalism and the Perspectival Character of Justification," *American Philosophical Quarterly* 40.1 (2003), pp. 3–18; "On Denying a Presupposition of Sellars' Problem: A Defense of Propositionalism," *Veritas* 50 (2005), edited by Claudio de Almeida, pp. 173–90; "Two Approaches to Epistemic Defeat," *Alvin Plantinga: Contemporary Philosophy in Focus*, Deane-Peter Baker, ed., (Cambridge: Cambridge University Press, 2007), pp. 107–24; "Propositionalism and the Metaphysics of Experience," *Philosophical Issues* 17 (2007), edited by Ernest Sosa and Enrique Villanueva, pp. 165–78; "The Rational Significance of Reflective Ascent," *Evidentialism and Its Discontents*, edited by Trent Dougherty, (Oxford: Oxford University Press, 2011), pp. 34–54; "Perspectivalism and Reflective Ascent," *The Epistemology of Disagreement*, edited by David Christensen and Jennifer Lackey, (Oxford: Oxford University Press, 2013), pp. 223–43; and "Epistemic Normativity," *Epistemic Norms: New Essays on Action, Belief, and Assertion*, edited by John Turri and Clayton Littlejohn, (Oxford: Oxford University Press, forthcoming 2014).

1

Epistemic Appraisal

Our project begins from the egocentric predicament regarding what to do and what to think, and abstracts from it. In particular, we note that a resolution of the perplexities involved in this predicament will be an all-things-considered resolution, issuing in imperatives such as, "Get up and go to work," "Quit doubting Obama's citizenship," "Commit to the idea of promoting democracy around the world," etc. Epistemic appraisal is just one dimension figuring into such all-things-considered directives, and before we can theorize about it, we need some idea of its scope and reach.

Though this topic is interesting in its own right, it is especially important in the context of our value-driven inquiry. For one threat to our project is the idea that multiplicity reigns in the domain of epistemic normativity. If multiplicity reigns, we will not be able to find an input that factors into all-things-considered resolutions of the egocentric predicament regarding what to do and what to think from the epistemic realm, for there will be no such single factor. So the beginning point of our inquiry will be to identify the epistemic landscape in question and defend a meta-theoretical account of its features that leaves open the possibility of a theory that speaks with a single voice.

We might begin as follows. The qualifier 'epistemic' gives us a clue. Whatever type of appraisal is involved in the kind of normativity to be addressed here, it is a type connecting to the enterprise of epistemology. That enterprise, at its most general level, is about the connection between mind and world: what types of connections, if any, are there between what is real and what we take, think, and believe to be real, and which of these connections count as successful or worth aiming for? The standard answers here are ones in which truth and knowledge appear: our goal is, or should be, to get to the truth, and the gold standard for success in this effort is knowledge. Whether or not these standard answers are correct is not the issue here, however. What matters instead is the general nature of the subject, the issue of the connection between mind and world. When thought of in this way, a natural starting point would thus be to carve off that part of the egocentric predicament concerning what to think from that part concerning what to do, and to identify epistemic appraisal with the former domain. We would conclude, that is, that epistemic appraisal does not apply in the realm of actions. Moreover, it applies only to one part of the mental realm. When we consider the connections between mind and world, there are two possible directions of fit to be considered. With respect to cognitive attitudes such as belief, the idea is to get the belief to map onto, or mirror, or be patterned after the way the world is. With respect to conative or affective attitudes such as desires and preferences, the guiding principle is in the other direction, where the idea is to get the world to conform to the attitude itself. So, given such a starting point, it is relatively easy to see how to get to this conclusion: epistemic appraisal applies to all and only cognitive states such as beliefs.

This story is roughly the approach recommended by Roderick Chisholm. He writes,

> We may distinguish epistemic requirements from other normative requirements by noting certain general features both of the objects of epistemic requirements and of their substrates. I will first put the matter somewhat loosely. Then I will present a more precise formulation.
>
> So far as the objects of epistemic requirements are concerned, there is a sense in which they all may be said to be "doxastic." We will say that a state of affairs imposes a doxastic requirement provided only that it requires a believing or a withholding of a believing, or that it requires that one prefer certain believings or withholdings to other believings or withholdings. (Chisholm, 1991, p. 122)

There are several reasons for concern about this approach, however. The first involves the substance of the Chisholm–Firth debates about the ethics of belief, for as Roderick Firth argued, there can be reasons for belief that are not epistemic reasons for belief.[1] Examples of this sort should not surprise: they can be found in Pascal's Wager Argument (Pascal, 1966[1669]) for believing that God exists and in William James's argument (James, 1897) against W. K. Clifford (1877[1999]) that when faced with live, forced, and momentous options, it is rational to believe even without adequate evidence. But there are other reasons for concern as well. Recently, there has arisen a cottage industry on epistemic constraints concerning assertion sparked by Williamson (1996) (see, e.g., DeRose (2002), Hawthorne (2004), Stanley (2005), Weiner (2005), Lackey (2008), Brown (2008), and Kvanvig (2009, 2011a), and it is an easy step to make to think that the Chisholmian view is overly restrictive: that epistemic appraisal applies not only to doxastic items but to certain types of actions, such as assertion, as well.

---

[1] See, e.g., Firth (1959, 1978).

In addition, there is the final element in the earlier Chisholmian quote that can strike one as mysterious. Chisholm counts a type of preference between doxastic states as itself a doxastic state: to prefer believing to withholding is counted among doxastic states. But if we take the usual approach to the distinction between cognition and conation, preferences are to be classified along with desires, hopes, and fears as conative states, answering to a direction of fit from mind to world, rather than cognitive states, such as belief, which answer to a direction of fit from world to mind. If we become convinced that Chisholm has misclassified here, but really does want some conative states to be subject to epistemic appraisal, why not more? Why not speak, for example, of epistemically justified fears or hopes or wishes?

I believe the Chisholmian approach has resources for addressing these concerns, but that there is a further concern it cannot handle. I'll defend the Chisholmian approach in the first section from the objections just raised, before introducing this further concern in the following section and tracing its implications for our topic. As we will see, the lessons to be learned by seeing the failure of the Chisholmian approach have dramatic implications for the theory of rationality to be developed here as well as for any substantive theory of justification (i.e., one motivated in ways that go beyond characterizing some notion that plays a functional role in the theory of knowledge).

1.1 Defending a Chisholmian Approach

The Chisholmian approach contained in the earlier quote claims that epistemic requirements can be distinguished from other requirements by pointing out two things: the first, noted previously, is the *objects* of epistemic appraisal and the second is the *substrate* of such requirements. In the passage quoted earlier, I included only the part about the objects of epistemic appraisal, and what he says about the objects in question leaves the view open to the concerns expressed previously. Once we attend to what he says about the substrate of such requirements, however, we can see how to address these concerns.

Chisholm writes,

And what about the substrates of epistemic requirements? Oversimplifying slightly, we may say that every such substrate includes something that imposes only a doxastic requirement. But we should make a slight qualification. Presumably everyone who is required to do anything is subject to such negative requirements as that of not inflicting needless pain and suffering. Hence it would be somewhat more accurate to say that, if an epistemic substrate imposes a requirement that does not include a doxastic requirement, then that requirement is imposed by anything that imposes a requirement. For example, there are considerations which (1) require me to believe that I am in a room with other people and which (2) do not impose any other requirement upon me—except for those requirements that are imposed by the fact I am a rational and responsible being. (Chisholm, 1991, p. 122)

This approach contains Chisholm's response to the Firthian challenge. Firth held that epistemic appraisal was analogous to, but independent of, moral appraisal, pointing to examples where a belief was morally required but epistemically irrational. Chisholm agreed that there are such cases, but held that this point is compatible with epistemic appraisal being a type of moral appraisal. He thus held that Firth's conclusion does not follow from his premises. To sustain this charge, Chisholm must be able to provide an account of epistemic duty, one that goes beyond merely implying that epistemic duties are duties but different from moral duties. As he says,

Can we say what an epistemic duty is without falling into a circle? It is not enough to say only that an epistemic duty "is not an ethical duty" or to say that an epistemic duty is one that "pertains to believing reasonably." And it would be obviously circular if we were to characterize epistemic duty in epistemic terms. (Chisholm, 1991, p. 121)

To resist the Firthian conclusion, Chisholm begins with a worry about how to characterize epistemic normativity in non-circular terms, and begins with the claim that epistemic normativity pertains to believing reasonably. He knows, however, that this remark is insufficient to identify epistemic normativity, since the justification of belief can have both an epistemic and an ethical (as well as a practical) dimension. The task of characterizing epistemic normativity thus takes the following form for Chisholm: begin from the starting point that it applies only to beliefs and other doxastic states, and then let the account of the substrates of epistemic requirement do the rest of the work.

There is a side issue here concerning Chisholm's view that the objects of epistemic appraisal are doxastic states that I want to note before proceeding to the main issue between Chisholm and Firth. There is no good reason to think that all cognitive states are doxastic states, and so no reason to adopt Chisholm's restrictive view that the objects of epistemic appraisal are all doxastic states. Here are some other cognitive states that a generalized version of Chisholm's view ought to include among the objects of epistemic appraisal: degrees of belief (credences), confidences (intervals on the degree of belief scale), assumptions, presuppositions, acceptances, what we assent to unhesitatingly, intuition, etc. And beyond these is the generic notion of a cognitive commitment, which one can make without certainty. Given the possibility of complexity here in our understanding of what it is to be a cognitive state and exactly which kinds of states are going to end up counting as cognitive states, there is no reason to be Procrustean here, assuming that everything cognitive can be forced on to the doxastic bed. But there is little to be gained for an epistemological project in pursuing these issues in the philosophy of mind and psychology. So I will speak of the cognitive realm as Chisholm does, using the language of belief and doxastic states, in spite of recognizing that the prospects may be dim for the reductive project of explaining the entirety of the cognitive realm in terms of belief. For the central present issue for the Chisholmian project does not concern what he says about the objects of epistemic appraisal, but rather what he says about the substrates of such.

Chisholm's claim about the substrates is indirect. He doesn't tell us what these things are but merely identifies them as the kinds of things that "impose" requirements. The simplest idea would be that certain substrates impose only doxastic requirements, and then we could distinguish moral grounds for belief from epistemic grounds merely by pointing out the different substrates in question. But Chisholm worries about moral absolutes: he presumes that anything that imposes any requirement at all also imposes any morally absolute requirement, such as not inflicting needless pain and suffering. So he grants that epistemic substrates impose requirements on things other than doxastic states.

But, he thinks, this is a merely technical problem. For there is nothing special here about epistemic substrates. Everything that imposes any requirement of any sort also imposes the requirements involved in moral absolutes. So we are entitled to refine the position to exclude this apparent counterexample. How do we do so? Chisholm seems to claim that we should say something conditional: *ES* is an epistemic substrate if and only if, if *ES* imposes a requirement that does not include a doxastic requirement, then that requirement is imposed by anything that imposes a requirement. But that is not Chisholm's intention: things like my truck don't and wouldn't and can't impose any requirements at all, and yet, for all that, are not appropriately classified as epistemic substrates. Instead, Chisholm says,

We will say, then, that a state of affairs imposes a *pure doxastic* requirement provided only (1) that it imposes a doxastic requirement and (2) that it includes no non-doxastic requirements other than those that are imposed by anything that imposes a requirement. (Chisholm, 1991, p. 123)

It is thus more plausible to attribute to Chisholm the following: *ES* is an epistemic substrate if and only if (i) *ES* imposes a doxastic requirement and (ii) if *ES* imposes a requirement that does not include a doxastic requirement, then that requirement is imposed by anything that imposes a requirement.

How does this account help in avoiding the Firthian conclusion? The idea, I think, is that the Firthian challenge is to explain how a person can be required to hold a belief on insufficient evidence, if epistemic requirements are a species of moral requirement. The answer is that the epistemic requirement arises from an epistemic substrate, which is itself part of a larger substrate that itself imposes a moral obligation. Given this point, the only worrisome remainder is when one and the same substrate imposes both an epistemic and a non-epistemic require-ment, and Chisholm thinks that this can only happen when the non-epistemic requirement is one imposed by absolutely everything that imposes any require-ment at all. The result is an account of the substrates of epistemic requirement that allows such requirements to be a species of moral requirement without con-flicting with the obvious fact that sometimes we are morally required to believe contrary to our evidence or in the absence of adequate evidence.

So the Chisholmian approach to epistemic appraisal can survive the Firthian challenge, but what of the other two difficulties raised earlier? One of them had to do with epistemic appraisal of certain types of actions, especially speech acts such as the act of assertion. The careful formulation of epistemic substrates helps here as well. If in a given circumstance, it is morally wrong to assert a given claim, and if the explanation of this appeals to something that Chisholm classi-fies as an epistemic substrate, that doesn't imply that it is epistemically forbidden to assert that claim. For the requirement in question could be a require-ment that any substrate whatsoever imposes. For example, suppose it is always and everywhere prima facie wrong morally to assert-p-without-knowing-p, or to assert-p-without-adequate-confirmation-for-p or to assert-p-when-p-is-false. Then, Chisholm might maintain, every substrate that imposes any requirement of any sort imposes these requirements, even though the epistemic substrates in question also impose epistemic requirements only on doxastic states. In short, finding moral requirements to involve passing epistemic scrutiny doesn't show that epistemic appraisal applies to non-doxastic states.

What of the concern about epistemic appraisal applying to conative as well as cognitive states? Chisholm includes certain *preferences* among doxastic states as themselves doxastic states. If generalized, this way of proceeding is clearly ob-jectionable: a preference for certain types of gustatory experiences is not itself a gustatory experience. And if we admit the obvious here—that preferences are conative, not cognitive, states—why should we restrict epistemic appraisal to just these types of conative states? Why not epistemic requirements regarding hopes, fears, wishes, and desires as well?

A first point to note is that we can say everything we want to say about the ep-istemic dimensions of non-cognitive mental states without endorsing epistemic appraisal of them, just as we can say everything we want to say about the episte-mic dimensions of various speech acts without making them objects of epistemic appraisal. Some hopes and fears are irrational because of certain epistemic features of the circumstances in question, but that doesn't require that those hopes and fears be classified as epistemically irrational.

Chisholm, in his typical minimalist fashion, does not say why epistemic appraisal of non-cognitive mental states is to be anathema. But I think we can hazard a guess, and it is a guess that points to a significant gap in the Chisholmian story, one that can be filled only by abandoning that story for a better one.

1.2 *Contra* Chisholm

The problem is this. According to Chisholm, we begin the story with three doxastic states: believing, disbelieving, and withholding. Suppose, then, that we say that epistemic appraisal applies exactly to just the three types of entities. If we think more generically about what the world is like and the information we have about what our world is like, there is a full generality here that an adequate epistemology needs to accommodate: for any proposition p, and given state of information I, I either tells us that p is true, tells us that p is false, or doesn't say either way. So if we want to line up the doxastic states in question with this full generality, and assuming that states of information are the relevant substrates of epistemic requirements, we should want to say that (i) when I says that p is true, then anyone S for whom I is their state of information, S epistemically ought to believe p, (ii) when I says that p is false, then anyone S for whom I is their state of information, S epistemically ought to disbelieve p (i.e., believe its denial), and (iii) when I is neutral with respect to p, then anyone S for whom I is their state of information, S epistemically ought to withhold concerning p.

Such a view is seriously problematic, however. For one thing, it imposes impossible demands on us. If correct, we have to take an attitude toward every proposition whatsoever, and that is impossible for a finite mind. For another, there is the problem of cognitive overload. For any belief we have that our state of information tells us is true, that state of information also tells us that either that claim is true or it is true. But the proposition p is not the same proposition as $p \lor p$, so we'd have an additional obligation of a sort, that if generalized, requires way too much cognitive overload (even if we grant that there is some way to avoid the application of this line of argument to infinity). There is no reason to *require* an attitude toward everything confirmed by our state of information.

So suppose Chisholm were to agree that the view just described is problematic precisely because it involves an untoward commitment to unconditional intellectual requirements. One way to proceed is to admit that there aren't any unconditional intellectual requirements, that every epistemic requirement is a requirement to take exactly one of the three attitudes if one takes any attitude at all.[2]

One might worry, however, that a person could meet this requirement too easily, just by never taking any of the three attitudes. But there is a deeper problem if one is a Chisholmian here, since it is no longer clear what the objects of epistemic appraisal are on this hypothetical requirement story. They are not actual cognitive or doxastic states of any sort, and so a real Chisholmian should find the language troubling and look for an actual mental state to make it possible to explain the hypothetical requirements in question without abandoning the view that the objects of epistemic appraisal are actual doxastic states. Appealing to preferences between believings, disbelievings, and withholdings allows just such a claim: the hypothetical requirements in question are now correct because of or in virtue of another purportedly doxastic state one is in, the state of preferring with respect to these three other attitudes.

Merely formulating this response reveals its flaws, for if the original view overreaches because it requires too much going on in the head, so does the enhanced view. The only difference is that the "too much" required is now in the form of preferences rather than (other) doxastic states, but that difference is clearly not a relevant one. I don't have preferences regarding doxastic attitudes involving propositions of which I can't conceive, nor am I epistemically required to (whatever that might mean for preferences). And there is no requirement that I take any attitude toward trivial complications of claims toward which I legitimately take an attitude, even when my state of information says that these complications are true.

Moreover, this explanation for introducing preferences into the Chisholmian story does nothing to avoid the charge that we are now epistemically assessing conative as well as cognitive states. Preferences, contrary to what Chisholm needs, are not doxastic states, so if Chisholmians need to find doxastic states to undergird and explain hypothetical requirements with respect to believing, disbelieving, and withholding, they will need to look elsewhere than at second-order mental states such as preferences between the former that fall on the conative side of mentation.

The failure of the Chisholmian approach shows that we need a deeper and more systematic investigation of the objects of epistemic appraisal. I turn to this issue in the next section, using a variety of terms of epistemic appraisal, terms

---

[2] Views of this sort will be discussed in Chapters 5 and 6, and are defended by Feldman (2007), White (2005), Fantl and McGrath (2009), and Feldman and Conee (2004).

such as warrant, positive epistemic status, rationality, confirmation, entitlement, etc. I will predominantly use the language of justification and rationality, but I want to remind the reader again that I'm using all of these terms as terms of art, and the relevant special context is merely that of attempting to determine which objects are to be included among the objects of epistemic appraisal. Since the history of epistemology over the past half-century or so has predominantly used these terms for addressing that issue, I'll follow that practice, using these terms as proxy for whatever favored term of epistemic appraisal one might prefer. The issues involved remain unchanged no matter which term of art we choose for discussing this issue.

It is also worth remembering our primary concern here. At the outset, we have assumed that a resolution of the egocentric predicament concerning what to do and what to think involves a variety of factors, one of them being epistemic. That assumption, however, requires that we have an account of epistemic appraisal that speaks with a single voice. Chisholm's approach comes readily to mind in this context, but as we have seen, it does not survive scrutiny. What we seek, then, is a replacement for Chisholm's approach that satisfies the strictures of our present project.

1.3 Objects of Epistemic Appraisal

There is the generic language of justification and rationality, language that applies to a wide variety of items, and then there is the qualified use of such language fitted for use in epistemology. At the generic level, actions can be justified, emotions can be irrational, organizational structures can be unwarranted, etc. But when it comes to epistemic appraisal, we should delimit the class considerably. The guiding principle for such delimiting is the nature of epistemology itself, which focuses on that aspect of the mind–world connection in which the governing story is one where the direction of fit runs from mind to world. It is for this reason that the concept of truth plays such an important part in the history of epistemology, for it is, in terms of semantic ascent, the feature of the world at which cognition aims or which it attempts to mirror. When we assess epistemically, we assess relative to the goals, needs, interests, or projects of a purely intellectual being.

This beginning point invites two kinds of restrictions on objects of epistemic appraisal. We find epistemic appraisal in the territory of things that have content, and the restrictions appear from both sides of this phrase: we can restrict the domain of appraisal to the *things* that have content as well as to the *contents* themselves. This first step fits well with our practices of epistemic appraisal, for we make such appraisals both of doxastic attitudes but also of propositional contents regarding which no attitude at all is taken. For example, the claim that Obama will run for a second term is a claim that can be epistemically reasonable for a person to believe even if that person takes no attitude whatsoever toward the claim. The evidence can confirm for a jury that a defendant is innocent even though none of them is willing to believe it. And there can be no justification for a claim that is believed by everyone, as skeptics have argued for centuries.

When we focus on the *things* that have content, the earlier beginning point invites a further restriction. Some mental states with content are not suitable objects of epistemic appraisal because they are not the kind of mental state satisfying the direction of fit that runs from mind to world. In this respect, I side with Chisholm: hopes, fears, wishes, and desires can be rational, can be justified, but they cannot be epistemically rational or epistemically justified. And the same should be said of actions as well, even those that have content, such as assertions, guesses, insinuations, assumptions,[3] and the like. We can say everything we need to say about the epistemic dimensions of acceptable speech acts without allowing that actions themselves are items of epistemic appraisal. We can use the same devices to re-phrase should someone inelegantly talk about epistemically rational hopes or fears. We can say that the content in question is confirmed by the information the persons in question possess, and that in virtue of this epistemic assessment, the hopes or fears are rational or justified (though not, strictly speaking, epistemically rational or justified). Moreover, there is a sound motivation for such re-phrasing, since the story of epistemology is about successful mind–world connections with a particular direction of fit.

Once we have reached this conclusion, we can easily appreciate the attraction of Doxasticism. For on this view, we exclude non-mental states from the items capable of epistemic appraisal and we exclude affective or conative states as well. In addition, we unify the two remaining restrictions, the restriction on the *things* that have content as well as to the *contents* themselves, for concrete doxastic states are the right kind of thing to appraise epistemically and they are also things with content. As we have seen, the Chisholmian version of Doxasticism has difficulty with the latter unification step, because of its focus on concrete doxastic states, but the motivation for the view is easy to appreciate.

---

[3] It is important to note that the notion of an assumption is ambiguous. Some assumptions are mental states, others are actions. I can assume that you'll be on time, and I can make an assumption in the context of doing a proof. The second is not a cognitive state, but an action, and so isn't within the realm of epistemic appraisal. The first is a mental state, and within the cognitive realm, so presumably is appropriate for epistemic appraisal.

The challenge from the epistemic evaluation of contents is that the Chisholmian picture has to be abandoned in favor of a view that allows epistemic appraisal of both items in the concrete realm and in the abstract realm. One might propose to defend a version of Doxasticism that can survive this point by insisting that when we assess a content that is not actually believed, what we are in fact doing is assessing a belief-type rather than a belief-token, where the latter are concrete actual beliefs while the former are abstract entities. For example, such a Doxasticist would hold that when we say that the statement or claim or proposition that Obama will run for a second term is one that is justified for a person, a more careful articulation of the remark would be that there is a type of belief state that is justified for that person.

Such an account is a bit strained, however. Why identify propositions with belief-types, as opposed to other mental state types? We might as easily have identified the types in question as intentional-state-types, and then claiming that the view defended is a version of Doxasticism would be a mistake.

Besides, what are we to make of this idea of *identifying* one thing with another? The relationship between a person and a proposition is an appropriate object of epistemic appraisal; someone now proposes that this evaluation is *really* an appraisal of a relationship between a person and a belief-type, because we can *identify* propositions with belief-types. The argument is absurd on its face. Propositions aren't belief-types. Instead, belief-types, like other types of mental states, are individuated (largely)[4] in terms of their propositional content. Given this explanatory claim, propositions and belief-types are distinct items in any decent ontology. Thus, once we have acknowledged the appropriateness of epistemic appraisal of items in the abstract realm, thereby noticing a multiplicity of kinds of things regarding which epistemic appraisal is appropriate, the proper

---

[4] There is a complication here that I will merely mention and not pursue. The language of propositions here is a technical use of the term, one whose primary sense derives from the semantic understanding of what it is to be a proposition: it is a bearer of truth value. When we ask about the content of a belief state or other intentional state, propositions play a central role. But there are good reasons, deriving from Fregean concerns, for refusing to identify the totality of the content of a belief with its propositional content. There are also good reasons for thinking that whatever else is needed besides propositional content is itself something semantic, and this complicates any attempt to say precisely what a proposition is and what additional semantic elements are needed to complete a full picture of the content of the belief. This problem, which lies at the intersection of philosophy of mind and philosophy of language, is one that I intend to sidestep here. I will continue to speak as if all there is to the content of an intentional state is its propositional content in spite of knowing that this view is false. The complications needed to replace this mistaken account with the correct account, however, will not affect the epistemological results toward which I aim. I will treat this fact as license for pretending that the propositional account of the content of an intentional state is the correct account in the rest of this work.

direction of inquiry is to ask about the possibility of unifying our theory of epistemic appraisal in terms of the explanatory priority of one kind of appraisal over the other. This task is especially pressing in the context of this work, since the goal of developing a theory of epistemic appraisal that speaks with a single voice is best served by finding a fundamental kind of epistemic appraisal, by which we can understand the remaining kinds in question.

We are thus faced with three possibilities. The first possibility is that neither kind of appraisal is more fundamental than the other, and the other two possibilities find one of the two to be more fundamental than the other. In the next section, I'll argue that one of the two is more fundamental than the other, and that this result has important ramifications for what an adequate account of epistemic normativity can look like.

1.4 Doxasticism and Propositionalism

I have just remarked that the issue is whether one of two kinds of epistemic appraisal is more fundamental, but this remark can seem inordinately restrictive once we attend to the variety of syntactic locutions in which the language of epistemic appraisal appears. Using the language of justification, for example, consider the following appropriate uses of that language as a term of epistemic appraisal: *B is a justified belief, S's belief that p is justified, p is justified for S, S is justified in believing that p, S justifiably believes that p, S's believing p is justified, there is justification for S to believe that p, there is justification for S's believing p, and S has a justification for believing that p.* In addition to these passive uses of the notion of justification, there are active uses as well: *S justified his belief in p, believing e justifies believing p,* etc.

The goal I have set is to show that this diversity is only superficial by arguing that there is a basic kind of epistemic appraisal. I'll do this by using the language of justification as proxy for the kind of appraisal in question, so the question is whether there is a basic notion of justification. I'll begin by arguing that our syntactic list can be systematized into three categories: propositional justification (as in *p is justified for S*), personal justification (as in *S is justified in believing that p*), and doxastic justification (as in *S's believing p is justified*).

We can begin by noting that the active uses of the notion of justification are easily understood in terms of the passive uses. Believing *e* justifies believing *p* just in case *p* is justified by *e*; a person justifies her believing *p* just in case she uses some other claim *e* in defense of believing *p*, and *p* is justified by *e* for her. So, the active uses of the notion of justification do not prove difficult for unifying the variety of locutions in which the notion of justification appears. We are left, then, with the passive uses of the notion of justification. An initial glance at the earlier locutions suggests, as we noted in the previous section, three different uses of the term 'justified'. In the propositional case, justification seems predicated of a proposition; for example, when we say that a proposition p is justified for S, we do not commit ourselves to S's believing p and so can at most be committing ourselves to a justification for the proposition which would be the content of S's belief were it held. In the doxastic case, justification attaches to the believing itself; for example, when we claim that S's believing that it is raining is justified. In the personal case, justification appears to reside in the person in question. One example of this appears in the claim that S is justified in believing B.

The multiplicity involved in the original list of locutions involving the notion of justification is no broader than the three just noted, for the other locutions can be explained in terms of one of these three. Two are easily explained in terms of propositional justification: there is justification for S to believe p just when p is justified for S[5] and S has a justification for believing p if and only if p is justified for S, and S believes or is aware of that which justifies p for S.[6]

Other cases are easily understood in terms of doxastic justification: B is a justified belief (of S's) just in case, where p is the content of S's belief B, S's believing p is justified; S's belief that p is justified if and only if S's believing p is justified and S believes p; and S justifiably believes p just when S's believing p is justified and S believes p.

The only remaining proposition from our original list is the proposition *there is justification for S's believing p*. This claim is type/token ambiguous in its reference to S's believing p. If the reference to S's believing p is read as a reference to a token believing of p by S, then this claim implies that S believes p. However, if the reference to S's believing p is read as a reference to a type of belief, then no implication is present regarding whether or not S believes p. Given the ambiguity of the sentence, our final example can be explicated in either of two ways: either it means that p is justified for S, and S believes p, or it means simply that p is justified for S.

The initial list is by no means exhaustive of the uses of the language of justification but I believe it is complete in the following sense. Any examples from ordinary language which would suggest multiple and irreducible kinds of justification are represented on that list. Thus, any examples ignored by the discussion

---

[5] Until a more formal approach is introduced below, let us understand 'p' to be a schematic letter whose acceptable substituends are declarative sentences, and 'p' to abbreviate the expression 'the proposition that p'.

[6] The last conjunct of this gloss is formulated to be compatible with the view that the mental states involved in sensation are not themselves belief states but can only be counted as awarenesses.

to this point can be easily construed in terms of the three kinds of justification noted earlier as the most basic kinds.

So, the issue before us is the relationship between the three kinds of justification noted earlier, and I will argue that propositional justification is the basic kind of justification. I'll argue later that personal justification is just a stylistic variant of doxastic justification, but the initial point to note is the simple and natural way in which doxastic justification can be defined in terms of propositional justification. We can say that a token of S's believing of p is justified if and only if either (a) that token of S's believing of p is based on something which justifies p for S, or (b) p is justified for S, but not by anything other than itself, and S believes p.

This definition claims that doxastic justification amounts to propositional justification plus proper basing, if the belief in question is not a basic belief. If the belief is a basic belief (i.e., not based on any evidence or anything else which might be taken to be epistemically supportive of belief), then doxastic justification is just propositional justification plus belief.

The left-to-right direction of this claim is easiest to argue for. In order to deny that the right side is necessary for the left side, one would expect the claim to be either that proper basing is not necessary for justifiably believing a proposition or that a believing could be justified even though that believing has a content which fails to be justified. Failure of proper basing, however, is just the classic example of a case in which propositional justification obtains and doxastic justification fails to obtain; hence there is ample reason to rule out the first possibility. Further, unless one is employing the notion of justification in two different senses, it is unimaginable what it would be like for a believing to be justified while its content failed to be justified. Hence, there is good reason for thinking that the right side of this account is necessary for the left side.

Furthermore, if a particular believing occurs when the content of the believing is justified and the believing is based on that which justifies its content, we should expect it to be impossible for the believing itself to fail to be justified. What plausible further condition would be needed? There is one possibility here, but it is easy enough to finesse. The possibility arises from cases of "bootstrapping" or easy knowledge.[7] Cases of this sort arise for knowledge derived from ordinary perceptual awareness. I look at the table and see that it is red. I look at another object and see that it is blue. By repeating this procedure I develop an inductive basis for concluding that my color perceptions are reliable, for in each

---

[7] Thanks to Scott Sturgeon for bringing this issue to my attention. The problem was first formulated in Vogel (2000) and Cohen (2002) and has been widely discussed. See, e.g., Klein (2004), Markie (2005), and Neta (2005).

case, I notice that the color of the object is X and it looks X to me. So I bootstrap inductively to the conclusion that my color perception is reliable.

Such examples are relevant to this account in the following way. We might agree that the evidential basis in question is adequate for propositionally justifying the conclusion that I have drawn, but think that I still shouldn't be basing my belief on that evidence. Thus, one might think, one can have a justification for a claim and base one's belief on it without thereby justifiably believing the claim in question. In short, propositional justification plus proper basing need not imply doxastic justification.

The problem that leads to this concern is a problem of a certain type of epistemic priority. In some sense, it is reasoning to a conclusion that is epistemically prior to the evidence used to get to the conclusion. This point allows us to finesse the problem for an account like the one in question without abandoning the operative idea that doxastic justification is easily explained in terms of propositional justification and without having to solve the problem of easy knowledge in the process. We shall need to solve it, then, in terms of some notion of epistemic priority: some pieces of information are epistemically prior to other pieces of information, and one can't use epistemically posterior information to arrive at doxastically justified beliefs regarding epistemically prior beliefs. Once the point is put this way, all we need to do is to insist that proper basing involves basing on something that justifies, where the justifier in question is not epistemically posterior for the person in question to the content of the belief in question, and then there will be no plausible further condition a believing must meet in order to be justified. Hence, we can thus affirm:

DJ: A token of S's believing of p is justified $=_{df}$ (i) that token believing is based on something not epistemically posterior to p for S, which justifies p for S, or (ii) p is justified for S, but not by anything other than itself and S believes p.

One might object to the idea of there being justified beliefs that are not based on anything other than themselves. This objection, however, is not an objection to DJ, but rather an objection to certain types of foundationalism. So, this principle is not threatened by this concern.

One other point is worth noting as well. When we claim that a believing is based on a justifier, there are two understandings of basing that might be involved. The first is psychological, involving causal and explanatory notions relevant to that particular science. The second is epistemic, and the difference shows up in cases of reasoning. One can, for example, conclude q from a set of premises that includes $p \rightarrow q$ and p, and in the psychological sense of basing, one will thereby be basing one's belief on good evidence for it. But it is possible that one is not epistemically basing one's belief on that evidence, since the link between the premises of the argument and the conclusion drawn might depend on something other than seeing the *modus ponens* connection. The mere fact that q follows from the premises of an argument doesn't show that one has properly inferred q from the information that supports it. A natural and tempting way to make this point is that one must *see* the connection in question and having that awareness play a role in the drawing of the conclusion in question, but that is perhaps too strong a requirement, since it requires that one be in an additional mental state for epistemic basing by inference. What is important here, however, is not the precise characterization of what it is to perform a *modus ponens* inference on a set of premises, but rather the obvious fact that which particular inference rule one is following depends on something more than the fact that the premises contain information that supports the conclusion by a given rule of inference. To epistemically base by inference is a function both of what follows from the information one has and what rules one is following in drawing the inference in question.[8] One way to think about this problem is that it is a deviant causal chain issue, where we need to separate out causal chains that generate epistemic basing from those that do not. Regardless of how we think about the issue,[9] however, we can solve it programmatically by insisting that the form of inference being used be part of the story of what individuates an inference of a conclusion from premises that support it, relying on the point that epistemic basing will need to involve patterns of inference licensed by an adequate theory of propositional support.

To defend the claim that propositional justification is the basic kind of justification, however, more would be required, but undertaking that task at present would detract from the main flow of the argument of this work. For the concern that we are trying to rebut is that the language of normativity is irreducibly ambiguous, and the argument of concern is one that points to the variety of syntactic constructions involved in the language of normativity. Our defense of DJ is enough to show that no such disturbing ambiguity is present concerning the relationship between propositional and doxastic justification.

Moreover, there is no reason for concern here regarding personal justification either. Our project involves epistemic appraisal of items that figure in a resolution of the egocentric predicament concerning what to do and what to think. If we

---

[8] This distinction between epistemic and merely psychological basing is important for addressing the criticisms raised by John Turri concerning principles such as DJ, in Turri (2010).

[9] Those who think epistemic basing can come apart from causation will not be comfortable characterizing the problem as one concerning deviant causal chains, and I am sympathetic with this viewpoint. See, e.g., Lehrer (1974), Swain (1980), and Pappas (1979) for discussion of such views.

arrive at a theory that speaks with a single voice regarding doxastic and propositional justification, we will have ammunition enough for such a purpose, even if there is some other dimension of epistemic evaluation that applies uniquely to persons. The latter point can be granted, so long as this other dimension is not involved in the issues regarding what to do and what to think.

It is interesting to note, however, that a proper understanding of the language of normativity makes propositional justification the basic notion. In Appendix A, I show how to reduce personal justification to doxastic justification, and in Appendix B, I show why doxastic justification must be understood in terms of propositional justification rather than the other way around.

For present purposes, however, DJ provides all the conclusion we need to resist the idea that ambiguity arises in the arena of epistemic normativity at the very outset because of the variety of locutions attributing some notion of epistemic propriety. As we have seen, the evidence for variety is strong, and no simple doxasticist account in the Chisholmian heritage adequately explains the variety in question. Thus, an alternative to this heritage is required, and DJ provides it. It is also worth noting that DJ's propositionalism harkens back to a more ancient tradition than the Chisholmian one, for the central disputes in the history of epistemology concern the notion of confirmation and degree of confirmation, with skeptics claiming that there can be no confirmation for claims about the external world or that the degree of confirmation for such is inadequate in terms of making such claims be candidates for knowledge. It is an interesting historical question how this more ancient focus was turned into the contemporary focus on doxastic states and entitlement for such, but that is a topic for another time and place. What is relevant here is just this: the possibility of a theory of epistemic normativity that speaks with a single voice is not undermined by the variety of syntactic structures involved in the language of normativity. DJ shows how one can develop a unified approach without introducing irreducible ambiguity.

There is a further argument for Propositionalism, however, that will introduce aspects that are crucial for developing the theory of normativity defended here. This argument is independent of the direction of reduction issue that affects DJ, and is addressed in Appendix B. For even if that argument fails—the argument that doxastic justification cannot be used to define propositional justification—there can be other reasons for adopting Propositionalism and rejecting Doxasticism. I will claim that there are such reasons, arising out of the concept of epistemic defeat. These reasons will give us both a reason for adopting Propositionalism in the development of the theory of normativity as well as some understanding of the nature of the theory itself. We thus turn in the next section to the argument for Propositionalism from the concept of epistemic defeat.

1.5 Propositionalism and the Concept of Epistemic Defeat

The concept of epistemic defeat, or some surrogate for it, is essential for any falli-bilistic epistemology. If knowledge or justification requires infallibility, then the epistemic grounds of belief have to be strong enough that no further information could be made available to the cognizer to undermine these grounds of belief. When knowledge or any epistemically normative notion requires no such infal-libility, however, grounds of belief can be undermined by further information, information that defeats the power of the original information to put one in a position to know that the claim in question is true. Even if some combination of conditions for knowledge are sufficient for truth, if there is a nonpsychological, epistemically normative condition that is not sufficient for truth, that condition will need to appeal to some concept of defeat (or a surrogate of it).

I mention here the notion of a surrogate for the concept of defeat only to ignore it in what follows, for the following reason. Reliabilists, such as Alvin Goldman, recognize that a belief can be produced by a reliable mechanism, without put-ting one in a position to know.[10] For example, one may form a perceptual belief in circumstances that one has good reason to believe are deceptive. This further information defeats the confirming power of the perceptual experience. Since re-liabilists wish to construe talk of reasons and confirmation in terms of reliable processes and methods, they cannot be satisfied simply to note that these rea-sons defeat the confirming power of one's perceptual experience. Instead, they must construct a surrogate for this language of defeat. Goldman, for example, talks in terms of alternative reliable processes available to the individual which, if displayed, would not have resulted in the formation of the belief in question.[11] Such a proposal is not adequate as it stands, and those familiar with the sorry credibility of counterfactual proposals in the history of philosophy can anticipate what the problems will be.[12] For example, suppose there is a competent cognizer who disagrees with you about something you know to be true. There is a reliable process which if you had used it would have resulted in a different belief: namely, belief based on testimony. All this, in spite of the fact that knowledge is possible compatible with disagreement by competent cognizers.

The alternative is to embrace the language of defeat but to attempt to explain it in fundamentally Doxasticist terms. We can compare this approach to one that begins with propositional relationships, describing the concept of defeat in terms

---

[10] See, for example, Goldman (1979).   [11] Goldman (1979, p. 13).

[12] The *locus classicus* for an account of the implausibility of counterfactual accounts in philosophy is Robert Shope (1978).

of propositional justification itself. Such a theory places information about defeat up front, not informing us of how the defeat relationships play out in the context of actual belief, at least not initially. The other theory takes a back-door approach to the concept of defeat, assuming a context of actual belief and an entire noetic system, and describing defeat in terms of what sort of doxastic and noetic responses would be appropriate to the addition of particular pieces of information. Where the house is the noetic structure itself, the front-door approach characterizes the concept of defeat in terms of the propositional contents a belief might have, thus characterizing defeat at the front door. It presumes that once let into the house, some changes will be required, but the characterization of defeat is logically prior to any account of such changes. The back-door approach characterizes defeat in terms of what leaves the house, in terms of beliefs that exit the noetic system in response to intrusions into the system, in terms of what the staff of a well-run household kick out the back door for making a mess of things. The best-developed example of a back-door theory is Alvin Plantinga's, and I will show why his theory and approaches like it will be unable to explicate accurately the concept of epistemic defeat. I will argue that a front-door approach is needed rather than a back-door approach.

The differences between these two approaches mirror fundamental differences in approaches to the theory of justification or warrant. The approaches are those seen earlier: the difference between propositional and doxastic, or Aristotelian, approaches in epistemology.[13] The Doxasticist wishes to characterize justification in terms of appropriate doxastic responses to input, without having to characterize some internal confirmatory relationship between the contents of input and output. The Doxasticist can describe the machine of justification solely in terms of the quality of the box that takes input and generates doxastic output: perhaps the box is a reliable one, or a properly functioning one, or one that displays the right sorts of intellectual virtues or excellences. The Propositionalist, however, tells a different story. According to the Propositionalist, there are confirmation relationships between contents independently of whether or not those contents are believed.

As already noted, given the truth of fallibilism, an account of justification will have to include an account of the nature of epistemic defeat, since that which makes for justification in one circumstance might be undermined in another circumstance. In the process of characterizing the concept of defeat, either theoretical perspective might sell its soul to find a good theory. That is, an explicit Doxasticist might characterize defeat in Propositionalist terms, and a

---

[13] See, e.g., Kvanvig (1996), Kvanvig and Menzel (1990), and Kvanvig (2003).

Propositionalist might adopt a Doxasticist account; in the language of the earlier metaphor, a Doxasticist might resort to a front-door theory and a Propositionalist to a back-door theory. This point in itself is no objection to such a mixed theory, but it is an objection to a theory that pretends to purity, whether Doxasticist or Propositionalist purity. Moreover, such a mixed theory faces an additional explanatory burden. If, for example, a theorist explicitly adopts a Doxasticist approach on the basis of expressed dissatisfaction with the usual versions of Propositionalism, such a theorist will need to explain why, after returning to feed at the Propositionalist table when trying to understand the concept of defeat, there is some special reason not to always and everywhere dine at the Propositionalist table when constructing an epistemological theory. It is worth noting, in this context, that the usual versions of Doxasticism express skepticism about the existence of the confirmation relationships between propositions needed to sustain the Propositionalist program, so if Doxasticists end up having to appeal to these very same relationships to clarify the concept of defeat, they have undermined their reason for looking elsewhere for a good epistemology in the first place.[14]

It is not surprising, then, that paradigm Doxasticists offer back-door approaches to the concept of defeat, since they need to do so in order to preserve their Doxasticism. I will argue here that such purity cannot be maintained, that a proper theory of the concept of defeat needs to be a front-door theory, and thus that the only pure approach available is a propositional one. As a result, Doxasticists will be in the position of needing to explain their aversion to Propositionalism without undercutting their appeal to that view when it comes time to explain the concept of epistemic defeat.

1.5.1 *Plantinga's back-door theory*

As I point out earlier, the best developed Doxaticist account is Plantinga's, so I will begin with the details of his account and some emendations of it. Plantinga's official account is:

D is a purely epistemic defeater of *B* for *S* at *t* iff

1. *S*'s noetic structure *N* at *t* includes *B* and *S* comes to believe *D* at *t*,
2. any person *S**
   a. whose cognitive faculties are functioning properly in the relevant respects,
   b. who is such that the bit of the design plan governing the sustaining of *B* in her noetic structure is successfully aimed at truth ... and nothing more

---

[14] One of the most forthright epistemologists in expressing this motivation is Ernest Sosa. See in particular his explanation for preferring a version of virtue epistemology to some Chisholmian collection of epistemic principles in Sosa (1991b).

    c. whose noetic structure is *N* and includes *B*, and

    d. who comes to believe *D* but nothing else independent of or stronger than *D*,
       would withhold *B* (or believe it less strongly). (Plantinga, 2000, p. 363)

This official account, however, does not represent Plantinga's full thinking on the matter, for he says,

> Still, argument is one way to give me a defeater. Is there another way? Yes; you can put me in a position where I have experiences such that, given those experiences (and given my noetic structure), the rational thing to do is to give up the purported defeatee. (Plantinga, 2000, p. 367)

This quote calls for a revision of the official account, since we shouldn't want to require that the person form a reflective belief to the effect that one is having experience *D* in order for that experience to function as a defeater. Clause (d.) requires such a reflective belief, however, so some change is necessary. The required change is obvious, though. Just change the beginning of (d.) to read "one who comes to experience *D* or believe *D*," and change clause (1.) in a similar fashion.

    Notice the back-door character of this account. The account characterizes a defeater in terms of epistemically appropriate responses to the presence of a defeater in a noetic system: we insert the defeater into the noetic house, and see which belief gets expelled out the back door.

1.5.2 The problem of defeater defeaters

Because of this back-door approach, this account has some difficulty with Plantinga's acknowledgment that defeaters can themselves be defeated (he calls them "defeater defeaters," and some defeaters are supposed to be immune from any sort of defeater defeater, and are called Humean defeaters in Plantinga's argument against evolutionary naturalism).[15] No adequate account of defeat can ignore this issue, since the possibility of such follows straightforwardly from an appropriate understanding of the fallible character of reasons for belief: defeaters are no more infallible reasons to abandon belief than is evidence an infallible reason to hold a belief.

    On the account in question, however, there is no talk or possibility of higher-level defeaters at all. If something that should count as a defeater is inserted into a noetic system containing a defeater defeater, the conclusion that follows on the account in question is that the purported defeater is not in fact a defeater at all

---

[15] The idea was first expressed in Plantinga (1991), but later refined in Plantinga (1993, 2000, 2011) as well as in Plantinga and Tooley (2008). See as well Beilby (2002), a collection of critical essays on the argument.

(since no belief exits the system if the system is properly functioning). This point leaves one wondering what to make of Plantinga's talk of defeater defeaters.

Other approaches to the nature of defeat face a similar issue. Michael Bergmann defines the concept of defeat as follows:

D1. d is a defeater at t for S's belief b iff (i) d is an experience or propositional attitude or combination thereof; (ii) S comes to have d at t; (iii) as a result of S's coming to have d at t, b ceases to be justified. (Bergmann, 2005, p. 422)

On this account of defeat, a defeater blocks a belief from being justified, but such an approach leaves us wondering what to make of the idea of defeater defeaters.

One way to deal with this issue is to treat talk of defeater defeaters on the model of talk of former senators and decoy ducks. A former senator is not a senator, and a decoy duck is certainly not a duck. So maybe a defeater defeater need not defeat something that is really a defeater; it need only block some item of information from being a defeater in the first place. As Bergmann says, "Thus according to (D1), if the defeating power of a defeater d is neutralized or defeated, d ceases to be a defeater." (Bergmann 2005, p. 422.)

Let us say, then, that when a defeater defeater is present, the original defeater is merely a potential defeater rather than an actual one. One way to understand this concept of potential defeat is suggested by the earlier discussion:

D is a potential defeater of B for S at t iff

1. S's noetic system N includes the belief B and the belief or experience D, and
2. There is some aspect DD of N which is such that, if it were not present, D would be a defeater of B for S at t.

Those familiar with the sad track record of counterfactual theories will know that this account is not going to work; those who believe that counterfactual theories hardly ever work may despair or salivate, depending on their attraction to the back-door approach exemplified here. Whatever the attitude, however, the approach in question cannot succeed as it stands, since DD might be entailed by other aspects of a noetic structure, or the noetic structure might contain other compelling grounds for DD. In such cases, dropping DD won't turn D into a defeater of B, since there is other information in the system that would still block this result. We can address these concerns by replacing the account in question with:

D is a potential defeater of B for S at t iff

1. S's noetic system N includes the belief B and the belief or experience D, and
2. There is some aspect DD of N which is such that, if it and any aspect of N giving adequate grounds for DD were not present, D would be a defeater of B for S at t.

We've now removed *DD* from the system, as well as anything that confirms it, in order to see if *D* is a defeater of *B* for *S* at *t*. Here's a possibility we need to be able to rule out, however.

Consider the implications of this account if the grounds for *DD* are also part of the grounds for *B* itself, so that in removing these grounds, we've made the grounds for *B* less than adequate. In that case, the definition under consideration counts everything in *N* distinct from *B* as a potential defeater of *B* for *S* at *t*.

It is important to note that such a possibility cannot be ruled out. Suppose Joe believes that the leaves on a certain tree are red on the basis of being told this by Jeff and Jimmy, a pair of complementary colorblind individuals who are known by Joe to be honest and sincere with him on, but only on, color reports: they are so self-conscious about being colorblind, they overcome their deceptive natures hoping to hide their colorblindness from others by a special display of sincerity and honesty. The ground of this belief for Joe is not their testimony alone, since Joe is like us in being suspicious of color reports by colorblind people. In this case, however, they both report that the leaves are red. Joe knows that the leaves have to be either brown, red, or green, and since Jeff confuses brown and red but not red and green and Jimmy confuses red and green but not red and brown, Joe comes to believe that the leaves are red.

The ground of Joe's belief is thus a complex combination of testimony and reasoning. If Joe just had the testimony of Jeff and Jimmy, he wouldn't believe them. If you add the information that it's a color report, Joe still wouldn't believe them, since they are colorblind. What grounds his trust includes his belief about their colorblindness, their self-consciousness about it, and the specific details about their colorblindness that confirm that the leaves are red.

In order to explain how their colorblindness is a potential defeater in this case, we must leave the defeater defeater out of the noetic system. That is, we must leave out the information about how their colorblindness combines to show that the leaves are red. But if we take this information away, Joe wouldn't believe that what they say is true. Not only is their colorblindness a potential defeater of Joe's belief, so is everything else that Joe believes (by the account in question of potential defeat).

Perhaps our difficulty here is the result of trying to characterize the notion of a potential defeater in terms of being an actual defeater. Perhaps what we should try to do is to characterize the grounds or reasons why the belief in question would be absent, if the actual defeater were removed. Here is a suggestion along these lines:[16]

---

[16] Thanks to Chad Mohler in his comments on the epistemology weblog, *Certain Doubts*, for this suggestion.

D is a potential defeater of B for S at t iff

1. S's noetic system N includes the belief B and the belief or experience D, and
2. There is some aspect DD of N which is such that, if it and any aspect of N giving adequate grounds for DD were not present (and nothing else were added to the system, and the system in question remained a properly functioning one with the operative aspect of the design plan successfully aimed at truth), S would withhold believing B on the basis of D.

That is, what would ground, or explain, the absence of the belief in question would be the presence of D in S's noetic system. This suggestion avoids the case of Joe, since not everything in Joe's noetic system will explain or ground Joe's withholding of belief in the conditions in question.

The concept of withholding here is ambiguous between mere absence of belief and the mental attitude of suspension between believing B and believing $\sim B$. Only one of these readings is helpful here, since requiring the attitude of suspension of belief is too strong. One need not take any attitude at all toward a claim one doesn't believe in order to believe that claim to be defeated for one, so we should interpret the notion of withholding in the consequent of the second condition given earlier in terms of mere absence of belief.

If we interpret the claim in this way, if we suppose that the withholding is not itself a propositional attitude taken by the person toward the proposition in question, the account in question requires the truth of the claim that the ground or explanation of a non-event involves the defeater in question. Both concepts yield problems. First, if we are thinking about explanations, then much of the noetic system will explain the lack of a mental attitude toward B by S, and so much in the noetic system beyond D will also count as potential defeaters of B for S. Yet, not everything in a noetic system that helps explain the absence of a particular belief is a defeater of that belief. To continue the example of Joe, Joe's noetic system contains the information that his only sources of information about the color of the leaves is from Jeff and Jimmy, and were their testimony removed, the loss of the belief in question would be partially explained by Joe's knowledge of his sources. But this knowledge about who reported the color of the leaves is not itself a defeater or potential defeater of the belief in question.

The other option relies on the concept of a ground of failure to believe. The appeal to grounds of failure to believe appears to be subject to the same problem as the earlier appeal to explanation, but there is a way to avoid that problem. It is natural to understand an appeal to grounds in terms of reasons, so that D itself gives S a reason not to believe B. Such an approach abandons the back-door character of Plantinga's theory, since D will constitute such a reason in virtue of confirming that the content of B is not true (or not supported by adequate evidence). By hypothesis, D is present in the noetic system but does not require a properly functioning system to abandon B, so if we characterize the rationalizing power of D with respect to B in a negative fashion, we will have to say that D disconfirms, or counts against the truth of, B. In short, the definition in question faces the dilemma of either being inadequate or abandoning the Doxasticist purity of a back-door approach to the concept of defeat.

So Plantinga's language of defeater defeaters is going to cause problems for his theory of defeat. These problems are a direct result of the back-door strategy Plantinga employs. The front-door strategy yields a straightforward solution: a defeater of the support generated for p by e is a claim d such that d&e does not epistemically support p; and a defeater of d is a further proposition dd where the combination dd&d&e does epistemically support p.[17] So one cost of the back-door strategy is that it threatens to undermine Plantinga's reliance on the language of defeater defeaters.

1.5.3 The Quine–Duhem issue

The problem that provided the focus of the last section is a foreshadowing of more general problems, problems faced by any back-door theory. In general terms, the problem is one that has been highlighted by Quine and Duhem regarding confirmation and disconfirmation for scientific theories and hypothesis. Their point is that when we test a hypothesis and get results in conflict with the hypothesis, the existence of auxiliary hypotheses involved in the testing prevents the test from forcing the conclusion that the tested hypothesis is false. Instead, there is a variety of rational responses to an anomalous experimental result. As a consequence, one may expect properly functioning noetic structures to display no single response to the introduction of a defeater. Instead, there can be a variety of changes displayed by systems that are both reliable and properly functioning.

In this way, introducing a defeater into a noetic system is the epistemic equivalent of a *reductio* argument. The *reductio* itself doesn't tell you which assumption is at fault, so information beyond the *reductio* itself is needed to determine what assumption to reject. Just so with defeaters. The defeater doesn't tell you how to fix the cognitive dissonance it introduces, it only tells you that something needs to be fixed. Any epistemological theory suitably sensitive to the difference between a permissible change to a noetic structure in light of further learning and

---

[17] This account of defeaters in terms of a hierarchy of overriders is articulated by John Pollock in Pollock (1986).

an obligatory change will have to allow that, when faced with a defeater, there will be cases in which there is more than one permissible option open for addressing the defeater.

It is tempting to say here that what is defeated is not a particular claim but a conjunction of all the claims that together conflict with the defeater. This temptation should be avoided, for two reasons. The first reason is that it forces our understanding of defeat to be modeled too strongly by the deductive analog of *reductios*. It is true that the only thing that follows logically from a *reductio* is that a conjunction of claims is false, but we shouldn't conclude from this fact that a defeater is only evidence against an entire collection of things with which it is incompatible. This point leads to a second one. In the case of a *reductio*, paralysis ensues at the end of the proof, if one's hope was to discharge one of the assumptions. The only conclusion that follows logically from a *reductio* is that the conjunction of all the assumptions is false. If we extend this analogy into the epistemic domain, a similar paralysis will ensue. We will tell cognizers that the only change they are entitled to make when confronted with a defeater is to abandon a conjunction representing all the different assumptions that might be abandoned in order to remedy the cognitive difficulty faced. This description, though, borders on incoherence: if there are multiple possible ways of accommodating a defeater, the notion of possibility here, one would think, would be normative, implying that each of the ways is permissible. The view in question, however, denies that any of them are permissible; only the disjunction of all possible accommodations is allowed as a response to a defeater.

Can we solve the Quine–Duhem problem by changing the last clause of the definition from a "would" counterfactual to a "might" counterfactual? That is, instead of saying that any person in similar circumstances would abandon the belief, can we say that any person in similar circumstances might abandon the belief?[18]

This change makes the account too weak, however, for on it, too many elements of the system of beliefs will count as defeaters. If we take the Quine–Duhem issue seriously, rational responses by properly functioning systems can vary quite considerably, but we don't want to disqualify your belief from counting

---

[18] One interpretation of this modal notion is in terms of the denial of a stronger, opposite counterfactual: to say that A might occur were B to occur is to say that it is false that $\sim A$ would occur were B to occur. More formally, using the standard notation for such conditionals, $A \diamondsuit\!\!\rightarrow B =_{df.} \sim(A \Box\!\!\rightarrow \sim B)$. For the source of this view, and more on the logic of counterfactuals, see David Lewis (1973). The primary alternative interpretation is an epistemic one, treating $A \diamondsuit\!\!\rightarrow B$ as equivalent to an epistemic possibility of $A \Box\!\!\rightarrow B$. Defenders of this view include Robert Stalnaker (1984) and Keith DeRose (1991).

as knowledge merely because someone might give up that belief in the process of making quite dramatic changes to their noetic structure in response to a given experience.

The proper response is not, then, to move to a weaker last clause in light of the Quine–Duhem point, but rather to look at the problem more carefully to see how to qualify the present account. To see how to do so, let's return to the scientific example that motivates the Quine–Duhem point. In that example, a contrary experiment prompts the need for making some changes regarding one's commitment to the combination of the hypothesis being tested together with the auxiliary hypotheses that play a role in the setup of the experiment. In response to the experiment, there are a number of rational responses that can be taken. The revealing question, however, is this: when we consider two different scientists who embody different rational responses to the experiment, what explains the difference in their responses? If we can answer this question, we are on the way to finding an adequate way to qualify Plantinga's account, since we can include this explanatory difference when describing how a properly functioning system of that sort would respond to the presence of a defeater. The point of the Quine–Duhem thesis is that the difference need not always appeal to background assumptions, beliefs, experiences, etc., of the two scientists. The differences would have to be able to be explained in other terms, at least in some cases.

If the difference can be explained, we should be able to refine Plantinga's approach to accommodate it. My concern here is not the precise nature of the explanation, but it is clear that the explanation will have something to do with the overall intellectual character of the different scientists. Some are disposed to seek originality more than others, some tolerate greater risk of error in their pursuit of the holy grail of truth, and others value precision and meticulous detail over grand visions. In each such case, differences in overall intellectual character are compatible with identical noetic structures prior to the anomalous experimental result, so we can accommodate the Quine–Duhem point by supplementing the account under consideration with a further condition requiring sameness of overall intellectual character.

There is a further restriction that is needed as well, and it will be more efficient to incorporate the changes together. Notice that the timeframe for the second clause can't be synchronic through all the clauses: clause (d.), where B is abandoned, must be later than the other clauses, since those clauses include the presence of B. Consider, then, a "road to Damascus" experience, an experience to which a response will occur, but where the response will not in any way be explicable in terms of rational strictures on belief change. In such a situation, nearly any change whatsoever might occur in a system which, up to the moment of change, was properly functioning. In such situations, however, the change to the system is explained other than in terms of the proper functioning of the system with respect to a design plan aimed at truth.

Because of this difference, we can accommodate this problem by including the restriction that the response itself is a display of a properly functioning system involving a part of the design plan aimed at truth. Putting these two changes together gives us the following revision of the official account:

D is a purely epistemic defeater of B for S at t iff

1. S's total intellectual character C and noetic structure N at t includes B and S comes to believe or experience D at t,
2. any person S^*
   a. whose cognitive faculties are functioning properly in the relevant respects,
   b. who is such that the bit of the design plan governing the sustaining of B in her noetic structure is successfully aimed at truth ... and nothing more
   c. whose intellectual character is C and noetic structure is N, including B, and
   d. who comes to believe or experience D but nothing else independent of or stronger than D and whose response to D is a display of a part of the design plan successfully aimed at truth of a properly functioning cognitive system,
   would withhold B (or believe it less strongly).

1.5.4 Deeper problems and learning one's lessons

The account in question is a proper response to the Quine–Duhem point about the openness of possible rational responses to anomalous experiential results. The developments that led to this formulation, however, include a number of possibilities relevant to our assessment of the back-door strategy, but not pursued in the last section. We saw that defeat needs to be compatible with a certain optionality in response; that sometimes a response is simply non-rational rather than rational or irrational; and this latter possibility of things being in good rational order prior to a response raises the question of what to say when things are not in good rational order prior to a response. As we have seen, it is essential to the back-door approach to imagine the prospective defeater as being "in the house," to see what emerges from the back door. The problem just noted is analogous to noting that houses come in various stages of disrepair just as noetic systems do. Sometimes the very belief regarding which a prospective defeater is being evaluated is part of what's in disrepair. Less metaphorically, one can acquire a defeater for a belief that is already unwarranted, already a display of improper function or of a part of the design plan not aimed at truth. Just as convicted felons can be guilty of further crimes, so can an unwarranted belief be guilty of further epistemic improprieties. In such cases, clause 2 of the account in question will be vacuously true since it is not possible to be characterized by the noetic system in question and also have the belief be the product of a properly functioning system whose design plan is aimed at truth. Furthermore, no account of defeat is complete without an account of this phenomenon; no account of defeat is complete when it limits the concept of defeat so that it is applicable only to systems of belief in good repair.

This problem is not one that calls for a bit more Chisholming away at a better definition of defeat. We can't consider the responses of systems in such disrepair, for the same reason that we don't follow the advice of the insane. The only option is to allow the noetic system of the properly functioning individuals in clause 2 to be different from the noetic system of the individual in question. This path is a deadend, however. There are too many possible remodeling designs for a house in disrepair to be able to determine what aspects of the house will, or would, be preserved. All we could hope for is some idea of what might remain, and we've already seen why such a weak modality isn't adequate. So even though our exploration of the Quine–Duhem issue found a path to a suitable response by back-door theorists to the particular difficulties raised there, that issue points us to a deeper problem for the back-door theory. That deeper problem is one that full reflection reveals to be insoluble.

There is a better approach to characterizing the nature of defeat. Instead of putting prospective defeaters in the house and seeing what comes out the back door, a better approach is to identify defeaters before they enter the front door. Instead of beginning with noetic structures and beliefs within them, we can begin instead with propositions and what is evidence for them. In a word, the better approach is a propositional rather than a doxastic theory of defeat. On such an approach, the fundamental notion will be the notion of evidence, and the fundamental form of defeat is where the conjunction of e and the defeater is not evidence for p.[19]

Such an approach handles the major problems we've seen here for Plantinga's theory. First, it allows a straightforward account of defeater defeaters. Where dd is a defeater defeater of d, the conjunction of any evidence e conjoined to d does not justify p, but the conjunction of e plus d plus dd yields at least as much justification for p as provided by e itself. Moreover, the Quine–Duhem problem ceases

---

[19] In the text, I ignore the issue of partial defeat, where a defeater lowers the credibility of a claim, but not so much as would require the loss of belief. We will explore these issues more fully in Chapters 2 and 6.

to worry as well, for even if d is a defeater of the $p|e$ relation (where e is the evidence for p), it need not be a defeater of the $p\&r|e$ relation. That allows rational adjustments to a system of beliefs in response to learning d that don't require abandoning p. All learning d requires (on the assumption that there are no restorers present) is that some evidentially suitable adjustment is made, one of which is abandoning p, but not the only one.

This way of proceeding is very much like that of John Pollock's,[20] though there are two important differences. First, he doesn't mention the Quine–Duhem issue and doesn't give a way to accommodate it. Second, his theory takes the relations of evidence and defeat to be relations between mental states rather than relations between the contents of mental states.[21] It is worth noting, however, that Pollock is not consistent on this point. To represent the concept of provisional defeat in his system, Pollock has to represent provisionally defeated conclusions in the system that can play a role in future changes of belief even though they are not believed—to quote, "Thus more than beliefs (undefeated conclusions) must be included in a representation of an agent's epistemological state." ((Pollock and Gillies, 2000, p. 82).) As a result of the need to represent provisionally defeated conclusions, a representation of a person's epistemological state will require representation of contents which play a role in determining the epistemic status of other beliefs. In such a case, there may be no mental state whatsoever with that particular propositional content, and hence no way for Pollock to represent all epistemic relations as relations between mental states.

This difficulty can be avoided by adopting Propositionalism. Pollock and his co-author Anthony Gillies note a problem for this view, however; they say,

Note that this makes the reason-for relation a relation between mental states, not the contents of the mental states. This is important because we reason quite differently from different kinds of mental states with the same content, e.g., the percept of there being something red before me, the desire that there be something red before me, and the belief that there is something red before me. (Pollock and Gillies, 2000, p. 74)

The worry here is that a thorough-going Propositionalism will not be able to explain why a desire that p is not a reason for belief, whereas a belief or experience that p is. This objection is important but not decisive. Here is how we can find an adequate reply to it. A first point to note is that we can distinguish between affective and cognitive states, and note that for the purely cognitive purposes in epistemology, the only kind of reasons that are relevant as a basis for a belief are

---

[20] See Pollock (1986, pp. 38–9).
[21] See Pollock and Gillies (2000). See, especially, p. 74, where they say, "…it must be borne in mind that it is really the beliefs, and not their contents, that are reasons for each other."

going to be cognitive reasons.[22] That still leaves a distinction between belief and experience, and it is a harder matter to say what the difference between these is, even though such a difference there must be (since no belief is a reason for itself and yet an experience of something red is a reason to believe that something is red). Recent work in the theory of consciousness and phenomenal content suggests a possible response, however, in terms of the self-representational character of phenomenal content.[23] On this view, intrinsic to the character of experience is an awareness that one is having the very experience in question, and if that is correct, we can account for how an experience as if p confirms a belief that p via the content of the awareness that is intrinsic to the experience itself without implying that a belief that p also confirms itself. In this way, the confirming power of an experience as if p will differ from the confirming power of a belief that p without having to abandon the Propositionalist view that confirmation is a matter of a relationship between possible contents of mental states rather than the mental states themselves.

Finally, this approach allows an explanation of the defeat of an already unwarranted belief. Such beliefs fall into two categories. The first is where there is some evidence for the belief, but enough counterevidence that the belief is not warranted. In such a case, one can possess a defeater in addition to the counterevidence, a further piece of information which, together with the evidence for the belief, fails to provide a justification or warrant for it. The second case is where there is no evidence at all for the belief. A further piece of information can be a defeater for such an unwarranted belief in several different ways. The primary way would be for the defeater to be evidence against the belief, but it could also be evidence that there are no reliable methods of learning that the belief is true. In either case, the front-door approach has resources that the back-door approach lacks.

The last possibility described earlier made reference to reliable methods and procedures, and it is worth noting that adopting a back-door reliabilist approach in place of Plantinga's back-door proper functionalist approach is not going to help with these problems. Such a reliabilist alternative will identify defeaters with reliable processes or methods whose use would have led to the abandoning of belief. Such an approach will face precisely the difficulties faced by Plantinga's

---

[22] It is worth noting in this context that a desire that p is not itself a reason to believe that one desires that p. Any reason for belief will need to be in terms of experience or belief, and we should explain the case in question as follows: one does have a reason to believe that one desires that p; but it isn't the desire itself, it is rather one's experience of having such a desire. After all, if the desire were subconscious or unconscious, its presence would give no reason for belief at all.

[23] See Uriah Kriegel (2006).

proper functionalist approach: it will have to address the problem of defeater defeaters, and it will have the same difficulties with the Quine–Duhem problem.

It won't help here to talk of reliable indicators rather than reliable processes, either.[24] Such a theory works best when it is a front-door rather than a back-door theory, as can be seen when we ask about the nature of the indicators in question. A front-door approach will take these to be a relationship between some piece of information and a proposition which may or may not be believed. The reliabilist component of the view, then, is simply a requirement that the indicator relationship be a reliable one, i.e., that it generate objective likelihood of truth. The theory could be given a back-door rendering as well: it could be claimed that the notion of a reliable indicator is to be clarified with reference to the proportion or percentage of true beliefs generated by a mechanism or process that takes awareness or belief in the indicator as input. Taken in this way, the reliable indicator theory has all the difficulties of the reliabilist approach cited in the last paragraph.

The lesson to learn is that if one is attracted to a reliabilist approach here, the best option is the front-door, Propositionalist option. The alternative, back-door version shares with Plantinga's account the fundamental problem of beginning with talk of *B* as a belief, trying to characterize defeat in terms of conditions under which a belief would be abandoned. Back-door approaches to the concept of defeat are bound to fail, precisely because of this core.

One final point by way of comparison of the two approaches, is a point especially instructive in the context of Plantinga's epistemological agenda. Some defeaters engender mental apoplexy, since they tell you that something has to be changed, but you can't tell what to change. Call these "paralyzing defeaters." Such was Russell's paradox for Frege regarding his set theory: he knew that something must be changed, but had no idea what to change. Plantinga thinks that something similar plagues the evolutionary naturalist.[25] Plantinga holds that such naturalists have an undefeated defeater for their view, but in order to sustain this conclusion, Plantinga must hold as well that those who understand his argument but do not abandon their view are somehow malfunctioning.

It's easy to see how a Propositionalist account of defeat could reach this conclusion: argue that there is a propositional defeater of which evolutionary naturalists are aware, show that there couldn't be a propositional defeater defeater for this defeater, point out that the evolutionary naturalists have been shown the evidence against their view but remain unpersuaded, and conclude that they must be

---

[24] For an example of such, see John Greco's "Holding Defeat to the Fire," presented at the Pacific meeting of the APA, March 2004.

[25] See Plantinga (1991) and Beilby (2002).

malfunctioning in some way.[26] It is interesting to note that this strategy is strikingly like the one Plantinga follows. Instead of addressing the question of proper functioning directly, his discussion focuses on the issue of whether the content of his argument gives a reason not to believe evolutionary naturalism. Once we see the distinction between front-door and back-door approaches to defeat, and the underlying distinction between Propositionalism and Doxasticism, we can see that Plantinga's actual practices fit well with a Propositionalist approach in spite of his official Doxasticist dogma. His practice shows all the signs of illicitly partaking of propositional fruit here, 'illicit' given the back-door Doxasticism of his official account of defeat.

In any case, the right approach is propositional, whether or not Plantinga is implicitly relying on one. This result is bad news for Doxasticists, since now they cannot remain Doxasticists and include the concept of defeat in their epistemological theory.

1.6 Conclusion

Our investigation into the syntactical, semantic, and logico-metaphysical status of epistemic appraisal has generated a pleasing result, the result that there is no basis in this arena for insisting that the language of epistemic appraisal must resort to ambiguity even prior to epistemological theory construction. As we have seen, there is an argument for the view that epistemic appraisal is fundamentally propositional and that other forms of epistemic appraisal can be understood in these terms.

This result is pleasing in another way, for one of the unfortunate developments in philosophy over the past century has been the separation between confirmation theory in the philosophy of science and the theory of epistemic appraisal in the theory of knowledge. This break is not surprising, for as specialization proliferates, generalists in the discipline—those who speak to multiple specialties—tend to decrease. So as philosophy of science came into its own, those who work on the theory of confirmation within the philosophy of science tended to generate their own community of inquiry, separate from that in general epistemology. One implication of the defense of Propositionalism presented here is that this break is not insurmountable, for the theory of confirmation has always been addressed to the question of which propositions, theories, and hypotheses

---

[26] I should note that my discussion of the strategy of the argument is not meant to be an endorsement of the argument or its conclusion. Those are topics for another day and time, so I will do no more than register my opinion that the argument fails and the conclusion drawn is false.

are best supported by the information available to us. In short, Propositionalism offers the best option available for seeing the theory of confirmation and the theory of epistemic appraisal as two sides of the same coin, which they surely are.

We turn then, in the following chapters, to the epistemological project itself, the project of constructing a value-driven theory concerning the fundamental egocentric predicament concerning what to do and what to think. The assurance of the present chapter is that there is no pre-theoretical basis in the syntax, semantics, or logico-metaphysical basis of epistemic appraisal that bars such a theory from speaking with a single voice.

2

The Egocentric Predicament and Normativity

2.1 Introduction

As noted already, our project begins within the arena of the fundamental human concern involved in the egocentric predicament. We often cannot tell what to do or think, what to be or become. When we begin investigating the non-descriptive aspects of reality, we can do no better than to begin with such fundamental concerns and the realities that arise out of these concerns. Our task in this chapter is to see how to carve out a normative domain that is motivated in terms of this fundamental concern.

2.2 A Double Double-Aspect Approach

When we consider the perplexity we all face at times about what to do or think, we begin by carving what is descriptive from what isn't. Such a perplexity involves noticing that what we actually do and what we actually think can't relieve our perplexity. We start, not from the world as we find it, but in the hope of something else.

Yet, as soon as we distinguish the descriptive from the non-descriptive, we notice immediately two non-descriptive features. What would be nice is to have a theory that always gives an answer that would resolve our perplexity, but one that honors the platitude that such a resolution is always relative to the perspective of the individual in question. So, for example, if I leave the airport knowing that there are two routes home, and resolve my perplexity in favor of the one that I know from experience is typically a few minutes faster, things still might not go well: the wreck on the chosen route might leave me stranded in traffic for three hours. While sitting there, I might begin kicking myself mentally: shoulda gone the other way. But such thoughts, while understandable, do not honor the perspectivality platitude. They are mistaken. It is simply not true that I should have gone the other way, though it would have been better if I had. If I had known of the wreck, then it would make sense to kick myself in this way. But I didn't know.

What the example shows is that there are two non-descriptive features to attend to. One is the feature of how to resolve the perplexity concerning what to do or think in a way that turns out *best*, and a second is a way to resolve the perplexity in a way that gives the perspectival platitude its due. For simplicity, I'll identify the former as the evaluative dimension and the latter as the normative dimension. When we face the egocentric predicament, we seek a solution in terms of the normative dimension, in hopes that the solution will also match a solution in terms of the evaluative dimension. We do so because we can do nothing less if we wish to give the perspectivality platitude its due.

Why such a role for this platitude? The story here is value-driven as well. When considering the egocentric predicament, it is important to notice two different ways of kicking ourselves after the fact. We always aim to resolve any perplexity in terms of what is best, and kick ourselves when we fail; but sometimes in the midst of the kicking is the realization that our failure to achieve the best is fully excusable because fully rational in terms of the right way to go about addressing the perplexity we face concerning what to do and think. We didn't know better and perhaps couldn't have known better—and understanding why this excuse is a full one is precisely what is involved in giving proper recognition to the perspectival character of an adequate resolution of the perplexity in question.

An alternative story here resorts to multiplicity immediately, identifying the normative dimension with the evaluative, demanding that the right thing to do is the best thing to do, and then introducing another non-descriptive dimension in order to explain the role of adequate excuses for normative failures. On such a view, taking the route in question is wrong, but excusable nonetheless. Such a position is best avoided at this point. When we face the perplexity in question, we want a theory to speak with a single voice. We don't want a theory that says, "It was wrong to take the route you actually took, but fully excusable." There are two reasons to resist at this point. First, what is needed is a final answer, spoken from a single voice. An answer that says, "There is no single answer: there are just different dimensions of non-descriptive evaluation to be found here. When in such a situation, whatever you do will be negatively evaluated along one dimension at least." Such a theory is not what we need from a theory designed in terms of the predicament in question. So we should resist it at the outset, even if we succumb to it at the end.

Moreover, it is a perplexing remark as a piece of advice to be told: "You should do X, but it would be fully excusable not to do X." What are we to make of such advice? If the first conjunct is true, there is no need for the second. And the fact that the second conjunct seems forced on us in such contexts should give us pause about the first conjunct, once we notice the difference between the quite different dimensions of the non-descriptive, the evaluative, and the normative. Confusion between these two dimensions leads to the vapid advice of a banal investment joke: buy low, sell high. As soon as we are sensitive to the difference between the evaluative and the normative, we can understand the perplexing advice. The first remark responds to the evaluative dimension, and the second to the normative dimension. In such a case, however, we should resist the inclination to use normative language regarding the evaluative dimension: if doing X is best, we should prefer that description to one that conflates what is best with what is required. We should do so, at least at this point in our inquiry, since we are trying to avoid responses to the predicament in question that involve cacophony. And there is a straightforward way to explain the situation while avoiding cacophony: the advisor knows more than the advisee, and there is a perspective shift between the conjuncts. From the perspective of the advisee, before input from the advisor, the fully justified course of action is not to do X, but once the perspective of the advisor is taken into account, the fully justified course of action is to do X. After all, once you know that doing X is best, it is the right thing to do. But we can affirm that link between the evaluative and the normative without endangering our need for a theory that speaks with a single voice regarding the normative dimension itself.

So the first element in our theory is to respect the difference between the evaluative and the normative, acknowledging this important double aspect regarding the non-descriptive features of reality. Regarding the normative dimension in question, we notice a further double aspect to it. We are immersed in the egocentric predicament at every conscious moment of our lives, and occasionally notice it and experience perplexity regarding it. For those who think of human rationality as exceptional from the rest of the natural order, it is tempting to identify the first experience as one we share with the beasts, which involves cognitive responses to our environment resulting from impingement on the senses and the adaptive responses we develop as we mature. The second, one might proclaim, is what is distinctive about humans: they reflect on their situation, they display not only consciousness but self-consciousness. They recognize their animal natures, and notice also that the rationality of beasts does not always result in what is best, and so we reflect, trying to improve our success rate in responding to what we observe. A full understanding of normativity will attend to both of these dimensions, the beastly as well as the reflective, the normative dimension involved in consciousness itself and that involved in self-consciousness.

I mention human exceptionalism not to endorse it but to use it to illustrate the way in which a two-dimensional approach to normativity is well motivated by the varieties of conscious beings who face the predicament in question. Nothing about the resulting theory relies on human exceptionalism, and that is a good thing, since to my mind at least, such exceptionalism is unjustified by what we know about the minds and behavior of animals. Since this is an essay in epistemology rather than cognitive ethology, however, I won't pursue these issues here but rather return to our focus on epistemic normativity itself.

Each dimension of normativity raises its own problems for theory construction. The primary difficulty in understanding the first dimension, what I am terming "the beastly dimension," is whether rational sense can be made of it. Let me explain. It is clear that there is causal interaction between human organisms and their environment, and it is also clear that this causal interaction prompts certain patterns of response in human beings, both in terms of action and in terms of cognition. For the time being, let us think of cognitive responses in terms of belief: our responses to sensory input include patterns of belief formation and sustenance. How are we to understand this connection? Perhaps we can do no better than to employ the language of dispositions: upon causal interaction involving a given sensory input, the organism in question is disposed to form or sustain a belief with a given content.

Such an approach makes no rational sense of the interaction, providing no intelligible link between the inputs and outputs. On such a story, if one's sensory appearance is that of a Bengal tiger, we have no story as to why believing there is a Bengal tiger near is an appropriate doxastic response as opposed to believing something else, other than to say that nature has so designed us that we are disposed toward the latter on the basis of the former. Such a story provides an *explanation* of the interaction, but does not make the connection between the two *intelligible*: from the point of view of the agent forming the belief in question, the mechanisms involved are impenetrable black boxes. There is no specific story as to why believing there is a Bengal tiger near is an appropriate response to the sensory input in question. There may be a *general* story of why this is appropriate. For example, perhaps it is part of a divine design plan for human beings that they respond in this way, or perhaps the presence of such disposition in our ancestors is part of the explanation of why they enjoyed reproductive success enough for us to exist. But these stories are not specific stories. They do not point to some connection between the individual appearance state in question and the particular resultant belief content that explains why that very belief content is appropriate to that specific appearance state, an explanation that makes it intelligible or understandable why that very belief content is a fitting, or the fitting, response to that precise appearance state.

The first part of the theory of normativity involves an exploration of this topic of natural rationality, but regardless of the conclusions arrived at, there is a deep perplexity facing any theory of natural rationality. If we suppose we can find a specific account that makes understandable why some beliefs are more fitting in a given circumstance than other beliefs, there is still the possibility of the organism in question reflecting on the situation in question and coming to the conclusion that a different belief is better in those circumstances. Such an organism may even engage in cognitive training, so that believing something else becomes a habit. If all we have is a theory of natural rationality, we must conclude that such an organism is believing irrationally, in spite of following the light of reason as best it can. In short, in addition to a theory that accommodates the beastly dimension, we also need a theory that accommodates the reflective dimension.

In schematic terms, the dilemma is this. The theory of rationality, if wholly constituted by the theory of natural rationality, yields rules for what to believe under what circumstances. Yet, one of the distinctive features of human rationality is the ability to reflect, and among the things we reflect on are the rules that guide us. Among the things we learn about are not only the features of the universe we inhabit, but the features of our own cognitive systems and how their functioning might be improved. But if the theory of natural rationality is theory enough, it is hard to avoid attributing irrationality to a large part of our reflective pursuits, since they often lead us to view our natural response styles as inappropriate and best replaced by more sophisticated response styles. Moreover, the theory will have the egregious defect of failing to recognize that among the things we learn about, are things concerning how to improve our success rates in interacting with our environment. In short, we need some notion of the rules of rationality that isn't completely rigid, but rather allows an initial set of rules to be replaced by more sophisticated ones as we adapt our approaches to the egocentric predicament on the basis of our personal and corporate etiologies.

One way to think about this double aspect of normative evaluation is in terms of finding a middle way between two extremes. One is where intellectualism reigns, thinking that rationality involves the kind of reflective deliberation distinctive of only some of our rational behavior. The other extreme discounts reflection, maintaining that all of rationality is just like the animal sort.

2.3 A Sketch of Double-Aspect Rules of Rationality

We begin with a characterization of the beastly dimension of rules of rationality. At a highly abstract level, the story of rationality is a function of four items: *conferrers, enablers, targets,* and *epistemic operators.* Each specific theory of rationality will fill in the substance of what each of these items involves, but we may begin here with what is common to them all. These four items function in the conditionals that constitute the epistemic principles in a theory of epistemic normativity. Here are a couple of examples of such principles with each of the items identified in terms of these four items:

- If S is appeared to F-ly without grounds for doubt,
  <u>conferrer</u>   <u>enabler</u>
  then it is reasonable for S to believe that something is F.
  <u>operator</u>   <u>target</u>

- If S's senses report that p and
  <u>conferrer</u>
  no defeater exists for the connection of this report to p,
  <u>enabler</u>
  then S is in a position to know that p.
  <u>operator</u>   <u>target</u>

Conferrers are what Roderick Chisholm termed the "substrates" of epistemic appraisal (Chisholm, 1991, p. 122). They are potential bases of a cognitive attitude toward the target proposition. As potential bases, it is important to note that conferrers in such epistemic principles must be thought of atomistically rather than holistically, since it would make a theory objectionable to require, for example, that a belief be based on everything epistemically relevant to its normative status.

The concept of basing just employed in this point is not a feature of the epistemic principles themselves, but rather a feature of the full theory of epistemic normativity. The principles give us the theoretical underpinning for a properly conducted intellectual life, and the full theory requires not only the presence of such underpinning but a psychological realization of the relationships so described as well. An intellectual life fully adequate in terms of this normative dimension is an intellectual life in which the mental states in question are held because of, or on the basis of, conferrers of such adequacy. The theory of basing doesn't require, of course, that the total basis of belief involve only the conferrers, and it doesn't require either that a belief is based on every conferrer that is available in a given set of circumstances. But the details of the theory of proper basing can be left for a later time, since our focus here is on epistemic normativity itself rather than on what types of psychological realization are needed.

The enabling condition is a function of two ideas: diminution of degree of rational support and defeat of rational support. There is a level of rational support offered to the target proposition by the conferrer of rational support, and the enabling condition tells us that there are no diminutives significant enough to surpass the threshold that turns a diminutive into a defeater.

Epistemic principles require such an enabling condition precisely for the reason that normative adequacy is a defeasible, non-monotonic affair. If the potential bases of belief were factors that could not be undermined by additional information, there would be no need for an enabling condition, since once present, such indefeasible grounds would always make for normative adequacy. Any remotely realistic epistemology, however, must recognize that the information on which we come to see the world as we do is capable of being undermined or defeated by further learning, hence requiring the presence of enabling conditions in the epistemic principles involved in a correct theory of normative adequacy.

It is also worth noting that the enabling condition will have to be hierarchical in structure, to accommodate the point that a given defeater of the support provided to the target by the conferrer may itself be overridden by further information. The resulting enabling condition will thus require that there is a stopping point in the hierarchy at which the absence of diminutives sufficient to defeat is not itself overridden by any further information. The example principles given earlier make no mention of this hierarchy, requiring that they be modified to accommodate it in order to have any hope of being correct.

The epistemic operator, as already remarked, sets an upper bound on the level of rational support available for the target, given the conferrer. Among the epistemic principles or norms that a theory is built out of, some will specify the complete absence of diminutives in their enabling conditions, and it is relative to these principles that the upper bound is set. Other principles will involve the same conferrer with the presence of some diminutives. Depending on how fine-grained the theory is regarding types of epistemic operators, different stories will result. For theories that are rather coarse-grained regarding epistemic operators, the conferrer in the absence of diminutives may connect to the same epistemic operator as the conferrer in the presence of some diminutives (so long as the diminutives in question do not cross the threshold for becoming defeaters). For other theories, a more fine-grained approach will be used, so that when a diminutive is present together with the conferrer, a weaker epistemic operator will need to be used in order for the norm to be correct.

Two examples from the literature may help to clarify this latter point. Chisholm's work in epistemology is an example of the former approach, while probabilists are examples of the latter approach. Chisholm's most elaborate vision contained six epistemic operators: something's being certain, being evident, being beyond reasonable doubt, being acceptable, having some presumption in its favor, and being counterbalanced. These levels are generated from the coarse-grained psychological attitudes that Chisholm employs in his epistemology:

believing, disbelieving, and withholding. So, for example, something is beyond reasonable doubt just when believing it is preferable to withholding; something is acceptable if and only if it is not the case that withholding is preferable to believing; and something has some presumption in its favor just in case believing it is preferable to disbelieving it (Chisholm, 1977).

For probabilists, the degree of support generated for a proposition can be measured on a scale from zero to one inclusive, in a way that satisfies, e.g., the Kolmogorov axioms. In such a case, we will have as many unique operators available to a theory as real numbers between zero and one.

For present purposes, we need not pursue the issue of whether one should prefer a fine-grained rather than a coarse-grained approach to epistemic operators. For the central point about their role in epistemic norms or principles is just this: they set an upper bound on the degree of support a given conferrer is capable of generating for a given target proposition. This level of support can be diminished or defeated, but not enhanced by anything implicated in the enabling condition. A symmetrical point holds as well when considering normative improprieties: a given source of impropriety will set an upper bound on the degree of impropriety, a degree that can be diminished or defeated by an analog of the enabling condition, but never enhanced by it.

The theory of epistemic normativity is thus constituted by a complete set of epistemic principles or norms, but is not itself a norm. Nor is there some über-norm to be found in the theory, a norm that itself summarizes the implications of what all the more specific norms say. The reason here is that the norms are built out of that which is cognition-guiding, containing in their antecedents potential bases of belief. The explanation for thinking about rationality in this way is, again, *value-driven*: we want an understanding of what to think and what to do that answers to our egocentric predicament of needing guidance regarding what to do and what to think. It is this crucial *guidance function* that the theory of fundamental norms or principles answers to. In spite of no existence of such an über-norm, we still get a complete theory here, one which summarizes what all the norms say, and includes a closure clause that there are no other ways to achieve epistemic propriety other than by reference to the norms.

It is worth noting the resources this approach has for dealing with the notion of excusability. Recall that earlier I was hostile to a call for multiplicity in the theory of normativity, where that multiplicity allowed for a belief to be irrational and yet excusable. The hostility arises out of a need for a theory that speaks with a single voice, and the theory as presented so far has abundant resources for explaining the notion of excusability without resorting to multiplicity. Irrationality, on this present approach, involves either the *violation* of a specific norm (as when the conferrer and enabler conditions are satisfied, and one believes the denial of the target), or *failure to conform* to a specific norm (as when one withholds or takes no attitude at all when the conferrer and enabler conditions are satisfied), or when one's circumstances fail to provide a ground for any attitude whatsoever and one takes one anyway. Given this background, degree of irrationality is, at first pass, a function of two things. The first involves the distance between one's attitude and the level of epistemic support for p. The second requires an additional measure on the difference between withholding and taking no attitude, when there is support for a withholding that involves pure indifference between p and $\sim p$. We also need a third measure here, but providing it is a bit more difficult, and I'll bypass it here. We need a measure of irrationality involved in taking the attitude of pure indifference when there are no grounds for taking any attitude whatsoever toward the target proposition. How to provide such a measure isn't clear, but this issue needn't detain us. The details can be worked out when the schema developed here is turned into a full-blown theory. What is important to note, instead, is that the role of diminutives in the theory allows a fine-grained account of excuses. One's level of irrationality has an upper bound set by the analog of a conferrer of rationality, and excuses can arise in the form of both diminutives and defeaters. In the former case, one's level of irrationality is diminished, and in the latter, it can be eliminated altogether. The result here is pleasing for those thinking that we need a theory of excuses. We do, and the schema shows how: when the prima facie irrationality of a given belief is diminished by some factor, we have a first type of excusing condition; and when the diminution is strong enough that it constitutes a defeater, the belief is excusable.

We might say, in such cases, that the belief in question is both irrational and excusable. But it is not ultima facie, or all-epistemic-things-considered both excusable and irrational. Instead, it is only prima facie, or pro tanto, irrational and not ultima facie or all-epistemic-things-considered irrational (because excusable).

To find a need for some independent notion of excusability, we would need to find a reason to think that excusability can be a function of something that cannot be explained in terms of diminishers and defeaters. We shall see such a reason in the next section, and it is a reason intimately linked to the need for a second aspect in the theory of epistemic normativity. Discussion of it is thus best done in the next section.

For the present, then, we can conclude the following: these resources give us an initial glimpse into the nature of epistemic propriety in beastly incarnations, one compatible with an insistence that a theory adequate to the demands of the egocentric predicament is a theory capable of speaking with a single voice. It is also a view that does not, by its very characterization, render the beastly dimension of rationality incapable of providing the requisite intelligibility between input and output. As noted earlier, the challenge for an account of the beastly dimension of rationality is how to describe it in such a way that from the point of view of the cognizer, the mechanisms of belief formation can be something more than mere black boxes characterizable only in terms of inputs and outputs.

But the schematic nature of the characterization in question of epistemic principles does not, by itself, sustain the demands of intelligibility here: such sustenance requires argumentation showing that the hope in question is actually defensible. The fundamental problem here concerns the role that experience plays in the story of rationality, and the tension between allowing experience its proper role while at the same time insisting that fundamental evidential relationships are content-based. I take up that issue in the following section, and the result I aim to achieve is a limited defense of Propositionalism about evidential support, to the effect that allowing experience to play an appropriate role in the theory of rationality does not present an irresolvable difficulty and allows for an understanding of the beastly dimension of rationality that leaves room for the intelligibility of the connection between evidential input and doxastic output, intelligibility from the point of view of cognizers themselves.

2.3.1 A defense of Propositionalism about evidence

To begin to see the problem caused for Propositionalism by allowing experience to play a role in the theory of justification, consider the propositional account of doxastic justification:

S's belief that p is doxastically justified iff (I) S believes that p; (II) S has evidence for *p* sufficient for justifying the claim that p; and (III) S's belief that p is properly based on S's evidence for *p*.

This definition counts as a version of Propositionalism because the fundamental items that are justified or not are propositions. To complete the story of justification, we need to know something of what occupies the other position in the relation of justification. There is the thing which is justified—a proposition—and the things which justify. To have a full Propositionalist theory, one would expect the following story about the things that justify: the things that justify are one's evidence; to have evidence is to be in relevant mental states such as the state of believing or the state of experiencing; but what it is for one thing to be evidence for another is a relationship between contents of possible mental states rather than being in the mental states themselves. So a fully propositional theory of justification will endorse not only the earlier account of doxastic justification in terms of propositional justification, but will also endorse the claim that:

All evidence is propositional evidence.

But why think that? Shouldn't we think that some evidence is propositional and some evidence isn't? Sometimes information exists that provides a sound argument for a claim; in such a case, the evidence for the claim may perhaps be thought to be propositional. Other times, the evidence doesn't fit well with the argument model, but instead arises in the form of experience. Worse yet, why think that when the argument model is appropriate, the evidence is propositional? Why not think, for example, that sometimes one's evidence is in the form of beliefs and sometimes in the form of experiences?

Let's start with the last question, the question about whether the evidence is best conceived in terms of beliefs and experiences rather than propositions. At one level, the claim is correct—the evidence you have is either in the form of beliefs or experiences, but that point doesn't undermine the Propositionalism I'm proposing. If we put experiences to the side for the moment, we need to ask what makes a particular belief evidence for whatever it is that it is evidence for. It is here that Propositionalism has the right answer. If you believe p, and that belief is evidence for q, which you may or may not believe, it is evidence for q in virtue of its content. So the straightforward answer is this: the having of evidence will certainly need to be understood in terms of mental states such as believing and experiencing, but the existence of evidence, what it is for there to be evidence for a given claim, need not be understood in terms of the mental state of believing but rather in terms of the content of a possible mental state. The important point is that the evidence one has is in the form of beliefs only when the content of the belief is itself evidence for certain claims and not for other claims. To have evidence is to have beliefs or experiences; to be evidence is, according to the propositionalist, to be a proposition.

Granting this point turns our focus to the other difficulty facing a fully Propositionalist theory, the difficulty of what to say about the role of experience in the story of justification. The problem a full Propositionalism faces here is much more difficult than the problem of what to say about the role of beliefs in the theory of justification. It is, however, central to the project of explaining the intelligibility of the link between evidence and what it is evidence for, for without such an account, we are left with the black box story, where input might explain outputs but not in a way that is intelligible from the point of view of cognizers themselves.

The difficulty experience presents for this account is, in large part, a matter of coming to grips with Sellars' Problem.[1] We can put this problem in the form of a dilemma. Either experience has propositional content or it does not. If it does not, then it cannot justify a belief. If that point is not compelling in itself, and it is not, it is compelling here, since the justificatory relation demanded by the present version of Propositionalism needs to render the truth of supported beliefs intelligible to the believer. But how could an experience generate intelligibility unless experiences have content? Without an appeal to content, all we have is some mindless mechanism of belief production, to which Father God or Mother Nature appends some feeling or sense of intelligible truth of belief. Such a story makes intelligibility an extrinsic feature of the justificatory connection between evidence and belief, but that is precisely what we don't want. The value of justification over true belief (and especially in the context of perplexity concerning what to think and do) is not a matter of such extrinsic appurtenances, but rather something intrinsic to the evidential relation between experience and belief.

The other horn of the dilemma, however, claims that if experience has propositional content, then it must be adjudged in some normative terminology before passing scrutiny for purposes of generating justification for belief. For example, suppose you are appeared to elephant-ly. In some circumstances, such an experience is fully appropriate to your circumstances (e.g., when there is an elephant in full view) and passes scrutiny for the capacity to justify a belief. But, Sellars' Problem would have it, not always. If you have that experience while focusing intently on the words of this sentence, you're a cognitive mess and your experience can't take you any way down the road from true belief to knowledge even if in fact you find you're appeared to elephant-ly and there really is an elephant in the room.

There are mistakes in this argument, but also a serious challenge. One mistake is in the claim that we won't get an adequate theory of knowledge if we let abnormal experiences of the truly clinical variety count as evidence. That point would be correct if we didn't have additional filters on what gets justified and which justified beliefs count as knowledge, but we do have such filters.

Experience doesn't automatically render a belief justified, since the evidence provided by experience must not be undermined by internal defeaters. Moreover, even when it is not undermined by internal defeaters, it may be undermined by external (non-misleading) defeaters, and hence not be a candidate for knowledge. So there is no particular reason to be found here for insisting that we sort experiences into those that provide evidence and those that do not.

---

[1] The *locus classicus* of this problem can be found in Sellars (1956).

In addition, even if the argument were correct that experiences are going to have to be sorted into those that have confirming power and those that do not, it is not clear that this point has any direct implications for Propositionalism. In the context of attempting to solve the regress problem regarding justification, the challenge from this horn of Sellars' Problem is central and unavoidable. But Propositionalism itself has no dog in this fight. A Propositionalist of the pure variety maintains that anything that justifies has propositional content, but the view certainly does not require that everything with propositional content has confirming power. So if some experiences lack that power, Propositionalism itself is not threatened.

Even given these points, however, there is still a challenge here. If we've reached the conclusion that experiences are evidence for belief only if they have content, the question is how to sustain this view and what the content might be. That there must be some relationship of content between experience and belief is required if we attend carefully to the lessons of the following example. We can call it the case of Hume and the missing shade of blue. Hume has never had an experience of the missing shade of blue, and has developed the following dispositions in every color experience he has. He always notices both the color in question and the distinction between it and the missing shade of blue, fascinated as he is with the fact that he has seen all colors except this one. So he is reliably disposed, tracks the truth in virtue of stable dispositions, functions properly in forming his beliefs, and satisfies any other non-content-based requirement one might wish to impose in the theory of justification, to the following effect: to believe that the object is the particular color it is perceived to be and in addition to believe that the object is not the missing shade of blue. After years and years of so believing conjointly, Hume finally encounters the missing shade of blue. What is the rational thing for him to believe? One thing is that the object in question is blue, but if he forms a rational belief involving the concept of the missing shade of blue, it had better not be the belief that this is not the missing shade of blue. His experience undermines the rationality of that belief. So he needs to form the belief, if he forms one, that the object is the missing shade of blue. What explains this distinction? It can only be something about the content of his experience. No information about truth-tracking, reliability dispositions, recognition skills, and the like that fails to advert to the content of the experience can explain why Hume should believe that he has finally found the missing shade of blue.

Even so, there's a further challenge, brought up already in the previous chapter. It is the Pollock challenge, and it is the difficulty of explaining why the very same content under different mental attitudes can't function to make rational a belief. For example, believing that Joe is married may be a reason to believe that

Joe is not a bachelor, but hoping that Joe is married isn't. If evidence is merely propositional, why is the having of evidence limited to what one believes and experiences?

A first point to note is that we can distinguish between affective and cognitive states, and note that for the purely cognitive purposes in epistemology, the only kind of reasons that are relevant as a basis for a belief are going to be cognitive reasons, ones for which the direction of fit runs from world to mind. Since epistemology is about successful, admirable connections between mind and world, where the direction of fit is of this sort, we have good grounds for ruling out other mental states as capable of providing reasons for belief when their direction of fit is otherwise. Hence, hopes and fears don't provide epistemic reasons for belief since they are affective states; beliefs and experiences provide such reasons because they are cognitive states.

Even so, a problem remains, since the evidentiary role of experience differs from that of belief. The simplest reason why is that the former is evidence for the latter, but the latter is not evidence for itself. So even once we have reached the present point of needing to find content in experiences that are capable of justifying, Pollock's challenge is still threatening since we must distinguish the justificatory role of a given content depending on how it is encoded mentally.

Recent work in the theory of consciousness and phenomenal content suggests a possible response, however, in terms of the self-representational character of phenomenal content.[2] On this view, intrinsic to the character of experience is an awareness of the very experience itself in addition to the outward awareness of the primary focus of the awareness. Consider the following expression of the idea:

> Suppose, for instance, that you suddenly hear a distant bagpipe. In your auditory experience of the bagpipe you are aware primarily, or explicitly, of the bagpipe sound; but you are also implicitly aware that this auditory experience of the bagpipe is your experience. That is, you are aware of yourself as the subject of experience.[3]

Notice that, as described, the experience of hearing is accompanied by an awareness of the experience as one's own. Moreover, the awareness of self has a particular content to it: it is an awareness of the self as "the subject of the experience in question." Of course, that is an external description of the awareness, meant to describe in general terms a phenomenon that has particular instances involving more particular descriptions. It is not intended to be a particular description that a given individual would give to himself or herself in the experiencing itself.

---

[2] Kriegel (2006).   [3] Kriegel (2003).

Perhaps we can capture the particularity of each by saying that it is an indexical awareness of oneself as the subject of this very experience. That is, the content of the awareness includes an essentially indexical awareness of the state itself.

It is this indexical character of experience, tying any conscious awareness indexically both to the existence of the individual having the experience and indexically to the very experience itself, that provides the type of content useful for a defense of Propositionalism. I cannot undertake here a defense of this approach to the nature of conscious experience, so in an important sense I do not offer it as a full solution to Pollock's challenge. Instead, the defense of Propositionalism here presented should perhaps be stated in conditional form: if the self-representing account of conscious experience can be defended, Propositionalism can be adequately developed so that the fundamental relationships of evidence in the theory of justification are relations between propositional contents.

A conscious experience, on this self-representational approach, is representational, making one aware primarily of the (typically external) object of awareness but secondarily of oneself as the subject of the experience. The full experience is thus a composite entity, including a representation R involved in the focal awareness in question, and an indexical awareness R* that includes R as a component in virtue of the fact that R* involves an indexical reference to itself that includes R. In virtue of this indexical character of R*, the content which is R* is propositional content, involving the following elements: R itself, the subject of the experience, and the total content of the experience R*. The content in question implies that an experience involving R is occurring in this very subject in virtue of this very R* experience. R* is thus evidence for a number of claims, including the claim that something exists having the character specified in R, that the subject of the experience exists, and that the subject in question is having the very experience which is the secondary focus specified in R*.

When R* is encoded in an actual experience of the relevant individual, the description of the case changes from there being evidence for such claims to the having of evidence for such claims. But what happens when R* is encoded in the form of belief? Must we say that the person in question has evidence then as well for the claims in question?

The answer is "no." There are two ways to conceive of R*. Perhaps R* intrinsically and essentially involves the experiential modality because of its self-referential character. Perhaps, that is, R* cannot itself be encoded in the form of a belief because it cannot be encoded in any mental state other than an experiential one because of its self-referential character. How could this be? one might ask. How could the content limit, metaphysically, possible encodings? I'm not sure it can, but here is a possible line of reasoning to that conclusion. In order for a belief to involve R^* in any way, the person in question will have to change focus. Recall that an experience having R^* as content involves a primary focus on R and a distal focus on the self as the subject of the experience. Perhaps in order to form a belief involving R^*, one would have to bring into primary focus the self-referential aspect specified in R^*, and in so doing will form a belief, not with content R^*, but with the content that R^* is the content of one of his or her experiences. So it may be plausible to maintain that the particular content R^* simply cannot be the content of a belief but can only be the content of an experience.

Perhaps this line of reasoning is correct, but I remain skeptical of it. Even if this line of reasoning is mistaken, however, so that R^* can be the content of a belief, the belief will be utterly incoherent. It will involve the obvious absurdity of confusing a belief and an experience. It will be a belief to the effect that this very experiencing is occurring in me, and the having of such a belief is a state of utter confusion and incoherence. In such a case, the propositionalist is under no requirement of treating the person in question as having evidence that includes R^*. Just because the evidence one has is in the form of experiences and beliefs is no reason for thinking that every belief one has is part of the evidence one possesses. It is typical in the theory of justification to insist that one cannot arrive at a further justified belief by inferring from premises that are irrational for one to believe, even if in fact one believes them. Given the obvious absurdity of the belief in question, there is no need for the propositionalist to hold that it is among the evidence one has, and in such a case R^* will be explanatorily otiose in the justificatory status of any claim for the person in question.

Whether such an approach to the theory of justification can be sustained has not been settled by these considerations, but that has not been my goal. The goal instead is to show that Propositionalism does not succumb in any immediate way to the fact that evidence comes in the form of both experiences and beliefs. The earlier appeal to a purported self-representational character in the content of experience is one way to address Pollock's challenge, but not the only one. Another is to endorse the view that an experience with content p and a belief with the same content are states containing precisely the same evidence. What is different about the two states is to be understood in terms of a restriction on the nature of evidence or on proper basing. One might insist, first, that one can't properly base a belief on itself (that would be epistemically circular) and experiences aren't appraisable epistemically so are neither properly nor improperly based. On this approach, then, a belief with content p is a belief in something for which there is evidence (namely, p) and it is evidence one has, but the belief can only be doxastically justified by the evidence one has when it is properly based on that evidence.

Alternatively, one might claim that the evidence one has is to be characterized in terms of a relation between two propositions (the evidence and what it is evidence for) and two types of mental state, where the latter two cannot be identical when the former two are identical. In such a case, the belief *p* is not evidence one has for itself.

One other option is worth presenting, since it has much to recommend it outside of epistemology. When addressing the problem of cognitive significance, it is difficult to avoid a Fregean conclusion that requires of mental states such as belief of both a propositional content and a mode of presentation (for argumentation to this effect, see Salmon (1989)). Moreover, there are reasons for thinking that modes of presentation are themselves semantic entities, as Frege held. They, for example, figure into explanations of action in just the way that semantic content typically figures into such explanations. Consider Hume and Heimsohn, both believing that Hume is hungry and Heimsohn is hungry, but only Hume believing of himself that he is hungry. The difference here, on the Fregean story, is one of mode of presentation, and the modes of presentation help explain why Hume feeds himself and not Heimsohn, and why Heimsohn feeds no one. Such a role in the explanation of behavior mirrors precisely the role that content plays when we explain Hume's raising an objection to Descartes that Heimsohn does not raise: Hume is characterized by a doxastic state with a propositional content involving some mistake in Descartes, while Heimsohn is not. Moreover, such an understanding of the Fregean position underlies attempts to give a two-dimensional semantics of the sort defended in Chalmers (2012), and such approaches give the propositionalist another possible way of replying to Pollock's challenge. For the mode of presentation, however construed, must be different for a belief that p and an experience as if p, and when semantically construed, this difference in mode of presentation can explain why the *relata* for the evidence relation need not involve beliefs and experiences themselves. Of course, that which does the justifying will have to be understood slightly differently than what has been stated so far, for it won't itself be a proposition. But as I pointed out in footnote 3 of Chapter 1, the discussion here glosses over the distinction between propositions and full semantic content needed for addressing the problem of cognitive significance. We can thus take it as a friendly amendment to Propositionalism to understand it in the more sophisticated guise of full semantic content, since the divide between doxasticists and propositionalists is a divide between the abstract and concrete realms, and not one between two varieties of semantic content that might be invoked to explain the fundamental items of epistemic appraisal.

There are thus several options available to a full Propositionalism for addressing Pollock's challenge, and we need not view that challenge as presenting an insurmountable obstacle for the view. By endorsing full Propositionalism, we can give an account of the beastly dimension of rationality that preserves the desired intelligibility from the cognizer's own point of view for how evidential inputs make rational certain doxastic outputs. What remains, then, is the other aspect of epistemic propriety, which concerns epistemic propriety under conditions of deliberate reflection on one's circumstances and the norms involved in epistemic appraisal.

2.4 Reflective Dimensions of Rationality

2.4.1 *The formal picture*

We begin with the formal structure of views that accommodate the double-aspect nature of epistemic normativity, addressing later the challenge that no such accommodation should be made. A theory that accommodates the second aspect begins from a base level with the kinds of principles described earlier involving conferrers, enablers, epistemic operators, and targets. When reflection occurs, however, different epistemic principles become involved in the explanation of the propriety of belief. An example of such a principle, with the relevant new element in its antecedent involving the level of reflective ascent achieved, is:

If

- S's senses report that p,
  <u>conferrer</u>
- under level of reflection n linking p and q,
  <u>ascent level</u>
  where n is the highest level of reflection achieved, and
  <u>ascent limit</u>
- no defeater exists for the connection of this report to q,
  <u>enabler</u>

then

- it is rational for S to believe that q.
  <u>operator</u>   <u>target</u>

   The idea that such principles accommodate is that rational agents can come to reflect on their situation, both about the information available to them and its significance. In the process of maturation, one not only acquires additional information but learns what to make of it as well. In learning what to make of the information available, whatever base level epistemic principles might have explained the propriety of belief no longer do so (so long as reflective ascent has the kind of rational significance we are at present assuming).

We can think of the process in question as follows. People do not ordinarily reflect in terms of the actual norms that govern their situation, but instead on an abstraction of such. They use and reflect on what I will call epistemic conditionals. We define an acceptable base-level epistemic conditional as the (ordinary, indicative) conditional we get when an epistemic norm is stripped of its enabling clause and epistemic operator, when in a situation in which the enabling condition is satisfied and the epistemic operator is at or above the level needed for rational belief: these are the *(context-specific)* conditionals that guide rational belief formation and sustenance.

No attitude needs to be taken toward such a conditional in order for it to play the role that it does, for the explanatory role in question can exist without reflection being triggered. Such a role for these conditionals is especially relevant to the beastly dimension connecting experience with beliefs based on it: the conditional in question plays a partial explanatory role in the cognitive transition from appearance state to belief, showing the way in which the organism in question is adapting cognitively and rationally to its environment. Once reflection occurs, however, different conditionals come into play. For example, if we begin with an unreflective situation involving a conferrer C and a target T, instead of $C \rightarrow T$, we might now have $C \& R \rightarrow \sim T$, where R picks out the type of reflection that has occurred.

Here is a fuller but still schematic example. Suppose S is appeared to F-ly, and believes that something is G. Given this specification only, we have a classic example of an irrational belief. S then reflects on the situation in question, coming to see the world, let's say, in such a way that his/her being appeared to F-ly reveals that something is G, still believing that something is G. In the first situation, there is no epistemic principle available to rationally explain the transition from potential conferrers to belief; in the second there might be. Or so we are assuming until the formal details of the position are fully in view. Once reflection occurs, n-level epistemic conditionals are those which involve both the original conferrer together with the linking principle arising from n-level reflection, whether consciously active at the time in question or present only dispositionally in virtue of leading to habituated transitions from one type of state of information to another.

For the account to be fully general, we place no limits on the level of reflective ascent that might occur. People can reflect about their (base-level) situation, and can reflect about it and their (first-level) reflection on it. They can wax even more reflective, wondering about both their situation and their reflection on it, whether it was the right way of responding intellectually. At each level of reflection, different epistemic norms and epistemic conditionals come into play in the story of epistemic normativity. The important point to notice, in order to accommodate the role of reflection in the story of epistemic normativity, is that the epistemic conditionals, and thus the epistemic principles that explain them, are different for each different level of reflective ascent, on pain of contradiction. In the schematic example in question, if both $C \to T$ and $C\&R \to \sim T$ were still relevant to the story after reflection has occurred, then by modus ponens twice we get both T and $\sim T$. The present approach derives the governing epistemic conditionals from epistemic principles that include in their antecedent a factor concerning level of reflective ascent, so the conditionals generated in any given context are those that acknowledge the level of reflective ascent achieved. The other conditionals, ones that would have been relevant without the reflection, are simply not present or acceptable in the reflective context in question. And it is the acceptable epistemic conditionals that are present in a given context that guide the intellectual life when it is normatively adequate.

The motivation for this view is fully general fallibilism.

2.5 Fallibilisms and Fully General Fallibilism

It is worth taking the time necessary to say what fallibilism is and what it means to endorse fully general fallibilism, for both notions are a bit opaque. We will take up the issue of fallibilism itself first, and then point out how fully general fallibilism differs from it.

2.5.1 What is infallibility?

As a first pass, we might try what we said earlier: infallibility amounts to being able to rule out every possibility of error. As Lewis says,

It seems as if knowledge must be by definition infallible. It you claim that S knows that p, and yet you grant that S cannot eliminate a certain possibility in which *not-p*, it certainly seems as if you have granted that S does not after all know that p. To speak of fallible knowledge, of knowledge despite uneliminated possibilities of error, just sounds contradictory. (Lewis, 1996, p. 549)

Lewis's view, however, remains murky, because of its reliance on the language of "ruling out." A natural interpretation of this phrase is in terms of knowledge itself: one rules out a possibility when and only when one knows, or is in a position to know, that it does not obtain. Yet, once we endorse a plausible closure principle about knowledge—that one can come to know the logical consequences of what is already known by competently deducing them (Hawthorne, 2005)—infallibility, on this construal of it, can be a consequence of epistemic closure alone, which is too weak an interpretation.

One might try to avoid this weakness by referring to the evidential basis of the knowledge in question, and require that the ruling out be done by it alone. Fallibilists, however, can still trivialize the view: evidence e rules out all $\sim p$ possibilities when and only when e provides an adequate epistemic basis for believing p. To avoid such trivialization of infallibilism, a retreat into the refuge of logic seems fortuitous: e rules out all $\sim p$ possibilities when and only when e entails p. Thus, it might seem, the heart of infallibilism is found in the demand for logical guarantees of truth in one's evidence base.

This characterization can only work if one insists on excluding p itself from e, but this restriction is appropriate: we don't want an account of knowledge that allows knowledge of p to arise in virtue of the fact that p entails p. Even so, this account of infallibility remains too easy to satisfy. It leaves open the possibility of cheap infallibilism.

One obvious example of cheap infallibilism arises from a disjunctive account of the contents of perception. One might hold that one is in a different perceptual state when one is actually seeing an elephant from the state one is in when no elephant is present, even though one's perceptual state is indiscriminable by reflection from the former state (for representative literature on this view, see Byrne and Logue (2009)). If we include the contents of experience in the body of evidence available, then this disjunctive approach is a version of cheap infallibilism, since the body of evidence in question could not obtain without the belief in question being true.

Another example of cheap infallibilism arises from the Williamsonian identification of knowledge and evidence (Williamson, 2000). If one's evidence is exactly what one knows, then one's evidence entails anything known to be true.

These infallibilisms are cheap because no self-respecting skeptic would allow that such an infallibilism is enough to solve the skeptical challenge. We don't need a careful account of exactly what it takes to solve that challenge to notice that the earlier infallibilisms do not solve it. Such approaches may be part of an adequate response to the skeptic, but they can't do so in the straightforward and satisfying way that, say, success of the Cartesian project in the *Meditations* would provide. In that sense, the infallibilism they provide is *cheap*, leaving any responsible epistemologist even slightly inclined toward skepticism wishing for more.

It is worth noting that there is a way to build an account of evidence where it is assumed that basic evidence itself doesn't guarantee truth, and yet which generates a version of cheap infallibilism. Suppose e is adequate (basic) evidence for p, and suppose we assume that our epistemic logic will include a Deduction Theorem, to the effect that if there is an adequate epistemic connection from e to p, then there is an adequate epistemic connection from no premises whatsoever for the conditional $e \to p$. Furthermore, suppose we insist that all such theorems of the logic are automatically included in one's total evidence. In such a case, one's total evidence will include both e and $e \to p$, yielding a cheap infallibilism on which admittedly fallible grounds are always part of a total body of evidence that guarantees the truth of what the fallible grounds support.

Such a cheap infallibilism will strike some as suspicious, since if the basic evidence alone doesn't guarantee truth, then this account of total evidence, gen-erated by the Deduction Theorem, will sometimes allow that $e \to p$ is among one's total evidence even though it is false. For those inclined to think that evi-dence is factive, that nothing false can be included among one's body of evidence, this cheap infallibilism is too costly.[4] But for those convinced by arguments such as those marshaled by Fantl and McGrath (2009) against the view that evidence must be factive, such a cheap infallibilism is readily available.

Since nothing in the current project requires settling the issue between fac-tive and non-factive conceptions of evidence, and since my only intent earlier is to give examples of cheap infallibilisms rather than defend any of them, we can set aside the issue of whether a cheap infallibilism is defensible. The primary concern here is not whether such a view is defensible, but how to distinguish such views from real infallibilism, for the difficulty of this problem plays out in major discussions of fallibilism in the literature. Consider the accounts of falli-bilism developed by Jeremy Fantl and Matthew McGrath (Fantl and McGrath, 2009). They identify three versions of (attempts at stating) fallibilism. The first, entailing the conception noted earlier, they reject because, among other things, it doesn't distinguish between cheap and real infallibilism. They then describe two other versions of fallibilism, strong and weak, which are:

Weak Fallibilism: a belief can be adequate without being maximally justified;
Strong Fallibilism: a belief can be adequate even though the epistemic chance of it being false is not zero.

To understand the difference, and ordering of strength, we need to know something about what maximal justification is and what epistemic chance is. About maximal justification, they first endorse the idea that no non-entailing

---

[4] For discussion and defense of this view that evidence is factive, see Littlejohn (2012).

justification is maximal, because an entailing one is better. But then they write something that also seems right, and which causes a problem:

[S]omething infallibly known in the logical sense can still be fallibly known in the weak epistemic sense. If you know *Plato taught Aristotle* on the basis of entailing evidence ... this is still compatible with your justification being imperfect. Your justification might not be enough, for example, to make you reasonable in investing [as much confidence] as you would in other propositions, e.g., *Plato is believed to have taught Aristotle*, let alone *here is a hand*. (Fantl and McGrath, 2009, p. 10)

This point seems right, and though I think Fantl and McGrath are thinking only about cheap infallibilisms here, the same point can be made about real infallibilisms. Take Cartesian certainty as the exemplar here: if you insist that one has to be metaphysically certain to know, or be justified in believing, you are a real infallibilist. But once you see what Fantl and McGrath say in the last quote, you should or at least might agree about the range of things a successful completion of the Cartesian project would generate. Thus, you might say,

Even though I'm metaphysically certain that I think, and metaphysically certain that I exist, and metaphysically certain that God exists, axiomatic systems work in such a way that one is not always in a position to be as confident about the theorems as about the axioms. So there are distinctions to be drawn between the claim that I exist and the claim that God exists, since the derivation of the latter involves a bit of complexity, even when the derivation makes the conclusion metaphysically certain for me.

That is, once one makes the Fantl and McGrath point about cheap infallibilisms and entailing evidence, it looks like there is no good reason to insist that the same can't be said of paradigm, real infallibilisms.

But if that is right, then one can be a weak fallibilist, in Fantl and McGrath terms, and a real, genuine-article infallibilist.

The same might also happen with strong infallibilism, unless one adds the proviso that anytime one is metaphysically certain, the epistemic chance of error goes to zero. In the first chapter, they never explicitly endorse such a claim, though I expect they think it is true. I myself can't tell if this claim is true, because I'm not yet sure what epistemic chances are. I think I have a better idea what objective chance is, or what objective or subjective probability is, but an epistemic chance isn't any of these. Moreover, it is easy to become suspicious of any attempt to define infallibilism in terms of a notion of epistemic chance, where we must understand that notion to be logically stronger than that of maximal justification. (If we don't—that is, if we identify epistemic chances with degree of justification—then the distinction Fantl and McGrath wish to exploit between weak fallibilism and strong fallibilism disappears.)

So perhaps strong fallibilism will turn out to be incompatible with real infallibilism, which would be a good thing. But that conclusion won't give us a full picture of fallibilism, since being a strong fallibilist isn't obviously necessary for being a fallibilist. For, even if all infallible beliefs have zero epistemic chance of being false, that claim doesn't yet tell us that all fallible beliefs have some non-zero epistemic chance of being false. Moreover, if we add the further claim that all fallible beliefs have some non-zero epistemic chance of being false, then we have secured the truth of strong fallibilism by stipulation alone, rather than deriving it from some prior account of epistemic chance. As a result, I don't think the Fantl and McGrath characterizations of various types of fallibilisms are sufficiently detailed to help us in our project of characterizing fallibilism in a way that counts cheap infallibilism as being a kind of fallibilism.

The approaches discussed so far try to explain the difference between fallibilism in terms of the notion of evidence itself or in terms of some degree of justification or epistemic chance that will rely on the notion of evidence or some surrogate for it, such as a reason for belief. Because of the difficulties noted earlier, it is unclear how to draw the needed distinction, and in the face of this issue, an alternative is to conclude that we shouldn't expect to find an adequate account of infallibility solely in terms of evidence and what it entails. Instead, we might turn to modal dimensions of knowledge, looking for an account of infallibility in terms of epistemic modal notions such as safety and sensitivity.[5] A belief is safe when it would normally be true when held (Sosa, 2007), and a belief is sensitive when it would not be held when false (Nozick, 1981). Mere counterfactual connections are clearly too weak for infallibility, so the inclination is to look for necessary connections instead: in some sense, the belief not only wouldn't, but couldn't, be held while false; not only would the claim be true if believed, it would have to be true.

It would be too strong, however, to interpret the necessity needed here in terms of metaphysical necessity. On such an account, infallibility would require immunity from error concerning the claim in question in every world in which the individual in question exists. One reason such a requirement is too strong is that some cognitive interests are optional, in the sense that there are worlds where the person in question need not consider the claim in question, and should not be disbarred from being infallible about it simply because in some worlds the

---

[5] This conclusion is importantly similar to that defended in Dutant (2007). Dutant, too, distinguishes between evidential and modal approaches to infallibilism, but his modal approach differs slightly from the present one, focusing on the basis of belief rather than the informational system in question. Because of the points raised earlier about the optionality involved in basing, I think the latter approach has more hope of success here.

individual never considers the issue. Another reason arises because of possibilities of massive disability and mental incompetence or confusion. Descartes thought that some beliefs not even an evil demon could render believed yet false, but that is compatible with a demon getting one to believe that the claim is false even though it isn't. So if we impose a modal constraint on infallibility, it will have to be restricted to something less than perfect correlation between truth and belief across all metaphysical possibilities.

The Cartesian project is useful for pointing us in the right direction when looking for such a modal dimension. We want an account of infallibility such that if the Cartesian project had succeeded we would all be in a position to have a wide range of infallible beliefs: avoiding error would be totally up to us, requiring only that we don't let our wills outrun our understanding when it comes to belief. If it were transparent to us whether our will were outrunning our understanding, then we would have an argument available that guarantees the truth of our belief—an argument that would be accessible in a wide range of worlds. Some individuals will access such available arguments across all the relevant worlds, and others will be more spotty, noticing the argument in some worlds but not others. What to say about the latter group isn't quite clear, but it is clear that those individuals who access the available argument across all the relevant worlds will have infallible beliefs for the conclusions supported by the available arguments (the ones available on the assumption that the Cartesian project succeeds).

The central points to note are these. First, there is no legitimate requirement on infallibility that requires safety and sensitivity across all metaphysical possibilities. Second, we want an understanding of infallibility that allows for it to be present if the Cartesian project had been successful. One way to achieve such a result is to find arguments available from premises that are infallibly known for each belief that is held, but our earlier discussion of cheap infallibilism raises a cautionary flag to avoid appeals to "cheap" arguments for the beliefs in question. We have not succeeded in finding out what makes arguments and evidence cheap as opposed to non-cheap, but even in the absence of such an account we can recognize that some arguments are cheap and some aren't. Uncertainty about cheapness and uncertainty about the scope of an appropriate modal dimension for infallibility each show that we don't have a precise understanding of infallibility. Even so, what is clear is that infallibility is both about having evidence and argument sufficient to guarantee truth and about having control over whether one lands in error or finds the truth. In the ideal infallibilist case, getting to the truth and avoiding error is totally within our control, and such control requires available evidence to guarantee the truth of our beliefs. But such entailing evidence is not sufficient for real infallibility. What more is needed is modal in nature, involving control.

This discussion gives us a clearer picture of fallibilism, and fully general fallibilism, the kind being assumed here, is an extension of it. We turn then to the characterization of this assumption.

2.5.2   Fully general fallibilism

To understand what a fully general fallibilism involves, a bit of groundwork is necessary. One kind of fallibilism simply notes that good evidence is no guarantee of truth, and that is part of what is involved in fully general fallibilism. Central to the theory developed here is that there are two dimensions to the theory, for there is both the evidence and what we make of it. Regarding the second feature, it is easy to introduce an element of infallibilism here, since one can begin to wonder how those who are doing the very best they can to get to the truth and avoid error could possibly fail to pass scrutiny from a purely intellectual point of view. If doing the very best one can provides such a guarantee, there is a dimension of infallibilism in the story. It isn't an infallibilism about the truth of the beliefs in question, but rather an infallibilism about something epistemic.

We can label the differences here by calling the first "alethic infallibilism" and the second "epistemic infallibilism." The former view is roughly about whether it is possible to have justified false beliefs or rational false belief and the answer to that question is clearly yes. The second view is about the conditions under which rationality is guaranteed. It is clearly true that in the ordinary course of affairs, where we unreflectively experience the world and form opinions about it, it is possible to conduct one's ordinary life in a way that results in having some irrational beliefs. It is also possible to conduct one's ordinary life in an unreflective way and fail to believe some things for which the content of such a belief is rational for one to believe. The question that epistemic infallibilists raise is whether our ability to reflect in the way that has rational significance changes this picture. Once we reflect, doing the very best we can to get to the truth and avoid error, are we then in a position so that whatever belief we form or do not form, we are guaranteed to be rational in believing, disbelieving, withholding, or taking no attitude whatsoever?

A fully fallibilistic epistemology will endorse that we have no guarantees anywhere. We have no guarantee of getting to the truth and we have no guarantee of being rational either. Fallibilists of the most general sort recognize that murkiness, seeing through a glass darkly, is part of the human condition. In the process of development, human beings not only try to figure out what the world is like, they try to figure out what to take as good or bad signs regarding what to think and what to do. They construct, that is, the theory of the world together with the theory of evidence or rationality. Once we recognize that the principles that compose the theory of rationality are not themselves fixed for all persons and all times, we should adopt a fallibilistic attitude so that the principles to which we attend and use when deciding what to think provide no guarantee of rationality.

Recall that when reflection occurs, the epistemic principles that determine whether a given cognitive response is rational are elusive. When we take an epistemic principle and reflect on whether it is a correct principle to use in our present context, deciding that it is, the principle that determines whether our cognitive response is rational is not the principle on which we reflect. If we then turn our attention to the meta-principle that lies behind or above the principle on which we were initially reflecting, that meta-principle is no longer the principle that determines whether our cognitive responses are rational either. There is a hierarchy of such principles, and the governing principles are always one step ahead of whatever level of rational ascent one employs. It is this elusive character of governing principles that allows the present theory to endorse epistemic fallibilism in a fully general way.

A theorist that looks for more in the way of guarantees might agree that alethic fallibilism is false, but disagree with the position endorsed here concerning epistemic fallibilism. For such a theorist, the potentially infinite hierarchy of epistemic principles is unnecessary. For once reflection occurs, involving doing one's best to get to the truth and avoid error, a guarantee of rationality is available. As such, a theory of this sort would only need two levels of epistemic principles, one for the beastly dimension, and one for the reflective dimension.

I don't think we are entitled to any sort of infallibilism in our theory, and thus reject this simplifying assumption. Moreover, I think our reflective experience belies this infallibilism. We not only reflect on how to improve our efforts at getting to the truth, but we also examine our own reflections. We become uncertain about our capacities to think well about how to improve, thereby expressing an implicit awareness that our reflective capacities themselves provide no guaranteed corrective for our beastly inclinations. In the process of such meta-reflection, we acknowledge not only our fallibility regarding getting to the truth but also our fallibility in recognizing exactly what attitudes and responses are rational, given our circumstances. We are, we might say, doubly fallen creatures: epistemically as well as alethically.

Such fully general fallibilism is thus an outgrowth of the second aspect of fallibilism noted earlier. There is both the aspect of evidence not guaranteeing truth, but also the aspect about control over whether our efforts yield success. The point I'm emphasizing here is one about loss of control. It is not up to us, it is not within our power alone, to be right or rational. Once we grant this point—and our experience as reflective beings makes it obvious—we can see the fundamental connection between alethic and epistemic fallibilism. When it comes to cognition, it is not up to us alone whether our views are correct and it is not up to us alone whether our views are rational. Our best efforts are no guarantee of anything, either alethically or epistemically.

Some will think that such a position overreaches, and that there are more certainties here than this bleak portrayal allows. For those who wish to embrace a form of epistemic infallibilism, the theory can be adjusted in a minor way to accommodate that point of view. The adjustment involves the collapse of the hierarchy of epistemic principles down to the first reflective principle, so that all reflection is encoded in one principle that makes it impossible to fail to be rational under ideal reflective conditions. The harder question is how to accommodate the fully general fallibilism endorsed here. It is here that the elusive character of the principles of rationality is central. Because the principles are elusive, because when one reflects one can only reflect on the principles that would have governed one's situation had one not reflected, the theory accommodates the possibility that the governing principles say one thing about one's level of rationality whereas the principles on which one is reflecting say something different. It is in this difference that we find the thoroughgoing fallibilism on offer here.

2.5.3 Degrees of fallibilism

Fully general infallibilism requires something to be true of all of our beliefs, whether it is in our control to get to the truth or in our control to be rational. We thus can interpret fallibilism as simply the denial of fully general infallibilism. But fallibilism comes in degrees depending on how extensive the rejection of infallibilism is.

The most general fallibilism denies infallibilism always and everywhere. It insists that it is never up to us either in terms of truth or rationality whether we succeed; more accurately, it is never completely up to us. In order to refute this fully general fallibilism, the infallibilist only needs to find one instance where fallibilism does not hold. This leaves open a vast intermediary region where fully general fallibilism fails and fully general infallibilism fails as well.

The history of conflict between foundationalism and coherentism is a history involving this issue of whether there are any counterexamples at all to fully general fallibilism. From a value-driven perspective, however, the issue isn't whether fully general fallibilism is true. The issue is instead whether it matters whether fully general fallibilism is true. Allow me to explain.

Even if we suppose that there are some infallible beliefs, this fact might not be significant to epistemology at all. One of the standard complaints against foundationalism is that there aren't enough foundational beliefs to support the superstructure. That is the kind of point I am making when I note that the mere existence of some infallible beliefs might not be significant. It might make no difference at all to the process of theory construction whether or not there are any infallible beliefs.

So when I endorse fallibilism here, it is not a mere denial of infallibilism in its most fully general form. Neither is it an embracing of fallibilism in its most fully general form. It is instead an embracing of the significance of fallibilism, the position according to which nothing of theoretical significance turns on the question of whether there are any infallible beliefs. If there are such so be it; if there are not any that is just fine as well. Hence when we construct our theory, we will need to construct a theory in such a way that it does not require any beliefs to be infallible.

It is for this reason that it is crucial to our theory that the process of reflective ascent be a process that doesn't introduce or require elements of infallibilism at any point in the process. The feature of our theory that allows us to avoid any element of infallibilism is the hierarchical conception of epistemic principles that are constitutive of the theory in question. This hierarchical conception allows that the epistemic principles governing the rationality of a given context are always elusive: whichever principles or conditionals one is reflecting about, those principles or conditionals are not themselves the ones that determine whether one is rational.

A critic might wonder why it is impossible to reflect on the very conditionals to which the rationality of one's beliefs answer. The answer here is not one that prohibits any kind of self reference in various claims in epistemology or elsewhere in philosophy. Self-referential propositions are clearly possible. The prohibition in question arises not out of any general inability of a proposition to refer to itself, but rather in the process of theory construction itself. This theory begins with base-level principles and introduces a hierarchy beginning from this starting point. The hierarchy is generated precisely by the process of what reflection involves. When we reflect on our epistemic situation, we consider both the evidence that we have as well as the connection, the conditional relationship, between that evidence and what we believe (or are considering). In such a context, there is an epistemic principle which underlies the conditionality relationship being reflected upon, but it should not be assumed to be the same principle that determines whether one's belief is rational.

A benefit of this way of conceiving of the theory of rationality is that it is compatible with significant fallibilism of a fully general sort. If it turns out that sometimes a meta-level principle is precisely the same as the object-level principle, such a result would sustain some degree of infallibility in the story of rationality. If the governing epistemic principle were not elusive in the way described, it would be within our direct and immediate control to make sure that we are rational: all we would need to do is to make sure that we believe in accord with what the principle we are considering tells us. For those who are attracted to some form of epistemic infallibilism, that result would be pleasing. Since I view this attraction as misguided, the strategy followed here is to construct a theory on which no such control is assumed.

One way to think about this fully general fallibilism is that it runs counter to the motivations for access internalism. Access Internalists think that we have some sort of a priori access to the factors that determine whether a belief of ours is rational. Among these factors are not only the evidence on which we rely but the conditional relationship between the evidence and what we believe. We thus have access not only to signs of truth but to the epistemic principles which connect these signs to the proposition in question. Fully general fallibilism denies both claims. According to fully general fallibilism it may generally be true that we have access to our evidence, but it doesn't matter to the question of whether we are rational that we have such access. According to fully general fallibilism it may also be true that we generally have access to the epistemic principles that connect our evidence to what we believe, but again it doesn't matter to the question of whether we are rational that we have such access. Just as before, the explanation here for the failure of access internalism—note that I say failure not falsity—is the hierarchical conception of reflective ascent involved in the theory that we have developed.

We can put this point more formally. The issue of dispute between fully general fallibilism and access internalism is over the following principle for an adequate epistemic logic:

Jp ⊣⊢ JJp,

where the 'J' operator stands for "It is justified for a given person in a given circumstance that." The issue of dispute is over whether we can derive Jp from JJp. Access Internalists say yes to this implication, but fully epistemic fallibilists say no. They say no, on the basis of the fact that we learn how to find the truth in the same way that we learn the truth: by trial and error. So reflection provides no guarantee of success, either alethically or epistemically. The theory developed here allows us to avoid having to side with access Internalists on this issue, favoring instead the more realistic assessment of fully general fallibilists.

2.6 Conclusion

The goal of this chapter has been to present a schematic outline of a theory of epistemic normativity that answers to a philosophical methodology. Most particularly, it is an approach that shows promise of allowing our normative theory to speak with a single voice, addressing the egocentric predicament in a way that honors the perspectivality platitude that what is appropriate to think or do is a matter of one's total perspective on the world and one's place in it. The rest is a matter of things going well or badly, and though the world is never as cooperative as we would like in lining up the good and the right, we can take comfort in this: there is nowhere else to go to find a solution to the predicament. A normative theory of this sort is indispensable from a value-driven perspective.

Carrying through on this promise of having a theory that speaks with a single voice, however, requires getting past a roadblock. It is the roadblock of excusability, for many will insist that some irrational beliefs are excusable or somehow propitious in a secondary normative sense. If so, our theory will not obviously speak with a single voice, since it contains no resources for addressing the issue of what to think when thinking in a particular way is both irrational and excusable. To the important issue of excusability we thus turn in the next chapter.

3

Excusability

3.1 Introduction

The normative theory presented so far aims to honor the perspectivality platitude that the degree to which a given attitude or behavior is rational depends on the egocentric point of view of the individual in question. It also aims to do so in a way that is derived from a value-driven approach to epistemology, thus attempting at a minimum to develop a theory that speaks with a single voice in response to the questions of what to do and what to think. There is, however, a challenge to this hope, one deriving from the nature of excuses. We are familiar with the importance of excuses from our ordinary experience with the legal system, for in some cases in which the law is violated, a notion of excusability is invoked to diminish or eliminate legal responsibility. Thus, one way to motivate the need for a theory of excuses that is logically independent of the theory of rationality or responsibility is through the legal analogy. Another way arises from the fully general fallibilism that is a background assumption for the approach to normativity presented here. In the glory days of epistemology, infallibilist assumptions reigned to such an extent that we didn't have to consider the implications for the theory of rationality of, e.g., someone not knowing the rules to follow, or getting confused about which rule applies in a given condition, or about a person conscientiously attempting to follow a rule and just not being up to the task. In these ways, and others, there is a common viewpoint in contemporary epistemology that whatever theory of normative status one adopts for cognition and practice, the theory will have to be supplemented with some notion of excusability that is logically distinct from the normative notion in question.[1] In short, a fully general fallibilism of the sort endorsed here is thought by many to imply that ambiguity of evaluation is unavoidable.

To show that there is a problem lurking here takes a bit more explanation, however, for the natural response is that the normative notion of excusability

---

[1] See, e.g., DeRose (2002), Weiner (2005), and Hawthorne and Stanley (2008). I discuss these views in Kvanvig (2009, 2011). For resistance on the ambiguity approach, see Thomson (2008).

doesn't compete with the normative notion of what one ought to do or think. In cases where a belief is excusable, that doesn't affect whether it is rational, but only has some other effect (perhaps, how much blame is legitimately placed on the cognizer in question). One way to make this point is to insist that the notion of rationality already characterized is *primary*, and that the other normative notion of excusability is *secondary*. The value of the legal analogy is apparent here: we don't think the *law* itself is under threat just because sometimes violations of it happen in circumstances that eliminate the need for or justification of punishment. So, once a theory of rationality is in place, excusability can be passed off as an independent but secondary consideration, generating no threat to the normative language of the theory already developed.

Such is not the case in our context, however. The threat of an independent normative notion arises, on the present approach, from noting the imperatival origins of whatever normative notions we use in our theory of epistemic appraisal of belief. The normative notions in question derive from resolutions of the egocentric predicament, in the form of imperatival directives such as "Believe p," or "Take no attitude whatsoever toward p." These imperatival resolutions are encoded in our favored term of epistemic appraisal: it is rational to believe p; it is not rational to take any attitude toward p. The threat of an independent notion of excusability is thus that we have two normative notions, rationality and excusability, and our only legitimate source of normativity is the imperatival origin in question. So if we have two independent normative notions, we have no basis for claiming that one of the notions is primary and the other secondary. What we are left with is, simply, perplexity: which normative notion is the correct one to use in resolving the egocentric predicament? It would be laughable in the extreme to insist that the primary one is the one developed first, to be identified with the results of the last chapter.

Moreover, this perplexity generates a direct conflict with the initial hope of developing a theory answering to the predicament in question that speaks with a single voice. When we take as our starting point the constraints of ordinary language and common intuitions, we introduce multiplicity in a quite natural way: some behavior and thinking is irrational but excusable. And then we try to characterize the differences between the multiplicities in question. Our starting point, however, is more restrictive. We begin from an important human need or interest, and try to develop a theory that answers to it. The sketch of such a theory was given in the last chapter, and the worry is that the single normative notion it identifies will be insufficient—that no matter what normative notion we begin with, the introduction of another one will be unavoidable. If so, the point made in the last paragraph shows that the result will be stultification, since we will have sound basis for claiming that either of the two normative notions is the one that is primary.

This chapter is devoted to disarming this threat to the present approach. The idea is to show that we can say everything that needs to be said about excusability without threat to our project. That is, we can give an adequate role for excuses within our theory of rationality that does not result in any conflict between what is rational and what is excusable, all things considered. We turn first to the legal analogy and then to the argument from fallibilism.

3.2 Excusability and the Law

A natural starting point when thinking about epistemic normativity is to consider analogies with moral and legal responsibility, and if we do so, grounds for introducing a secondary notion of excusability can arise quite easily. Most especially, such grounds arise when we think of epistemic rationality as being governed by principles that resemble strict liability laws. A strict liability law is one for which appeals to context and possible excuses is never germane; all that matters is whether the law was violated. In such cases, a person will be held liable with no regard whatsoever for whether the person was at fault, or morally responsible, for the violation and damages which result. In criminal cases, a strict liability law is one for which proof of a violation involves no *mens rea* requirement, i.e., the prosecution bears no burden of proving that the person had a "guilty mind" with respect to the action in question. Thus, a conviction can be obtained even if the defendant was understandably ignorant of the factors that made their behavior criminal. In this way, a person may fail to be culpable, or blameworthy, and yet be found to have violated the law. Even the weakest *mens rea* requirement, that of criminal negligence, need not have obtained in cases where the law in question is a strict liability law.

Here are all the aspects for needing disunity in a normative theory. One normative notion is defined in terms which leave open the possibility of failing to live up to the demands of that normative notion in a way that is perfectly understandable, or excusable, or blameless. In the usual criminal case, there must be a concurrence of *actus reus* and *mens rea*, between the external elements of a crime and the relevant mental elements.[2] The usual common law standard

---

[2] Here the Latin term *actus reus* has the unfortunate implication that the act can be guilty independent of whether the mind is also guilty. It is instructive that in Australia now, these Latin terms have been replaced with the language of Fault Elements (corresponding to the *mens rea* requirement) and Physical Elements (corresponding to the *actus reus* requirement), keeping the proper perspective that the external, physical elements involved in action need imply no guilt of any sort.

for criminality is expressed in the Latin phrase *actus non facit reum nisi mens sit rea*, meaning "the act does not make a person guilty unless the mind is also guilty." If we have a strict liability law, however, this standard does not apply, leaving open a judgment of guilt even though the action in question might not be blameworthy.

One type of ground for positing epistemic excusability, then, is when epistemic principles are conceived on the model of strict liability laws. One way to put this point is to think of epistemic principles as completely perspective-free. For example, one might think of the epistemic principles involving logical or mathematical theorems in this way, insisting that anything provable from no premises whatsoever can never be rationally disbelieved. Conceived in this way, it is easy to see why we would want some notion of excusability in addition to that of rationality, since we want to be able to say something nice and comforting about poor Frege's mistakes in logical meta-theory.

There is a better response, however, and it is to find fault with the perspective-free conception of epistemic principles involved in this argument for such disunity in normative theory. When we think of epistemic principles in terms of principles of logic, we become tempted to the strict liability model and the subsequent demand for a notion of excusability that is different from that of rationality itself. The lesson to learn here isn't that we need an independent theory of excusability but rather that we need to think of epistemic principles in terms other than that of strict liability laws.

In considering what an alternative approach might look like, it is worth noting here the varieties of *mens rea* possibilities in the law. The weakest type of *mens rea* requirement is that of negligence, with recklessness being a slightly stronger requirement, followed by knowledge, and finally intention or purpose. In crude and oversimplified terms, the difference between a law with only a negligence requirement and one with a recklessness requirement is that recklessness requires knowing the risks in question, though not desiring that they be realized, while negligence requires neither such knowing nor desiring. The distinction between laws in which negligence plays a role from strict liability laws is typically explained in terms of whether a reasonable person so situated would have recognized the risks involved.

These characterizations are nowhere close to an adequate degree of precision needed if we wished for full understanding, but we can bypass these issues here since our interest is more in where epistemic principles or norms fall than in the category scheme itself. (Recall that what we are interested in here is whether the legal analogy gives us reason to posit an independent normative notion in our theory, and the force of any such analogy will trade on whether it is plausible to think of the epistemic principles involved in our sketch of a theory in the last chapter as appropriately like certain types of laws.) What we have seen to this point is that if we think of the relevant principles in terms of strict liability laws, we confuse the rationality of ideal agents with the rationality of ordinary agents, yielding a need to introduce an additional notion of excusability to account for legitimate confusion about the ideal principles of logic, explanation, and evidence. The question I wish to pursue here is what happens when we move past strict liability conceptions of epistemic principles, introducing some type of *mens rea* requirement, somewhere on the continuum from weak to strong requirements encompassing the categories beginning with negligence and ending with full intention and purpose.

In order to address this issue, it will be helpful to focus our understanding on the nature of such requirements in the law. As noted already, the distinction in the law is between physical and mental features of wrongdoing, between *actus reus* and *mens rea*. Thinking of the former in terms of the physical elements of wrongdoing helps us avoid the temptation to think of the behavior in question as itself prohibited by the law, except in the case in which the law is a strict liability law. A better approach is to think of the physical elements—the behavior in question—as something that the law has an interest in extinguishing. In short, it is behavior that is disvaluable in legal terms. We thus separate the theory of legal value from the theory of legal obligation, allowing an account of legal wrongdoing that adverts both to the theory of value and the continuum of *mens rea* options. In the simplest case in which a law is a strict liability law, there is a convergence between what is disvaluable and wrongdoing; in other cases, wrongdoing is a function of what is disvaluable and the continuum in question.

An alternative, and perhaps more common, way to think of the relation between *actus reus* and *mens rea* aspects is to view the behavior as itself prohibited, with the *mens rea* clause interpreted in terms of an alternative normative notion of excusability. In our context, however, such an interpretation is problematic, since it makes it too easy to show that no unified account of normativity (within a specific domain) is possible. That is the position we are evaluating, so when there is an alternative account that leaves this question open, we should adopt it rather than endorse an account that settles the issue by fiat. On the alternative account, we begin with a theory of legal (dis)value, and interpret what is prohibited in terms of *doing something disvaluable while satisfying the relevant mens rea standard*. It is not important here whether the laws themselves are formulated in terms of such language or whether they are formulated in other terms. What matters is whether this way of regimenting the various factors involved in legal liability is possible and theoretically fruitful, or whether the only defensible picture is one that immediately and self-evidently entails a need for multiple normative notions.

Our question, then, is what the implications are for this way of thinking of the continuum of *mens rea* involvements in wrongdoing within the context of fundamental epistemic normativity. In particular, I want to address the issue of how these various involvements lend credibility, or not, to the multiplicity claim regarding epistemic normativity, according to which, whatever primary notion of appraisal is used, there will be a need for an additional, secondary notion such as excusability or blamelessness in order to provide a complete account of epistemic appraisal.

3.3 *Mens Rea* and Epistemic Appraisal

Begin with the strongest *mens rea* requirements, one that says no belief is irrational except when people both intend and know that they are flouting the relevant truth-related considerations, or even merely know that they are doing so. With respect to such conceptions of epistemic appraisal, two implications arise. Such a requirement can easily be seen to undermine any need for theoretical disunity since it leaves no need for an independent notion of excusable behavior. After all, the person in question is aware of what's wrong with their cognitive behavior. Yet, if such requirements are needed for irrationality, it will be rare that we find irrational beliefs. From the point of view of fundamental normativity regarding what we should do or think, it shouldn't be this easy to pass epistemic muster. One needn't intend to violate the norms or know that one has done so in order to have an irrational belief.

Something similar can be said of *mens rea* involvements for anything stronger than negligence, though some explanation is needed to make this obvious regarding the recklessness standard. In legal contexts, recklessness requires a prior awareness of what counts as legally disvaluable behavior. In the epistemic context, however, the usual approach to epistemic value involves a double goal, perhaps the goal of getting to the truth as well as the goal of avoiding error.[3] In such a context, the risks involved in recklessness would have to be cast not only in terms of what is disvaluable, but also in terms of what is valuable. So a recklessness standard would first have to specify an appropriate balance between the two goals, and then specify what level of risk is tolerable for failing to achieve

---

[3] I prefer the starting point of James (1897), focusing on the centrality of not being duped and not missing out on something important, but the differences between this starting point and the truth-related goals are not significant in the present context.

an appropriate balance. The problem here is that requiring that any person capable of rationality of this sort would then have to know in advance what it takes to balance appropriately the competing goals in question, and such knowledge is rare and, perhaps, non-existent. Epistemologists sometimes presume a particular balance between these goals, perhaps that they are equally important, while others weight one as more important than the other (see Chisholm (1991)), but it is too much to claim that they have knowledge here. So, arguably, nobody knows what an appropriate balance is, even if there are some who have rational opinions on the matter. Moreover, even if some sophisticated epistemologists have such knowledge, it isn't broadly shared enough to undergird an account of irrationality in terms of recklessness of the sort requiring such prior knowledge or even belief. Given such a requirement, the recklessness standard leaves little need for excusable but irrational beliefs since nearly all beliefs would be judged rational on such an approach. So once again, any analogy argument for the legal sphere based on such a recklessness standard is far too generous in terms of its understanding of appropriate epistemic norms, and so can't be useful for the task of using the legal analogy to generate a need for an independent notion of excusability in the epistemic sphere.

We are left, then, with approaches that take the notion of epistemic rationality to be appropriately modeled after laws with weak *mens rea* requirements. It is easy to see here why it is tempting to think that an independent notion of excusability may be needed. Suppose, through no fault of your own, you simply don't see certain logical consequences that a normal, reasonable person would see in your circumstances. Maybe, for example, you were just given by your captors that horror to all clear thinkers everywhere, the blue logical-confusion-inducing pill, and *modus ponens* no longer seems valid to you but affirming the consequent, at least sometimes, does. So cognition operates in ways that yield irrational results, because they involve affirming the consequent, even though these results are excusable.

But once again, just as before, the need here is chimerical. The problem with such a conception is that it doesn't adequately honor the perspectival character of rationality, and thus provides a poor argument for disunity in the theory of rationality. We only need excusability because we are substituting the perspective of a normal, reasonable person for that of your own drug-induced perspective. After all, the appropriately perspectival notion here takes a change in how things seem to you to be central to the explanation of why certain attitudes are rational and others are not. It may be that for certain purposes, we want a different normative theory that is not perspectivally sensitive in this way, and such a theory might be appropriately modeled on laws whose only *mens rea* requirement is that of negligence. But for the fundamental normativity that addresses the primary concern of what to do and what to think, we need a perspectival theory that doesn't evaluate one person's rationality from the perspective of another person.

As we have seen, however, stronger *mens rea* requirements make it too easy to pass the test for rational belief, and thus cannot be embraced. The question is how to find a position without the flaw of substituting a different perspective for the relevant one, and which doesn't require the kind of awareness involved in stronger requirements such as recklessness or full intentionality to violate the norms. The appeal of such a theory should be obvious by now, since an approach that makes rationality distinct from excusability tends to be a view that is insufficiently attentive to the perspectival character of rationality. It is this point that lies at the heart of the New Evil Demon Problem (Cohen and Lehrer, 1983), where accounts of epistemic norms that do not take sufficient account of the perspectivality platitude run the risk of having to say that the inhabitants of evil demon worlds have irrational but excusable beliefs, in contrast to our own situation, in which the same beliefs by the same individuals are both rational and excusable. The central lesson of this problem is that such approaches to rationality are insufficiently perspectival.

Such a criticism provokes the philosophical tendency to solve a problem by drawing a distinction. Here, one might say that there is a subjective notion of rationality that treats denizens of demon worlds just as actual world inhabitants, and there is another, objective notion of rationality that distinguishes the two in terms of rationality or justification (see, e.g., Goldman (1988)). In our context, however, such a maneuver must be rejected. If we want to understand the fundamental notion of epistemic appraisal, one that honors the perspectival character of rationality, we shouldn't say that denizens of demon worlds are any more irrational than we are, since their perspectives are the same as ours. In this context, drawing a distinction of the sort in question doesn't undermine the probative value of a counterexample, as can easily be seen by considering the device of preserving the idea that the earth used to be flat by distinguishing objective from subjective truth. At most, such a drawing of a distinction only has rebutting power, showing how to preserve an alternative approach to rationality while maintaining logical consistency among one's commitments. It doesn't show that the example isn't strong enough evidence against an approach to reject it. And here, the example retains this power even in the face of the distinction, since the distinction leaves untouched the obvious point that the best analogy with fundamental moral and legal responsibility for an account of epistemic appraisal is one that makes rationality perspectival enough to require more *mens rea* involvement than any such objective notion allows.

So what we need in order to defend unity regarding fundamental epistemic normativity is something weaker than the recklessness and full *mens rea* requirements characteristic of some types of legal responsibility, but strong enough that mere ignorance of the standards isn't sufficient for rational belief. One way to avoid this result appeals to the negligence standard incorporating what a rational person would recognize in the situation in question, but we have seen that this approach is insufficiently perspectival. So what is needed is an approach that is more attuned to the perspectival character of rationality than a negligence standard is, but not in such a way that stronger requirements such as recklessness or full *mens rea* are required. In consequence of this conclusion, the argument for multiple notions of epistemic appraisal based on some analogy with the legal sphere must be judged inadequate: to put it simply, the notions at work in various levels of legal responsibility are not fine-grained enough to provide any such argument.

This conclusion, however, provides fodder for a very strong argument that unity in the theory of rationality is simply not possible, and thus that we must choose between adequate perspectivality in our theory and unity. In the next section, I'll first explain how our conclusion about where to locate appropriate perspectivality in our theory in terms of the levels of *mens rea* requirements in the legal context leads to the dilemma and then how the dilemma can be avoided.

3.4   Excusability and Fully General Fallibilism

The conclusion of the last section commits us straightforwardly to an implication of our own fallibility, to the effect that whatever the norms of rationality are, they are not automatically known to us and we are not immune from error regarding them. This fact forces on us the conclusion that unknown violations of such norms are possible, and unknown violations of norms appear to leave us with the possibility of an irrational belief that is nonetheless excusable in some sense, thereby undermining any possibility of the unity we seek in the theory of fundamental epistemic normativity. Hawthorne and Stanley give voice to the fundamental argument for such multiplicity:

In general, it should be noted that intuitions go a little hazy in any situation that some candidate normative theory says is sufficient to make it that one ought to F but where, in the case described, one does not know that situation obtains. As Tim Williamson has emphasized, cases of this sort will arise whatever one's normative theory, given that no conditions are luminous. . . . In general, luminosity failure makes for confusion or at least hesitancy in our normative theorizing. . . . After all . . . excusable lapses from a norm are no counterexample to that norm. (Hawthorne and Stanley, 2008, pp. 585–6)

Hawthorne and Stanley note rightly the hesitance that arises when norms are unknowingly violated, and this hesitancy can incline one to accept the following type of argument: irrationality is displayed by violating a norm, but when the violation is not a known violation, there is something excusable about the violation, so there needs to be a secondary notion of propriety for any theory, since no theory can deny the possibility of unknown violations of norms (on pain of having to endorse the idea that we have infallible recognition of the governing norms).

This position of multiplicity is echoed quite widely in contemporary epistemology. In discussing a counterexample to his knowledge norm of assertion, a case in which one doesn't know that it is snowing outside but rationally believes that one knows, Timothy Williamson says,

The case is quite consistent with the knowledge account. Indeed, if I am entitled to assume that knowledge warrants assertion, then, since it is reasonable for me to believe that I know that there is snow outside, it is reasonable for me to believe that I have warrant to assert that there is snow outside. If it is reasonable for me to believe that I have warrant to assert that there is snow outside, then, other things being equal, it is reasonable for me to assert that there is snow outside. (Williamson, 2000, p. 257)

Williamson's distinction is not between rationality and excusability, but between warrant and reasonability, and his point is the same as that of Stanley and Hawthorne: a distinction between two types of normativity is useful and, presumably, unavoidable.

Keith DeRose concurs:

The knowledge account of assertion would lead us to expect that though such speakers are breaking the rule for assertion, their assertions are warranted in a secondary way, since they reasonably take themselves to know what they assert. Thus, our sense that such speakers are at least in some way asserting appropriately does not falsify the knowledge account of assertion. (DeRose, 2002, pp. 199–200, n. 23)

Matthew Weiner concurs as well, though in defense of the truth norm of assertion, in contrast to the knowledge norm defended by Williamson and DeRose:

If an act is governed by a norm, primary propriety is determined by whether the act conforms to the norm, and secondary propriety is determined by whether the agent has reason to believe that the act conforms to the norm. Thus, if assertion is governed by the truth norm, an assertion is secondarily improper if the speaker does not have reason to believe that it is true. (Weiner, 2005, p. 239)

In each case, the argumentative support for such endorsements of multiplicity come from the underlying fallibilism or anti-luminosity to which Hawthorne and

Stanley point. The challenge to our approach to normativity is thus the challenge of how to allow our theory to speak with a single voice without abandoning the fully general fallibilism which we are here assuming.

The schematic outline of the theory of rationality developed in the last chapter has the resources for avoiding this argument from fully general fallibilism to multiplicity. It does so by allowing two places in which a notion of excusability has a place, and allowing the conclusion that no further notion of excusability is needed beyond these two places.

Begin with the first place in which excusability can arise. Within the beastly dimension of rationality, the principles of normativity involve only *conferrers* of rationality, *targets* of belief toward which the conferrers are directed, *epistemic operators* that govern the target in question, and *enablers*. The latter is a function of diminishers and defeaters of rationality and requires that no diminisher that is present passes the threshold sufficient for defeat. One example of such a principle within the beastly domain is a classic Chisholmian principle:

If I'm appeared to F-ly and have no grounds for doubt that something is F, then it is reasonable for me to believe that something is F.

Here the conferrer of rationality is the appearance state, the enabler is the absence of grounds for doubt, the target is a proposition of the form *something is F*, and the level of rational support provided by the conferrer for the target is at the level sufficient for rational belief.

Such norms for the beastly dimension allow an initial notion of excusability without sacrificing unity. Suppose an individual violates the above norm in the following way: upon being appeared to F-ly, the individual believes that something is G, where G is not F (nor related to it in any way that would explain how believing that something is G is appropriate to the circumstances). Such a case divides into two: in one case the person knows the principle and that it is being violated; in the other case, such knowledge is absent. In the former case, the irrationality is not excusable; in the latter case, it may be.[4] But this fact alone provides no fodder for the multiplicity conclusion, since the principle under consideration, and all the principles relevant to the beastly dimension, have an enabling condition in them. In situations in which irrationality is present, the analogous condition to an enabling condition is one that includes an excusing condition. When the enabling condition is fully satisfied, the analogous case on the negative

---

[4] It is important to note that mere lack of knowledge isn't itself an excusing condition, but can be if the remark about not knowing is meant to indicate some sense or understanding of the situation that would explain in a positive light why the belief in question was formed. It is the latter kinds of cases where we find lack of knowledge involving excusing conditions.

side is when there are no excusing conditions. So, the relevant analogy here, for cases when an excuse is present, are cases in which the enabling condition is triggered in some way by diminishers of the level of rationality, perhaps to the point that the diminishers are full defeaters. So on the positive side, we can say that a conferrer has a certain level of epistemic potency that can be blocked by the diminishers or defeaters in question; and on the negative side, we can say that the explanation of irrationality (which, of course, involves the violation of a norm) can be diminished or defeated as well. Such a resource is already present in the story concerning the rationality of the beastly dimension and triggers no need for multiplicity at all. For the resources of that story already encode in the function of the enabling condition an aspect that allows an analogous notion of excusability which can explain simple cases of the difference in culpability between known and unknown violations of norms.

What such principles cannot explain, however, are more sophisticated types of violations of norms, for there are two other types of excusing conditions that such an account fails to accommodate. In the first category are the "drugs or disability" excuses. When our rational capacities are compromised by the presence of drugs or disability (including insanity and other mental difficulties), both our intellectual and other behaviors might be fully excusable. Don't such cases require a notion of excusability that is conceptually independent of the normativity that is the focus of the present approach? In short, aren't disabling excuses quite different from diminishers and defeaters of irrationality?

Perhaps they are, but not in a problematic way. One way to keep such a recognition from being problematic is to keep the two logical spaces distinct. We might say that when behavior, intellectual or otherwise, is excusable in this way, the behavior in question is neither rational nor irrational, normatively adequate nor normatively inadequate. Instead, the best way to think of such cases is to categorize them as outside the bounds of normative appraisal altogether.

If we take this route, the distinction between rationality and excusability is present but never overlapping. That is, there is never a case where an irrational belief is excusable nor any case where a rational belief is inexcusable. With this wall of separation between the two, our understanding of normative propriety, as developed here, would not fail to speak with a single voice to the egocentric predicament of what to do and what to think. All that would result is that in some cases the theory had nothing to say at all, and some other theory would be needed for whatever falls under such exemptions from epistemic appraisal of cognition. That would be a limitation on the theory here, but not fatal to it, since fatality, in the present context, would be a matter of failing to speak with a single voice. Failing to have anything to say at all is not a failure to speak with a single voice.

To accommodate this way of thinking, the sketch of a theory in the last chapter would need to be amended. Doing so would involve adding another condition to the antecedent of our epistemic principles, to the effect that no exemption from epistemic appraisal is available in the circumstances in question. Such an emendation would have the requisite effect of guaranteeing that assessments of rationality and assessments of excusability were never jointly correct.

This route, though possible, is nonetheless not a fully satisfying one. The reason is that the phenomenon of disabling excuses doesn't remove the individual in question from the egocentric predicament, but rather simply changes its form. The answer under consideration would be a fine approach if all disabling excuses changed the person in question from agent to patient, no longer capable of the kind of response to environment distinctive of the former as opposed to the latter. Mere patients face no egocentric predicament: the carrots in my garden don't have the capacities relevant to such, nor do the flu viruses that I hope to avoid this winter. Responsiveness to environment is not what is distinctive about an egocentric predicament, but whatever is, is something not always removed by a disabling excuse. So we should not presume that the value-driven grounds for the present approach to normativity can be so easily set aside.

If we refuse to build a wall of separation between normativity and disabling excuses, however, we must allow that, e.g., insanity doesn't by itself imply normative impropriety. The complex conceptual schemes of some paranoid schizophrenics, for example, may strike us as irrational. But they are constructed in response to the same egocentric predicament we all face, and though for certain purposes, legal and social, we shouldn't treat such people as responsible for their behavior, we don't need to generalize here and require our theory to treat their beliefs as irrational in the sense under investigation here. Part of the readiness to accept such negative characterization of the beliefs of those suffering such challenges is paucity of vocabulary, instanced by adolescents when everything they don't like is characterized by a single term.[5] So, when disability excuses are present, even conceptually resourceful philosophers sometimes sound like inarticulate adolescents. There is no need for such, at least from this particular value-driven orientation. We can grant the possibility of full rationality for paranoid schizophrenics while noting the negatives. We can avoid calling their beliefs irrational while still noting that they are delusional, out of touch with reality, that

---

[5] Unfortunately, "gay" is the most recent favored term of which I am aware. "Unfortunate" is an understatement here, since the term is also associated with bigotry and discrimination, and the connection between the latter and the use of the term in question is not accidental. I much prefer the slang of my generation, where "cool" and its denial could always be relied on in every context without having such unfortunate political, social, and ethical consequences.

they suffer from social and occupational dysfunction, that they reason in ways that can easily lead to incoherence, etc. But they also face the same egocentric predicament more normal people face, and our theory should not allow whatever excusability conditions that are present and which legitimately affect other normative domains (legal and moral responsibility, for example) to carry sway here. The inclination to do so is certainly present in ordinary language and thought concerning the notion of rationality, but we are dissociating from that evidential base for our approach. Once we do so, the inclination to treat disability excuses as signaling irrationality always and everywhere needs to be recognized for what it is: it involves a loss of focus on the value-driven underpinnings of our investigation combined with an acquiescence to the lexical paucity displayed in ordinary language.[6]

We should not be misled into thinking that the theory will be so permissive about beliefs under conditions of drugs or disability that it will count nearly all, or at least most, such beliefs as rational. Such an assessment is incorrect. The challenge of the reflective level, for example, is its generality. It is simply not that easy, on the basis of reasoning about what to make of one's evidence, to endorse principles that never lead to the kind of incoherence that undermines rationality.[7] Moreover, principles endorsed yesterday, but not rejected today, can serve to undermine one's rationality because of the conflict between the two. It takes an incredible amount of ingenuity to maintain, for example, a paranoid picture of reality, and the strategy of asking for more information to find out exactly what is involved in such a conception of the world is quite regularly a good strategy for revealing the incoherence of the picture. So leaving open the possibility of full rationality for such delusional conceptions should not be thought to open the floodgates, making it too easy to be both rational and delusional. There is no reason, I think, to suppose that the world and our experience of it is likely to be so epistemically kind.

It is this latter approach that I prefer, refusing to restrict the domain of epistemic appraisal, but in either case, the existence of these types of excuses will not pose a problem for our project. In neither case do we find a reason for thinking

---

[6] My whining here is thus double-edged. One part is about the value-driven origins of this project. The other part, though, is directed at projects that have underpinnings in terms of ordinary thought and talk. Such approaches need to be careful not to ignore the possibility that their theories simply incorporate limitations on vocabulary instead of something of more semantic or metaphysical interest (say, the meaning or essence of the concept). I will leave it to others more interested in such projects to determine how to avoid this difficulty.

[7] I qualify the kind of incoherence in question because of the lessons of lottery and preface paradoxes. The lessons there are that certain types of incoherence are unavoidable for fallible beings, even for those who are perfectly rational.

that our normative theory cannot speak with a single voice, and it is that threat alone that forces us to say something about excuses. There is, however, one further kind of excuse that our theory to this point does not address. This type of excusability reveals the limitation of the approach to excuses that adverts only to principles governing the beastly dimension. This type of excusability arises when we consider pairs of related cases such as the following:

- Case 1: S believes a target on a given basis for which there is no epistemic principle that treats the basis as a conferrer with respect to that target.
- Case 2: Add to Case 1 that S believes the target as a result of intentional deliberation about how to find the truth, following the light of reason as best S sees it.

In terms of the resources developed in the section on base-level principles, we can say that the two cases are the same in terms of the prima facie irrationality of the beliefs, but not the same in terms of (level of) ultima facie irrationality, because of the presence of diminishers that may be strong enough to constitute defeaters, thereby rendering the belief excusable (and thus not irrational). But this story may appear too weak. One might object, claiming that "We need a *positive* epistemic notion to describe the second case, not one that is merely equivalent to lessening or denying ultima facie irrationality."

If we agree on this point, then we need a further condition for excusability beyond what has been developed so far. And I believe we should agree, for if we attend again to the earlier example, what is important to note is the shift in total perspective between Case 1 and Case 2. Recall that the concern toward which our theoretical efforts are directed is one arising out of the egocentric predicament and which requires a resolution honoring the perspectival character of what to do and what to think. Since the perspectives are significantly different in the two cases, theories are implausible when they treat the cases the same. In Case 1, there is only irrationality with no hint of excusability. In Case 2, the perspective is dramatically different, leading to a different assessment, perhaps one in terms of excusability but also perhaps one in terms of full rationality.

Accommodating this additional element of excusability requires a theory of the sort that grants the rational significance of reflective ascent. Hence the theory outlined in the second section provides precisely the needed resources for accommodating this additional notion of an excuse. It does so by pointing out that engaging in reflective ascent can turn an irrational start into an adequate finish. In such a case, there is still a scent of irrationality in the air, since the information alone, apart from the enabling clause and the reflective condition, provided no adequate conferrer for the target in question. But whatever element of irrationality is present in such a case, it can be fully excusable. And all this without any need to resort to a theory that refuses to speak with a single voice.

Reflective ascent can thus affect violations of base-level epistemic norms in two ways: by diminishing the degree of irrationality involved, and by introducing different principles which explain how the original irrationality is replaced by some positive level of rationality, including the possibility of full rationality. Some defenders of Perspectivalism will want something stronger, so that when one does one's best to follow the light of reason as one sees it, full rationality is guaranteed. For such approaches, an element of infallibility or luminosity will be part of the view. It is important to note, however, that nothing in the picture presented here is incompatible with a thorough-going fallibilism. Defenders of such fallibilism might cite the ineliminable possibility of unnoticed incoherence at every level of reflective ascent, and insist that incoherence can always generate impropriety in an intellectual life. Fallibilists might also point out the possibility of guidance by epistemic conditionals for which there is no underlying episte-mic norm, as happens when one has a "drugs or disability" excuse. Fallibilists might also point out the possibility of defeaters not incorporated into the reflective perspective, but present in the total information available to the agent in question.

In these, and probably others as well, there is no requirement that the present approach endorse any infallibility or luminosity. There is also no reason at this abstract a level to insist that the theory reject infallibilism either. That decision must be made on other grounds at a different time, but what is important here is to have the sketch of a theory in hand that doesn't require any amount or degree of infallibility. If good defenses of some degree or amount of infallibilism are found, it will be a relatively simple matter to revise the sketch to accommodate the infallibility. The harder task we have set is to make the sketch compatible with fully general fallibilism, and that, I claim, we have done.

One might also worry that accommodating reflective ascent in the story of normativity exposes a theory to the important objection raised first by William Alston concerning levels confusion in epistemology (Alston, 1981). Alston rightly argued that various skeptical strategies trade on levels confusion, first asking for evidence for what you believe, and once given, asking for meta-evidence that one's first-order evidence is actually a reliable guide to the truth of the claim believed. Alston rightly pointed out that the meta-challenge need not be met in order for the first-order evidence to confirm the proposition believed. That is, he insisted that one could have adequate evidence for a claim, even if one didn't have adequate evidence that one has adequate evidence for that claim. The skeptic's strategy is thus rejected as illegitimate.

The present approach, however, doesn't join forces with the skeptic against Alston on this point. What is correct in Alston's response is that *absences* of information at the meta-level don't undermine what is present at the base level, but nothing in this response to the skeptic tells us what to make of *presences* at the meta-level. The present approach focuses on the latter, and thus remains untouched by Alston's proper response to certain skeptical challenges.

Moreover, it is important that Alston's objection not be turned into a general prohibition against anything at the meta-level affecting any assessment at the object level. For it is well known that at least some involvement has to be present between the two. One type of undercutting defeater is when one acquires information that undermines one's confidence that the information one possesses is a good guide to the truth of the proposition one believes on its basis. Such an undercutter is evidence that one's information is not evidence for p. It is thus information at the meta-level, but if not overridden by further information, it defeats the rationality of believing the claim in question on the basis of the base-level information.

In the schematic outline presented here, no substantive commitments have been made, however, about exactly when and where meta-level information is relevant to object-level assessment. That is a matter to be decided in the process of turning schema into theory, which will be addressed later. The only point to note, then, is that there is no good objection arising from the concern about levels confusion to block this type of approach, leaving intact the positive case for such an approach.

3.5 Conclusion

The conclusion to draw here is that the notion of excusability introduces, by itself, no need to abandon hope that our theory can speak with a single voice. It is easy, however, to think that this univocity requirement is stronger than it is. It arises in the context of a particular value-driven conception of epistemic theorizing, beginning with a particularly fundamental human concern, and deriving a normative theory that answers to it. Given different starting points, the demand for univocity might be unsustainable or even undesirable. For example, it is fairly obvious that it will not be required in any theory attuned to ordinary language. As is well known, there is, at least, the "ought" of practical deliberation in ordinary language as well as the "ought" of general desirability (see Wedgwood (2007)), the first an epistemically constrained notion of what is required of us and the second one insensitive to this factor (see Sher (2009) and Thomson (2008)). More generally, there is the possibility that first-person assessment might come apart from third-person assessment, and perhaps second-person assessment as well (see Darwall (2009)), and there are the arguments for relativism and contextualism about normative language that generate disunity in a theory as well.[8]

It is worth noting that there is an important challenge to each such alternative project. In each case, we may ask why anyone would bother with constructing such a theory. Perhaps it is justification enough to have a free afternoon with little to do, but that puts such theories at the same level of philosophical significance as a long game of Solitaire. The discipline of philosophy deserves better, and to do better, each such theory needs to be motivated in some way in terms of something that matters. There is thus an underlying methodology for theory construction in philosophy as well as other theoretical projects, that is best satisfied by providing a value-driven explanation of why we engage in such work in the first place. Ordinary language projects in philosophy came into currency in such an environment—in a context in which there was an explicit meta-philosophy that limited the scope of what philosophy could be expected to accomplish and what it couldn't. J. L. Austin is noteworthy in this regard, maintaining that the distinctions found in ordinary use are much better as guides to reality than the invented vocabularies preferred by philosophers.[9] Such a meta-philosophy is explicitly value-driven, and projects that aimed at a descriptive grammar of some range of ordinary discourse could be justified in terms of it. Without such an underlying meta-philosophy, however, it is unclear how and to what extent the development of ordinary language projects in philosophy has any significance beyond that of counting blades of grass in one's yard.

It is worth noting that such an explicit value-driven meta-philosophy can be iterated as well. If one inquires why one should philosophize in the way that value-driven approaches recommend, this meta-philosophical question is appropriately answered in terms of what "meta-matters": we move to the meta-metaphilosophical level and talk about what matters at the first meta-level. And when further, higher-order queries of the same type arise, we answer them in the same fashion: for any n-level query about how to philosophize about level $n - 1$,

---

[8] For excellent discussion of these various grounds for disunity in theory, and strong resistance to such, see Thomson (2008, especially chapters X and XI).

[9] "...our common stock of words embodies all the distinctions men have found worth drawing, and the connections they have found worth marking, in the lifetime of many generations: these surely are likely to be more numerous, more sound, since they have stood up to the long test of survival of the fittest, and more subtle, at least in all ordinary and reasonable practical matters, than any that you or I are likely to think up in our armchair of an afternoon—the most favourite alternative method." (Austin 1961, p. 182.)

the answer will be in terms of what $meta_n$ matters. And there is no escape from the hierarchy of what matters.

So any ordinary language investigation of our use of 'ought' and its cognates needs to be buttressed by an explanation of why it is important to construct such a theory. And any approach to normativity that distinguishes between first-, second-, and third-person assessments needs to tell us why distinguishing these various perspectives answers in any way to what matters or what is of fundamental human concern. Finally, any approach that faults the present theory for failing to be able to generate an adequate account of moral authority should be able to say why such a failure is significant. Merely insisting that morality matters isn't enough. Answers here are not difficult to imagine, since the history of ethics is full of such answers. Perhaps morality matters because well-being is important, because we need solutions to coordination problems with other individuals, or because morality can be generated from relatively uncontroversial constraints on rational thinking and willing. Such answers would ground moral theory in a way independent of the present normative theory, and thereby eliminate any objection to the present theory arising from a concern that it can't provide a foundation for morality. If an independent account of the significance of morality couldn't be offered, and the present approach can't provide a foundation for morality, then so much the worse for morality: it would be as groundless as ordinary language projects pursued without the underlying ordinary language meta-philosophy that gave it its point.

Our present concern, however, need not become embroiled in such meta-philosophical issues, since the point of the present chapter is not to generalize the methodology used here to motivate a theory of rationality that speaks with a single voice. Instead, the point of this chapter was to investigate the plausibility of various challenges to the very idea of such a theory. The challenge of disunity is that, even given the theoretical starting point of the present project, we will be forced to posit a further, secondary notion of propriety relative to the purportedly fundamental notion. As we have seen, this concern does not withstand scrutiny: there is no need for our theory to speak with anything but a single voice in response to the issues of what to do and what to think.

4

Rational Disagreement

4.1 Introduction

We are now in a good position to reflect on what has been accomplished so far and what remains. The project undertaken here is, as I've been repeating, value-driven, arising out of the fundamental egocentric predicament of what to do and what to think. The schematic outline of the theory that answers to this concern is the double double-aspect approach that relies heavily on the difference between a non-perspectival value theory and a perspectival normative theory, one that distinguishes norms and principles appropriate to the beastly dimension from those appropriate to the reflective dimension. What remains to be done is to describe the manner in which the changes from one dimension to another are accomplished, and what is the mechanism driving these changes. Before engaging in this final segment of the project, however, we may take a brief interlude to show the power of the schematic approach generated to this point to address two important implications for matters of current epistemological controversy. The first one concerns the nature and possibility of rational disagreement, and the second one the scope and possibility of epistemic obligations. The present chapter will engage the issue of rational disagreement, with the defense of what I will call Epistemic Optionalism taken up in the next chapter.

We can approach the controversy in question by noting first how absurd it would be to deny that there can be rational disagreements, *tout court*. One way to arrive at such a position would be to endorse that everyone has an obligation to believe the truth, defining rationality in terms of satisfying such an obligation, and deriving from these two claims the conclusion that rational disagreements are not possible. But from the results achieved to this point, it is easy to see where this argument goes wrong: to hold that we ought to believe the truth is to confuse the theory of normativity with the theory of evaluation. While it is a good thing, perhaps the best thing from a purely intellectual point of view, to believe the truth, it is simply false that we ought to believe the truth. The reason we need to retain this distinction between the theory of normativity and the theory of evaluation is precisely because our normative theory needs to honor the perspectivality platitude, and no theory that insists on the inability of a false belief to be normatively adequate pays this platitude its due.

Slightly less implausible, perhaps, are approaches to rationality that rely on factive elements of some sort, such as those that endorse the claim that the norm of belief is knowledge. On such views, it is always irrational to believe something you don't know to be true, and if so, no case of disagreement could ever involve rationality by both parties.

Such views, construed as responses to the predicament of what to do and what to think, overreach. For one thing, it is doubtful that any endorsement of the requirement could itself be rational—philosophical knowledge is a very rare commodity, except in the case of negative information, such as that knowledge isn't justified true belief or that Descartes' proof for the existence of God fails in the context of his epistemological project. More importantly, such factive elements in the theory of rationality allow too much intrusion of the theory of epistemic value into the theory of epistemic normativity. What is right to do or think is deeply perspectival, whereas what is best isn't. To return to an earlier example, an analog of every factive approach to rationality will sustain the kicking of self when things go badly, as when one gets stuck in traffic for hours on a route that is typically faster. As we have seen, that is a mistake, one arising from a confusion of the theory of value with the theory of obligation. If one knew, or was aware, that things would go badly by choosing that route, the kicking would be appropriate. But one didn't know, and it isn't (even though regret certainly is).

Moreover, if one is attracted to the idea of conforming what one believes to what one knows, there is a better way to do so than to claim that knowledge is the norm of belief. The better way is to think of knowledge itself as the (or a) goal of belief, replacing (or supplementing) the standard truth goal with that of knowledge. Doing so makes knowledge itself what we aim at, or what drives cognition, rather than simply getting to the truth. Such a position has its attractions, and doesn't succumb to the problems noted earlier for the idea that knowledge is the norm of belief.

The same points would apply to any other factive controls on rationality, and all such approaches should be rejected precisely because they make rational disagreements impossible. Since it is a direct consequence of the perspectivality platitude that such disagreements are possible, we need to look elsewhere to find limits on the scope of rational disagreements.

There are more plausible stories than those just considered that suggest that if we control for certain differences between people, we can honor the perspectival character of rationality while still insisting that certain kinds of rational disagreement are impossible. Some say that such aren't possible once one has controlled for differences in total evidence and for known differences in competency.[1] Others say that there is no need to insist that all parties of such disputes are irrational, but only that at least one is.[2] If disagreement remains even after controlling for the differences just mentioned, then at most only one of the two is satisfying the rules of rationality, but so long as one is satisfying these rules, one is rational, even if it is equally obvious to each that they are satisfying the demands of rationality. The point of this chapter is to use the resources of the schematic outline of a theory of rationality developed to this point to consider the question of the possibility and scope of rational disagreement.

4.2 Mollificationism and Its Discontents

Let us call the position that views disagreement as a sure sign, albeit defeasible, of irrationality "mollificationism." Mollificationists see harmony in viewpoint as the equilibrium point in the theory of rationality. The rational expectation is that people will agree, at least under certain conditions, so when they don't, perplexity arises that needs to be explained in one of three general directions: either there is some difference related to possession of relevant information or the ability to process it, or somebody is being irrational.

Mollificationism faces serious problems, however. Notice, first, what happens when one insists that agreement in attitude is the only natural point of equilibrium in the theory of rationality. Mollificationists like to attend to cases of disagreement in which one person believes p and the other $\sim p$, but this is only one kind of attitudinal distance between people. There are, at the coarse-grained level, four possibilities: believing, believing the opposite (disbelieving), withholding, and taking no attitude at all. And if we move to the fine-grained level of degree of belief, there are as many possibilities as there are real numbers between zero and one.

Mollificationists hold that differences in attitude are always and everywhere rationally suspicious, and once we see the variety of attitudes possible, this view should look strange and bizarre. Even if we restrict ourselves to the coarse-grained level, the Mollificationist has strange demands. If you and I disagree about p, it is not enough that each of us gives up our beliefs. If you give up your belief and come to withhold concerning p, but I give up any attitude at all because I don't know what attitude fits my evidence any longer, the Mollificationist is still

---

[1] Representatives of this view include Christensen (2007) and Elga (2007).
[2] A view of this sort is defended in Kelly (2005).

unhappy. We still disagree in attitude: you withhold and I take no attitude at all toward *p*. What are we poor creatures, desirous of being rational, to do now? One of us must defer to the other, but we'd better not both do it at once! The same issue arises if you withhold and I believe. One must defer to the other, but which to which?

The fundamental point here is one about the paralyzing effect that comes from thinking of sameness of attitude as the equilibrium point for rationality. In some cases, no movement to an intermediate stance is possible: all that is possible is for one of the two to adopt the stance of the other.

There is a strong temptation at this point to appeal to the language of compromise to minimize the significance of this difficulty. The response I'm imagining is one that insists that there is no special problem here, that what is highlighted earlier is just a matter of how compromises work in some extreme cases. In lots of cases, there is an intermediate position available, but in other cases there isn't; in both kinds of cases, however, the demands of rationality still impose a requirement of compromise in the face of disagreement in attitude.

The language of compromise is rhetorically useful here for the Mollification-ist, and it is important to see why it is inappropriate language to use to describe the view in question. To see why, consider first how ordinary compromises occur and what they involve. Suppose two politicians disagree about policy. In the end, some resolution is necessary, since unending paralysis is intolerable (for whatever reason). So they compromise. Both think the result is less than ideal. To understand the result, we need to know not only the history of the process, what they used to think and why, but also what they presently think and why. They think that the compromise is best, in some sense, but also, in another sense, that it is not. Without some such internal conflict, we don't yet understand the political process in question or the full nature of the accommodations that have been made by one or both parties. Such compromise requires some such internal conflict, whereas, had one of the two convinced the other of the correctness of his or her view, no such conflict would be present and no compromise would have occurred.

Mollificationism can be pleasingly put in terms of the language of compromise, involving the claim that when two cognizers disagree about some claim *p*, there is rational pressure for compromise. Such language is misleading, however, since situations of cognitive compromise are different from situations of full resolution of disagreement or conflict. When resolution occurs, the story we tell has present agreement as the outcome of past disagreement, as when a husband and wife start with different priorities for a daily schedule and resolve their differences by adjusting their priorities in light of the preferences of the other. Such accommodation in solving a coordination problem introduces new information about the preferences of others, and thus differs from cases of political compromise. When cognitive compromise occurs, we expect something akin to what we found in the political case. As the disputants become more aware that they are converging on a point where rationality compels them to abandon their beliefs (as Mollificationists would have it), they may view the approaching event with consternation. They may view it as an intellectual loss to mollify their attitude, and this sense of loss will not leave once the convergence point is reached. Just as in the case of political compromise, some present mark will remain in place to distinguish it from cases of simply becoming convinced that one is mistaken. It is not enough to note only that the two used to disagree and now no longer do, since that doesn't distinguish compromise from mere change in view.

It is difficult to see what decent answer the Mollificationist can provide here to explain the difference. After compromise, the two now agree about p: they both withhold judgment, let us suppose. How did this come about, in a way that makes compromise different from mere change in view? One might try to account for the difference by saying that they still assess the force of the evidence differently. But this can't be the story if rationality requires compromise, since then X and Y still disagree: one's assessment is that the evidence supports p and the other that it doesn't. In order to be rational, the two will have to give up this view as well. If all we can say is that they used to disagree but no longer do, we have no difference at all between compromise and mere change in view.

Perhaps, though, the Mollificationist can go internal here. Each can hold that from their own point of view the claim in question appears true or false, respectively, and that this appearance doesn't disappear when compromise occurs. Putting the point in this way threatens to undermine Mollificationism almost immediately, however, for rationality is perspectival in just the sort of way that, if the two points of view differ in the way imagined, then a difference in rational attitude is to be expected. What the Mollificationist needs here is a distinction between total point of view (on which rationality supervenes) and some more partial point of view on which differing appearances remain in place. Such a distinction, however, is present in cases of fully resolved disagreement as well, however, since when you convince me that I've made a mistake, I can still see the aspects of the situation that led to my mistake. So the difficulty remains of distinguishing a situation of compromise from one involving a more ordinary resolution of disagreement through change in view, and I see no way to defend the use of the language of compromise here.

So the language of compromise can't be used to rhetorical advantage in support of Mollificationism, and the difficulty concerning the requirement that attitude agreement is the equilibrium point in the theory of rationality remains. Mollificationists might attempt to argue that this problem arises from our antiquated and coarse-grained psychology, one put in terms of the attitudes of belief, disbelief, and withholding. They might claim that a more fine-grained psychology, appealing to degrees of belief or levels of confidence, has the resources to avoid the problems raised.

Such is not the case, however. Even on such a fine-grained approach, there is no guarantee that attitude agreement is always possible. For there is quite a variety of possible psychologies to which our epistemic theory must be applicable. For truly gifted cognizers, a full range of attitudes, representable by the real number line from zero to one, is possible. But other possibilities abound. Some cognizers are not capable of credences, where a credence is represented in terms of a real number between zero and one: such cognizers have attitudes representable only in terms of intervals of real numbers between zero and one. Call the point-like cognizers "credencers" and the interval cognizers "intervalers." Credencers and intervalers are always guaranteed to disagree in attitude. Even among credencers, however, there might be limitations on the range of credence states possible. For example, some possible credencers are capable of only eleven possible credence states: $0, .1, .2, .3, \ldots, 1$. So when two credencers disagree by having adjacent attitudes (one has credence .1 and the other .2, or one has credence .5 and the other .6), there is no intermediate position of agreement available. Similar points can be made about confidencers as well, and once we note the possibilities for cognitive architecture, it becomes clear that the move to a more fine-grained psychology and epistemology isn't going to help. In some cases of disagreement, an intermediate position can be found, but for other cases, no such intermediate point will be available. In such cases, the only options are acquiescence by one of the parties to the dispute or irresolvable disagreement automatically judged irrational.

Moreover, even for fully gifted credencers, there is a difference between taking no attitude at all toward a proposition, and taking some attitude represented in terms of a real number between zero and one. When a credencer with an attitude meets a more laid-back credencer—one who lacks an attitude—disagreement exists. And it is a disagreement for which no intermediate position is available that would count as intermediate between the two. Once again, the only option is for one of the two to acquiesce to the point of view of the other, if Mollificationists are to be believed.

So, moving from coarse-grained belief to fine-grained degrees of belief offers no help on this issue. Mollificationism faces other problems as well, one of which is its tendency toward self-defeat.[3] To see the problem, begin with the hyperbolic thesis that whenever people disagree, they are both irrational. This view is obviously false, or so I believe anyway. This fact about what I believe together with the hyperbolic thesis in question implies that no one can rationally believe the hyperbolic thesis. It is a philosophical thesis undermined by a quite prosaic fact, the fact that some of us think that disagreement is at least as expected in matters philosophical as elsewhere. Moreover, consider the implications of this epistemological hyperbole. When tempted to such a view, a responsible cognizer should always check to see if others disagree. In cases of philosophical views, finding such evidence will always be quite easy. E-mail a few friends in philosophy and you will have it. But then not only the hyperbolic thesis itself cannot be rationally believed, neither can any disputed thesis in any part of philosophy or elsewhere.

We should not label the horribly hyperbolic thesis "self-defeating," however, at least not necessarily so. It isn't, since it is possible that everyone agrees with the thesis. A nice analogy here is with two versions of the Liar Paradox. The direct version of the paradox occurs when we have a sentence such as "this sentence is false." But there are indirect versions, such as when a shirt has the following sentences on front and back, respectively: "the sentence on the other side of this shirt is false," and "the sentence on the other side of this shirt is true." Here we have a kind of contingent undermining of each sentence. If we want to say that each sentence is a liar sentence, defeating its own truth, we will have to say the self-defeat is contingent rather than necessary as in the former case. Perhaps the language of self-defeat isn't the right language here, but terminology isn't really the point. What matters in both cases, semantic and epistemic, is that the view is problematic because of contingent factors that are in place. In the semantic case, it is the sentence itself that is defeated; in the epistemic case, it is belief in the hyperbolic thesis the rationality of which is defeated. In the epistemic case, what matters is that these contingent factors are so obvious and predictable that one needs a really serious epistemic blindspot not to take such a factor into account before endorsing the horribly hyperbolic position. We may want to say that the position is contingently self-defeating in the way the shirt sentences are, and I will adopt that terminology here, with the forewarning that contingent self-defeat may not be a form of self-defeat at all together with the additional proviso that

---

[3] This self-defeat argument is used against a version of Mollificationism in Plantinga (1999). I believe the first printed version of it is Peter van Inwagen (1996), which was presented at the Chapel Hill Colloquium in 1993, but wasn't published until 1996. It is instructive to note that defenses of Mollificationism since these pieces were published typically ignore this argument from self-defeat.

the object of defeat is the truth of a sentence in one case and the rationality of belief in the other. What matters most is the clear point that the flaw in question is debilitating to any theory endorsing such a claim.

Contingent self-defeat doesn't only apply to the hyperbolic position, however. For those who detect a scent of irrationality and try to confirm it by additional factors, the same problem remains. If you think that scent and reality converge when the disputants are epistemic peers, the same problem remains; if you think such convergence occurs when epistemic peers share all and only the same direct evidence, the embarrassing problem is still present. I will not offer my own e-mail address for proof, but will now relativize a bit, in case I'm not your peer or your knowledge of epistemology exceeds mine. The thesis may not be contingently self-defeating for absolutely everyone, since there may be an epistemologist who is either smarter than all the rest or who has better information than all the rest. So the claim could be believed by the smartest or best informed, but by no one else. For everyone else, though, the thesis is so likely to be contingently self-defeating that it is no better off than the horrible hyperbole itself.

Perhaps we could put the point this way. There are too many assumptions needed for the amended hyperbole to be adopted. One assumption is that you are smarter or better informed than anyone who disagrees with you about the amended hyperbole. But there is another assumption that even the most arrogant among us will have trouble with. There will be lots of epistemologists in the future. Many of them will be really smart. Many of them will know lots more about epistemology than we do. And, right now, Mollificationists should agree with the result of us that some of these incredibly smart and well-informed epistemologists will think the amended hyperbole is false. But maybe I'm wrong. The point, however, is that it is an assumption needed for the amended hyperbole to avoid contingent self-defeat that I'm wrong. No one should be so intellectually arrogant as to commit themselves to the view that there will never be an equally informed and bright disputant of the refined hypothesis, nor that there will never be a brighter and better-informed disputant of the amended hyperbole.

Moreover, going down the hyperbolic path should seem, once we begin investigating it, a completely wrongheaded way to proceed intellectually. We want to get to the truth and avoid error. How to do so is often not clear, but it is easy to describe things at a very abstract level in terms of the concept of evidence or indications of truth or signs of truth. We seek indications of truth and falsity, and adjust our views to such signs. We want to be the kind of individual who looks for evidence of truth and follows the evidence where it leads. Nowhere in this story of the intellectual life does our neighbor enter in. When we want to know whether p is true, we don't turn to surveys to find if there are people who think *p* is false. Because we don't, we don't in turn try to sort these naysayers into more or less intelligent, more or less informed. At best, other people are repositories of the evidence we seek, not a source of basic evidence itself. That is how we behave when seeking the truth, and any account of the epistemic significance of disagreement needs to take account of this practice.

One might object that this description is woefully inadequate because it leaves out the role of testimony. In the course of finding the truth and avoiding error, our neighbor plays a key role as a source of information. This point should be acknowledged because others are repositories of evidence (or else there is a chain of testifiers leading back to such a repository). Once we learn, however, that the person speaking has no information about the matter beyond what we also have, that person's word ceases to have the ordinary power of testimony, which the word of others has in virtue of our lack of information on the subject. We can no more find out that the moon revolves around the earth by an opinion poll than we can that all ravens are black by looking at more sheets of white paper. The lesson is that we can easily supplement the story under consideration about truth-seeking to accommodate a place for testimony without coming anywhere close to Mollificationism.

There are complications that would need to be addressed in a full discussion of the relationship between the epistemology of testimony and the epistemology of agreement and disagreement, but my point here is simple enough that we can bypass the complications at present. We are considering the self-defeating character of simple views on which disagreement undermines rationality. In response, I pointed out that we don't engage in inquiry by taking surveys as seriously as such views would require, and the response to this simple point was that this simple point ignores the importance of testimony. My response is that we don't need to place the kind of importance on opinion surveys that the self-defeating views imply in order to take testimony seriously in our epistemology. Refining this point to make it precise would be an interesting detour here, but the point is so obvious that no such detour is needed to appreciate it.

Here a note of caution is in order, however, about this self-defeat argument. I have been careful to avoid characterizing this argument as an argument that Mollificationism is false. The kind of self-defeat in question is not with respect to the truth of the view, but with respect to the rationality of endorsing it. The argument is not intended to show that Mollificationism is false. It is only intended to embarrass defenders of the view. It embarrasses them because it shows that it is hardly possible to rationally endorse it. The worst cases of such self-defeat are cases where it is impossible to rationally endorse the view. Mollificationism isn't in this predicament but is still in a situation one shouldn't be sanguine about.

The facts that lead to the kind of self-defeat in question are fairly ubiquitous and obvious, so as a matter of contingent fact Mollificationists should abandon their view.[4]

There is a more direct complaint as well to lodge against the idea that compromise is the default order of the day in the face of disagreement. The more direct complaint concerns what I will call cognitive self-alienation. To see what cognitive self-alienation involves, let me begin indirectly. Each of us has certain cognitive abilities and disabilities. Some of us are better at math, some are better at noticing small details, some are better at visual detection, etc. In addition to these differences in cognitive abilities, there is also the matter of our own view of ourselves as to the level of ability we have in a given domain. This perspective on self can lead us to demur on changing opinion in the face of disagreement and can also lead us to defer to others in certain circumstances, such as when we view them as in a better position on the matter. Whether to demur or defer is, in part, a matter of our perspective on ourselves.

In between demurring and deferring is desisting in belief, which is perfectly sensible from each of our points of view when our view of ourselves falls between a view calling for one to demur or for one to defer. To defer and to desist both involve a change in view, but all three responses are often to be understood in terms of the relationship between a first-order response to disagreement and a meta-level perspective on oneself that makes sense of the various responses of demurring, deferring, or desisting.

The notion of compromise championed by Mollificationists, however, is different. Recall that we are supposing that compromise is required in such a way that points of view can differ in the way imagined between X and Y (so that from X's point of view p is true and from Y's $\sim p$ is true). Since resolution of disagreement has failed by ordinary means, each is aware of the presence of someone who disagrees, and neither has a perspective on self that removes the disagreement. We thus have individuals involved in a disagreement whose views of self are incompatible with desisting or deferring, but rather call for demurring on the issue of changing opinion. And yet, compromise is required, according to the Mollificationist. Such a requirement, however, insists that the perspective on self taken by the two individuals be abandoned or ruled irrelevant. Neither is allowed to take into account a perspective on self that calls for demurring, no matter how they came to such a view of self, and instead must respond in a way

---

[4] Elga (2010) responds to a version of the self-defeat argument. His response focuses on the issue of truth, however, and it is clear that the threat of self-defeat is not a threat to the truth of Mollificationism.

that would occur quite naturally if their perspective on self supported a response of desisting or deferring. The Mollificationist position thus requires cognitive self-alienation, where one has a view of oneself and one's abilities that coheres fully with all of one's prior experiences and one's total conception of things, and yet which cannot rationally play a role in what attitude is legitimate at the first-order level. Instead of a happy union and coherence between first-order belief and meta-level attitude toward self, we have alienation and hostility between these levels required by the theory of rationality in question. A theory that insists that rationality requires such cognitive self-alienation has a serious burden of explaining how the theory is appropriately sensitive to the perspectival character of rationality.

So the problem of cognitive self-alienation is a problem of failing to honor appropriately the obvious perspectival character of rationality. The Mollificationist emphasis on compromise requires discounting aspects of a perspective in determining what attitudes are rational. In any case of disagreement, part of what needs to be assessed is whether attitudes of deferring, desisting, or demurring are most appropriate. The mere fact that someone has one of the three attitudes doesn't by itself make that attitude appropriate, but which attitude is appropriate should be a matter determined from the point of the view of the individual in question. That is the lesson of the perspectival character of rationality, and the implication of it is that the Mollificationist's demand for compromise will often require cognitive self-alienation because the perspective of the person in question makes demurring the appropriate attitude when the Mollificationist insists on desisting or deferring.

4.3 Testimony and Disagreement

All of these points might seem so obvious and compelling that one can begin to wonder how one could favor the view that disagreement imperils rationality at all. There are two concerns here that might give pause. First, there is a concern about levels confusion, thinking that the argument under consideration concerning cognitive self-alienation is best addressed by carefully distinguishing between the rationality of belief and the rationality of meta-beliefs about the initial belief. Second, there is a legitimate worry from the fact that sometimes we do reasonably abandon a view because we find others who disagree. Both issues need to be addressed in order to make sense of the significance of disagreement. We shall also find important implications in addressing these concerns, implications regarding the idea that there is no optionality in rational opinion and regarding the idea that rationality is a matter of one's total evidence.

We can begin this sorting task by considering how to understand the epistemic significance of disagreement. Here we might model the epistemic effects of disagreement in two quite different ways. One way is to take opinions of others as evidence regarding the target proposition.[5] Another way is to treat the opinion of another as a way in which people typically signal that they have information that shows that the claim in question is true.[6] On such a model, the word of another isn't immediately and directly evidence for the claim in question, but rather (on the reasonable assumption that ordinary folk are typically reliable) evidence that there is good evidence regarding the claim in question. If we add to this model some account of how to detach the evidence operator, some account of the conditions under which the move from "there is evidence that there is evidence for p" to "there is evidence for p" is epistemically appropriate, then the model tells us conditions under which the opinion of another is evidence for the claim in question, though only indirectly so.

The difference between these two models concerns whether the word of another is evidence or meta-evidence, and there are various subtypes for each. Some subtypes appear when we think of disagreement in terms of defeaters. In the theory of defeat in epistemology, the usual view is that of John Pollock according to which there are two fundamental types of defeaters: rebutters and undercutters.[7] Since a rebutter of the evidential relation between A and B is just evidence against B, we get a distinguishable model only by treating disagreement in terms of undercutting defeaters. An undercutter for my evidence for p is a claim that supports the view that the evidence isn't a reliable indicator of the truth of p. For example, suppose you know that if you seem to see a pink elephant, your eyes can't be trusted. This information functions as an undercutting defeater for the usual evidential support relation between seeming states and related beliefs in the context in question.

There is theoretical pressure to model testimony and disagreement in similar terms, so it would be theoretically awkward to adopt an evidence model for one and a meta-evidence model for the other. Some may also argue that we get a more elegant model if we ignore undercutting defeaters, so that the word of another is either evidence for the claim in question or evidence against. For example, if the evidence model of testimony is accepted, such a requirement would force us to model disagreement in terms of rebutting defeaters (i.e., evidence

<hr>

[5] I believe it is fair to say that the evidence model is the default position in the literature on testimony and in the literature that endorses some version of what I am calling Mollificationism. See, e.g., Feldman (2006, 2007), Christensen (2007), Elga (2007), and Elga (2010).

[6] For a defense of such a view, see Kelly (2005). See also Moffett (2007).

[7] An early account of the distinction can be found in Pollock (1974).

against the claim in question). This second requirement, however, encounters difficulties when we think in terms of the meta-evidence model. To model testimony meta-evidentially is to hold that the word of another is first and foremost evidence that there is evidence for the claim in question, so modeling disagreement as a meta-level rebutting defeater would be to insist that disagreement is evidence that there is good evidence against the claim in question. Such a view is obviously too strong. At most, disagreement can only be meta-evidence that whatever evidence exists for the claim in question is not adequate to support rational belief in the claim in question. Once put in this way, however, it is clear that the best meta-evidence model will treat disagreement in terms of undercutting, rather than rebutting, defeaters, since an undercutter aims at undercutting the quality of the connection between evidence and what it defeasibly supports. The lesson, then, is that treating disagreement in terms of rebutting defeaters fits best with the evidence model, while treating disagreement in terms of undercutting defeaters fits best with the meta-evidence model.

At first pass, modeling the epistemic significance of testimony and disagreement at the meta-level seems to have an advantage. First, when one hears an utterance of "Bismarck is west of Fargo," the initial and basic epistemic significance of such an experience is to make reasonable the claim, not that Bismarck is west of Fargo, but that someone is saying that this is so. The nature of the sensory experience in question is best understood in terms of the latter claim rather than the former one. Given ordinary circumstances, the utterance also supports the claim that the person saying this believes it as well, and also that what is said is true. Thus, in ordinary circumstances, such an utterance provides rational support for the claim that Bismarck is west of Fargo. But the latter claim, at first glance at least, doesn't receive rational support in the immediate and direct way that the claim that something is F is immediately and directly supported when one is appeared to F-ly.

Such a meta-level view also fits quite naturally with our attitudes toward devices built to gather data. Imagine that you want to know the range of light conditions shining on a particular window in your home, from sunup to sunset. You don't have time to watch all day, and besides, if you look down to record an observation, you'll miss some information. So you want to build a detection device that records the observations automatically.

Of course, you don't just construct the thing haphazardly and then take its word for the truth (the idea, let's say, is to build a device that generates a continuous graph plotting light wavelengths against time). You construct it according to what you take to be a good design plan and then calibrate it to make sure that it is accurate. Prior to calibrating it, it didn't provide undefeated evidence about the matter in question. Prior to calibrating it, you had insufficient information to conclude that the machine was reliable. You need reason to trust it to use it to acquire information about the target of inquiry. Now, in general, failing to have any such meta-information is not itself a defeater of the confirming power of first-order information: I don't have to have information that I'm reliable before acquiring reasonable beliefs on the basis of inquiry. Moreover, calibrating the machine doesn't change its capacities with respect to my inquiry: it doesn't somehow turn the machine into a first-order evidence generator when it was only a second-order evidence generator before. Clearly, prior to calibration, the graph generated is evidence that this machine is responding differentially to different lighting conditions. We have evidence that the device is responding to information about the target of inquiry; it is a relay device, relaying information about something I want to know about. The information relayed is, of course, evidence: it is the information relevant to the question of what to believe about the target of inquiry. The question is how best to understand this production of evidence, and as described, the best model is fundamentally in terms of meta-evidence: its readings are evidence about the evidence regarding the target of inquiry.

Viewed in this way, we have a nice story to tell about the machine before and after calibration. Prior to calibrating the device, we aren't in a position to detach the evidential operator: we don't have a system of information that allows us to conclude that there is evidence for a given claim on the basis of the machine readings which give us evidence that there is such evidence. Prior to calibrating the device, we can't rely on the machine in arriving at reasonable beliefs about the target of inquiry, but after calibration, such a possibility exists, and the difference between these two situations is just the difference between only having evidence that we have evidence for the claim in question and actually having evidence for that claim.

I conclude then that the meta-evidence model of testimony and disagreement has an initial advantage over the evidence model. There is, however, a concern that might undermine this advantage. Such a picture may seem to conflict with the basic trust necessary for early learning and the rationality involved in it. Much of what we know depends on taking the word of others prior to having anything like the information generated by the calibration process described earlier for measuring devices. In being rational animals, we come equipped with default cognitive mechanisms and as learning progresses we come to adapt these default mechanisms in various ways, including the development of wariness about sources of information. So the description of calibrating a detection advice is relevant once a certain level of sophistication is achieved, but it can't be the basic description that applies to all testimony.

This point about early learning appears to threaten the meta-evidence model in the following way. On the meta-evidence model, there are two stages needed to use testimony as a guide to belief. In the first stage, detachment of the meta-evidence operator must be appropriate in order to get the information that there is evidence for the claim in question, and in the second stage, a second detachment of the remaining evidence operator must be permissible in order to arrive at the conclusion that the claim in question is true. On the evidence model, only one detachment step is needed.

Once seen in this way, there is some pressure to view the meta-evidence model as an overly intellectual model of how learning by testimony occurs. Take your favorite 3 year old, and consider what it means to say that this small child is detaching an evidence operator twice over. Isn't it all a bit silly to think of 3 year olds engaging in the practice of detaching evidence operators?

No it's not, once we are careful in our understanding of what epistemic operator detachment involves. We can see this point most clearly by considering the evidence model itself, on which only one instance of detachment occurs. On the evidence model, the child just hears what is said and detachment is just a matter of taking the word of the person in question: it is to come to believe the claim that is asserted by the source. What legitimates this detachment is the absence of grounds for doubting what is communicated. The epistemic engine of rational belief operates on its own, independent of awareness or inference by cognizers.

A simple perceptual case makes this point obvious. Consider the epistemic principle that licenses believing it is raining when it seems to be. The principle says something like "when it seems to you that p, and you have no grounds for doubting that p, it is reasonable to believe that p." There is an epistemic operator on the consequent of this conditional, and detaching it involves nothing more than believing p when the antecedent conditions are satisfied. One doesn't reason first to the conclusion that it is reasonable to believe p, and then detach in a further step of reasoning. But detachment must be legitimate, in spite of not being some step of reasoning encoded in one's psychology.

The meta-evidence model may still seem objectionable even given this point, since there must be a first detachment involving the conclusion that there is evidence for the claim in question. Surely it is implausible to view this child as forming beliefs about evidence prior to forming beliefs about what is asserted. So the meta-evidence model still seems to over-intellectualize the process of belief formation on the basis of testimony, even when the language of detachment is understood to require no step of reasoning from operator-governed content to operator-free content.

I think this criticism misconstrues the meta-evidence model, however. On this model, in order for testimony to make a belief rational, an intermediate explanatory step is required in which one moves from having evidence of evidence for p to having evidence for p. But the intermediate conclusion need not be present in the cognitive system in question in the form of belief. A common approach to detachment rules begins from the idea that high probability, or a high degree of evidential support, is not sufficient for rational belief, but it is in the absence of defeaters.[8] Defenders of the meta-evidence model might transpose this idea into the present context by claiming that the presence of evidence that there is evidence for p is itself evidence for p when there are no defeaters present to undermine the connection between the claim about meta-evidence and the claim about evidence. Thus, when the small child hears a parent say, "There are cookies on the table," evidence exists in the form of an experiential state in the child. This state, on the meta-level model, is initially only meta-evidence, but in the absence of defeat, it is also evidence; and once we reach the point that it is evidence, it makes the belief of the child rational so long as there are no defeaters to undermine the connection between it and p itself. Given this approach, two types of defeaters must be absent, one kind concerning the relationship between the existence of meta-evidence and the existence of evidence itself, and the other kind concerning the relationship between the existence of evidence and the object of belief.

The key to avoiding the over-intellectualization charge, then, is to refuse to treat the model in terms of inference structures that require an additional piece of information in the head of the child before allowing rational belief in the claim in question. Instead, the evidence claims themselves are cast in terms of properties of the state itself that is evidence. Thought of in this way, the experiential state in question has the property of being evidence for p always and everywhere on the evidence model, but it has this property on the meta-evidence model only when there are no other pieces of information internal to the agent in question that defeat the supports relation between the state in question and the claim that this state is evidence for the target proposition in question. This supports relation, however, is not a relation between an experience and some further belief or experience, but is simply a relation between the experience and a proposition.

Once we adopt the meta-evidence model, we are in a better position for understanding the differences between testimony and disagreement. Merely hearing "huh-uh" from the back of the room after reporting a low opinion of Bush as president isn't first and foremost evidence that he's a good president. It's not

---

[8] For discussion, see Williamson and Douven (2006).

always clear what counts toward being a good president, but what is clear is that merely having Joe Bozo (construing this name as a mere Millian tag, of course) in the back of the room on Bush's side isn't such evidence. Disagreement may give us pause about what we believe, and such pause is most naturally understood in terms of an initial role of undercutting legitimate confidence about the adequacy of our grounds for belief. In special cases, it may combine with other information to function in stronger ways, as when one acquiesces to greater expertise or more information. What is common to all cases of disagreement, however, is that such disagreement first and foremost provides a meta-level defeater: in short, an undercutting defeater of some sort.

Such a view of testimony and disagreement gives us resources for addressing arguments with Mollificationist tendencies. Consider David Christensen's discussion of such a case in which he and his friend are dividing up their respective shares of a bill at a restaurant, and they come up with different answers:

Given that my friend and I are generally reliable thinkers who have studied the same evidence, the fact that we disagree will be explained by the fact that at least one of us has made a mistake in the case. But intuitively, the explanation in terms of my friend's mistake is no more reasonable than the explanation in terms of my mistake. And I should acknowledge this by moving my belief toward hers.[9]

The argument here begins by assuming that both parties are equally competent and have the same evidence (and, we may assume, both reasonably view the matter in this way as well), and concludes that both parties are required to abandon belief in the conclusions they reached. The key claim in the example involves the idea of explaining the disagreement. There are two ways in which the disagreement can be explained: either in terms of one person having made a mistake or in terms of the other person having made a mistake. The key claim here is that neither explanation is more reasonable to adopt than the other.

The idea here, I take it, is that if your information includes parity of evidence and parity of competence regarding one with whom one knows that one disagrees, then a change in view is required. The passage itself actually employs the stronger position that the mere fact of parity itself requires a change in view. This stronger position should be avoided, however, since the facts may be as stated and yet it be rational to deny them (to say nothing of being unaware of the disagreement itself). So we should focus on the weaker position, that includes among your background evidence the parity in question and the disagreement itself.

---

[9] Christensen (2007, p. 196).

The example is well chosen to make plausible the principle enunciated, that parity information plus knowledge of disagreement requires attitude adjustment. The example, however, does not require Mollificationism, interpreted in terms of requiring compromise of attitude even when one's view of self supports demurring. In this case, demurring is not the natural attitude assumed to be present in each party, and hence the case is not a case of intellectual compromise at all. The contrast between Christensen's case and cases in which demurring is appropriate helps with the task of separating the theory of testimony from the theory of disagreement. The difference concerns the defeasible character of epistemic support.

Testimony provides reasons for belief because, in the usual case, no internal defeaters are present concerning the evidentiary power of testimony. But in cases of disagreement, the default position is that the power of testimony is in conflict with the belief in question and whatever evidential support there is for it. The testimony in question is meta-evidence that threatens the relationship between whatever evidence one has and the conclusion drawn from it, and thus is an undercutting defeater of some sort. Undercutters can appear in various guises here, but the view I find the most promising is that disagreement threatens the idea that enhancements of one's own epistemic position with respect to the claim in question would still confirm what one believes. In a context in which one has formed a rational belief on the basis of evidence available, the evidence not only must favor that belief over other attitudes, it must be evidence that is adequate for some given attitude such as belief. For evidence to be adequate evidence, it must not only confirm the claim in question but it must do so in a way that makes reasonable coming to a conclusion on the claim in question rather than refusing to take an attitude until more information is found. Of course, it is not necessary to form a belief to this effect, but if the total information available to one doesn't license closure of inquiry, then one shouldn't believe the claim in question even if one has good evidence for it.[10] This distinction between the quality of one's evidence and the question of closure of inquiry gives us two different types of undercutters that might be present. One sort threatens the confirmation relationship itself, and the other threatens the connection to closure of inquiry, and the approach that is quite intuitive here is that disagreement undercuts in the second way.

Either way, however, cases of disagreement are cases in which we have conflicting meta-evidence, with disagreement (on my preferred approach) providing

---

[10] For further discussion of this point, and application to the issue of norms of assertion, see Kvanvig (2009).

a defeater of the claim that one's evidence is adequate evidence, evidence sufficiently telling to warrant concluding inquiry. It does so in a context, however, in which one's total body of information also provides rebutting meta-evidence against the defeating power of disagreement, since we are assuming that until encountering the disagreement, the body of information in question made the belief in question rational, made closure of inquiry on the issue rational, and thus also provided warrant for the claim that anyone who disagrees must be mistaken. The result is that cases of disagreement are cases with conflicting defeaters, and some sorting is required to determine which defeat relationships take priority.[11]

Such cases are not limited to cases of disagreement, but arise quite generally when we confront new information that flies in the face of rational opinion. What is distinctive about disagreement is that the conflict occurs at the meta-level, at a level that affects the rationality of the target proposition only indirectly. In the ordinary case of new information, everything is occurring at the object level itself, and the interaction between old information and new information is merely a matter of replacing one body of evidence with another. In cases of disagreement, however, the conflict is occurring essentially at the meta-level, and meta-level information only affects object-level rationality when certain conditions are met.

The issue here is related to a point made by William Alston, a point about levels confusion in epistemology. Alston argued that it is not a good idea to let the skeptic use second-order claims to undermine the epistemic status of first-order claims.[12] For example, when the skeptic asks how I know that it is raining, and I cite some evidence for it, the skeptic may question how I know that this evidence is a reliable indicator of rain. That's an interesting question, but one that is irrelevant to whether I know that it is raining, according to Alston. It may be relevant to the question of whether I know that I know that it is raining, but if we hold that evidence needs to reliably indicate in order to generate knowledge, we do not also need to hold that we must know that evidence is a reliable indicator in order to know. Keeping clear of such levels confusion helps avoid a very quick regress argument for skepticism, since skeptics can always ask about meta-level $n + 1$ when we answer their query about level n.

As we saw in outlining the form of epistemic principles that are sensitive to the role that reflection plays in the story of rationality, Alston's arguments are all directed at a position that finds significance in *absences* at the meta-level, and as such, have no direct consequences for the position developed here that insists

---

[11] The requirement of sorting helps explain why dogmatic rejection of those who disagree is not always rational, in spite of having evidence, going into the situation, that those who disagree must be wrong.

[12] Alston (1981).

that *what is present* at the meta-level is epistemically relevant. This point leaves us with a satisfying result that, even though we can't automatically treat facts at the meta-level as having significance for the lower level, there are circumstances in which significance filters down to the object level.

That result still leaves disagreement, however, stuck at the meta-level. In cases of ordinary testimony meta-evidence becomes evidence through absence of defeaters, and evidence secures rational belief because of the absence of defeaters at this level as well. But disagreement is meta-level evidence that often cannot filter down on this basis because of the problem of conflicting defeaters.

In such cases, the only way to go is up: conflict is resolved at the next meta-level. It is here that one's perspective on oneself as a cognitive being provides an arbiter in the form of an overrider in one direction or the other. That is the lesson of the discussion of deferring, demurring, and desisting connected with the problem of cognitive self-alienation for Mollificationism. Which of these options is the rational one to adopt depends on the full development of the schematic outline of the theory of rationality developed to this point, so we will need to remain silent at this point on exactly how and when meta-level information allows for rational disagreement even when controls are in place regarding intellectual peerhood and quality of evidence.

The upshot of this account of the difference between testimony and disagreement is insight into the degree to which rationality is a subjective and perspectival matter. In slogan form, the claim being defended concerns the rational significance of reflective ascent. As a person loses trust in self as a cognitive being, rationality dissipates in the face of disagreement, and an adequate theory of rationality needs to honor this point. What is rational depends on one's total perspective, and a theory that treats two perspectives as identical even though one perspective contains significant self-trust that is not irrational and the other does not is a theory that doesn't rightly treat the perspectival character of rationality.

4.4 Implications for Evidentialism and Optionalism

These results about rational disagreement threaten two important positions. The first concerns the degree to which optionality is found in the domain of epistemic rationality. The most restrictive view is one that proclaims that there is one and only one attitude toward any given claim rationally compatible with any body of total evidence.[13] The other position threatened is evidentialism itself. In order

---

[13] In Feldman (2007) Feldman labels this position the Uniqueness Thesis. David Christensen, in Christensen (2007), speaks of Rational Uniqueness, and Roger White, in White (2005), argues extensively for the view though he never fully endorses it.

for these two positions to be consistent with the role that reflective ascent plays in the story of rationality, reflective ascent will have to change one's body of total evidence and change it in a way that is mandated by prior evidence.

Begin with the latter worry, the worry about evidentialism itself. We can escape the worry by trivializing the view, by insisting that one's total evidence is everything relevant to the rational status of one's cognitive attitudes. Evidentialists, however, do not typically think of their view as an utterly trivial one, so suppose we do not wish to trivialize the truth of evidentialism in this way.

If we do not, then there are difficulties accommodating the rational significance of reflective ascent, precisely those difficulties noted earlier concerning the relationship between object-level bodies of evidence and meta-level factors. Once we grant the mundane fallibilist point that meta-evidence isn't evidence, we face the possibility that meta-evidence might affect the rationality of belief without itself being part of one's object-level body of evidence regarding the content of that belief. These points thus leave the door slightly ajar for the claim that reflective ascent is relevant to rational status but not in virtue of changing one's total body of evidence with respect to the target proposition.

It is worth comparing the role of reflective ascent in the face of disagreement with undercutting defeaters. Undercutting defeaters are meta-level claims, threatening the relationship between evidence and belief, but typically add to the body of evidence in question in virtue of being a defeater: where e is evidence for p, an undercutter d is typically a defeater in virtue of the fact that $e\&d$ is not evidence for p. (Compare: a visual experience is evidence for the claim that a given object is a particular color; but that very same visual experience, combined with knowledge that lighting conditions are abnormal, provides no evidence for that object being that color.) It is thus clear that adding an undercutter of this sort to the story changes the total evidence with respect to the claim in question. That is, in the case of typical undercutters, a meta-level claim filters down into the body of evidence in question precisely because an undercutter is a defeater and hence alters the total evidence with respect to the claim in question.

There are two important differences between typical undercutters and the role of reflective ascent in the face of disagreement. The first is that the type of undercutter provided by disagreement is unique. It is a type of undercutter that threatens closure of inquiry, which is not the same thing as an undercutter that threatens the evidential support relation itself. As noted already, in cases of epistemically rational belief, the body of evidence in question needs to provide support both for the content of the belief and for the claim that further inquiry into the matter is not necessary before forming an opinion (though, of course, there is no need for the individual in question to form any belief toward this claim or even to have considered it). In order for this type of undercutter to filter down to the body of total evidence, one will need to maintain that a defeater with respect to legitimate closure is also a defeater with respect to the target proposition itself. That is, where e is one's total evidence for B(p), then if u is such that $e\&u$ fails to support the claim that there is no need for further inquiry concerning p, then $e\&u$ fails to support p. This claim, however, I think is false, and its falsity is revealed by the lottery paradox. In such a case, one's background of the setup of a fair lottery provides evidential support for the claim that one's ticket will lose (assuming a lottery of sufficient size). But there is also information blocking the conclusion that no further inquiry is needed concerning whether one's ticket will lose: that is why it is a mistake to give the ticket to me, and why people check the newspaper to see whether they won.

The concern raised by this point thus goes as follows. Critics of evidentialism might claim that there is a levels confusion occurring when evidentialists count undercutting defeaters in the body of total evidence concerning a given claim. The response, for typical undercutters, is that such undercutters are defeaters of the support relation between the evidence and the claim in question. But the kind of undercutter provided by disagreement is not of this sort. It is an undercutter relevant to the rationality of belief, but some further argument would be needed to show that it is an undercutter of the support relation between the evidence and the claim in question, since lottery cases are examples in which an undercutter with respect to closure of inquiry is not a defeater of the support provided to the claim in question.

Similar remarks apply to the reflective ascent information that resolves the conflict of defeaters that occurs when disagreement is introduced in a context of rational belief. Such information is relevant to the rationality of belief, but it is not obvious that it is legitimately included in one's total body of evidence relevant to the target proposition. One way to put this point is that such reflective ascent information is not exactly evidence itself, but information relevant to how one should weigh the evidence one has. Such a result is a fitting one as well, since it is something close to a truism for a perspectively sensitive theory of rationality of the sort developed here that *there is both the evidence and what we make of it*. To the extent that what we make of the evidence we have is a function of a perspective with healthy doses of reflective ascent, there is pressure to think of rationality not solely in terms of one's total body of evidence regarding a target proposition, but also in terms that are less sanguine to the claims of evidentialism. To say that rationality is a function of one's evidence and what one makes of it is, in this way, to say something that goes beyond evidentialism itself.

The role of reflective ascent also presents problems for highly restrictive views about epistemic rationality. Once we specify a given body of evidence and a given proposition in such a way that disagreement is part of the story, individual differences in how to weigh the available evidence in determining what level of self-trust to display seem inevitable. Restrictivists might insist that such individual differences must be eliminated because only one particular type of reflective ascent is rationally possible, but such a claim is implausible. Some egos are fragile and others are not; some people have a higher degree of self-confidence than others. In the arena of action, it would be indefensible to maintain that there is some precise attitude toward risk that all must display or that there is some precise level of self-confidence required of each person. In our intellectual lives, at the level of reflective ascent, such restrictions are equally implausible. Even when we engage in the most deliberative type of reflective ascent in attempting to sort out whether to defer, demur, or desist, the only hard data we have comes in the form of multiple reference classes. Is this case of disagreement one of mathematical competency? Or is it a case of disagreement arising because I voiced an opinion in the presence of a contrarian? There is evidence relevant to this sorting, to be sure, but the process clearly involves a weighing of the evidence one possesses as well. What is needed is an evaluation of which reference classes are the most relevant for the particular issue at hand, and the idea that such evaluation can be done in an algorithmic fashion on the basis of the underlying evidence plus acceptable rules of inference is a position that needs a powerful argument on its behalf, given how doubtful such a claim is in itself. Such deliberation requires judgment, and though some such judgments are better than others, that is a far cry from saying that there is a uniquely acceptable position that must be adopted. A more realistic account of such cases is that in precisely the same overall evidential situation, some people are more intellectually timid and others are more intellectually self-confident, and that neither character trait is somehow irrational or epistemically inappropriate.

As a result of these trait differences, reflective ascent plays out along different paths, with the result that a given belief is rational for one but not the other. The best explanation of the phenomenon in question is that the role that reflective ascent plays in the story of rationality provides a strong argument in favor of some optionality regarding rational belief, but we will have a chance to investigate this issue more carefully and in more detail in the next chapter.

4.5 Disagreement and Deference

The lessons for disagreement, whether by intellectual peers, superiors, or inferiors, are straightforward. One tempting mistake is to address these questions while assuming the epistemic insignificance of reflective ascent, arguing that if deference is warranted it will have to be so on the basis of information unrelated to the issue of disagreement itself. No such universal rejection of the epistemic significance of reflective ascent is warranted, however, and once we grant this point, it is easy to see why a refusal to adjust one's opinion in the face of disagreement need not be justified in terms of information unrelated to the issue of disagreement itself. One loses grounds, that is, for any straightforward or general conclusion to the effect that rational disagreement among equally competent and informed peers is impossible.[14] One's ability to reflect on the situation and assess whether the general competence and informedness of one's interlocutor is decisive in the present circumstances can't be ruled out as epistemically significant for what is reasonable to believe, and if it can't, there will be no general conclusion available that equal competence and informedness by someone who disagrees requires revision of belief by either or both parties to the dispute. Equally true is that disagreement with cognitive superiors and the better informed can't by itself rationally force revision of belief, for the same reasons. Finally, there is also no justification for a dismissive attitude toward all disagreement by those less informed or less intellectually competent, on the same grounds. It is perhaps true that it is a common vice among intellectuals to resist the pressures of disagreement more than is wise, given an interest in getting to the truth and avoiding error, but such resistance, even if unwise, need not be irrational or unjustified, and a fully perspectival approach to rationality and justification can explain why.

It is worth noting here that embracing the epistemic significance of reflective ascent doesn't require holding that the reflective perspective is always definitive of rational status. An example will help illustrate this point. Suppose you have a rational belief and then reflect on your situation, coming to the conclusion that your belief isn't rational. Nothing about persectivalism or the epistemic significance of reflective ascent forces us to say that the combination of a rational base-level belief is incompatible with a rational meta-belief that the base-level belief isn't rational. One might develop a particular version of this approach that has this implication, but one need not. These issues will be explored more fully, however, in the penultimate chapter.

It is worth comparing this idea of a fully perspectival approach to the use of metalevel information with a related view recently endorsed by David Christensen (Christensen, 2010). Christensen defends a "bracketing" approach to meta-level information, according to which one must fail to give one's evidence its proper "due" in order to be rational (Christensen, 2010, p. 198). For example, if one has a proof of p, but learns that one has just been given a logical-confusion-inducing drug, the proof can't by itself make one's belief in p rational if one

---

[14] Feldman (2009) and Kelly (2010) offer defenses of such a view as well.

continues to believe it, ignoring the new information. Or, again, if one has formed a belief on the basis of a compelling inference to the best explanation (IBE), and learns that one has been slipped the dreaded IBE-confusion drug, the evidence involved in the explanation, in spite of its virtues, can't be given its proper due any longer.

Christensen claims that cases that require bracketing are different in kind from ordinary cases in which undercutting defeaters are present. He says,

> Nevertheless, it seems to me that this second case is very different from the one in which I learn I've been drugged. In the second case, my reason for giving up my former belief does not flow from any evidence that my former belief was rationally defective. (Christensen, 2010, p. 198)

Christensen thus claims that some undercutters show that a belief previously held was "rationally defective," thereby requiring bracketing of present information in a way that isn't present in cases of ordinary undercutting, as when one learns that there is a black light shining on an object regarding which one has previously formed a color belief.

The notion of not giving evidence its proper due, and the related claim concerning rational defects in beliefs, is clarified best by an example Christensen uses, where E is adequate evidence for H, and D is a claim that requires bracketing, such as that an evidence-assessing-confusion drug will be slipped into one's coffee tomorrow. Christensen says,

> I can now see that, should I learn ($E\&D$), I'll have to bracket E, and not become highly confident in H. But I can also see that in not becoming highly confident of H, I'll be failing to give E its due, and I can see that in that situation, H is actually very likely to be true! This accounts for the sense in which the beliefs it would be rational for me to form, should I learn ($E\&D$), are not beliefs I can presently endorse, even on the supposition that I will learn ($E\&D$). (Christensen, 2010, p. 202)

This bracketing picture of higher-order evidence is, we might put it, a position slouching toward a full perspectivalism. One can know in advance that if I learn $E\&D$, H will be likely to be true, just as it would if one only learned E. But upon learning $E\&D$, things change. It is no longer rational to endorse either of these conditionals, and it is not rational to believe H either. But the explanation here is not that one is failing to give E its epistemic due, after learning $E\&D$. It is, rather, that learning $E\&D$ has harmed one epistemically by destroying the evidentiary basis for the conditionals in question. One thus learns, in this situation, not only $E\&D$, but also that the grounds for the conditionals ($E \rightarrow H$ and $E\&D \rightarrow H$) are not adequate for rational belief.

Of course, a fully perspectival approach will need to note that an adequate basis for these conditionals could be restored by further reflection. For example, one might remember one's prior epistemic condition of yesterday, and recall one's rational belief then that these conditionals are true, and that one's knowledge today of E&D is thus misleading evidence regarding H.

Christensen recognizes these points, including the point of how close he is to a full perspectivalism, noting that he has no argument against such a position (Christensen, 2010, p. 203). He resists such a description in favor of the bracketing picture for three reasons. First, he wishes to highlight the way in which the first-order evidence involves epistemic ideals that won't be highlighted apart from the bracketing picture, and second, that the bracketing picture allows a special focus on the role that higher-order evidence plays in the story of rationality. These first two grounds are easy to accommodate within a full perspectivalism. The ideals of being logically and explanatorily omniscient are fully preserved even if we grant that fallible cognizers can sometimes rationally contravene such principles, and it is central to a fully perspectival account of rationality to highlight the epistemic significance of reflective ascent.

Christensen has a third reason as well for preferring the bracketing picture. He says,

Finally, it seems to me that we should continue to recognize a sense in which there is often something epistemically wrong with the agent's beliefs after she takes a correct account of HOE [higher-order evidence]. There's something epistemically regrettable about the agent's being prevented, due to her giving HOE its proper respect, from following simple logic, or from believing in the hypothesis that's far and away the best explanation for her evidence. (Christensen, 2010, p. 204)

On this point, full perspectivalism is in complete agreement. Inferences that preserve truth are, in some sense, failsafe practices to follow in belief formation, and acknowledging the relativity of rationality to full perspectives has the regrettable consequence that rationality is not as intimately connected to truth as would occur if rationality were a function of logical or (objectively) probabilistic inference patterns. Moreover, when we note that, in some sense, the point of epistemic assessment has to do with the goal of getting to the truth and avoiding error, it is easy to see why there would be, in the air, a scent of epistemic failure when the implications of a fully perspectival approach to rationality are acknowledged. The proper response to these points, however, is not to abandon full perspectivalism or to reject the idea of bracketing central to Christensen's view, but rather to note that the appearance of epistemic wrong arises because of imprecision in specifying how rational assessment is related to the goal of getting to the truth and avoiding error. In particular, as Foley (1986) argues, it is crucial to distinguish the goal of truth over error from the goal of truth over error *now*. Moreover, whereas getting to the truth and avoiding error now is ideal, the ideal falls within the domain of epistemic evaluation, not epistemic normativity. It is best to get to the truth, and following simple logic is clearly the best way to do that. But normativity is a different matter, and honoring the perspectival nature of it forces us to recognize that what to do and what to think isn't controlled by what is best. Careful precision on this point will not eliminate epistemic regrets about having to endorse forms of cognitive assessment that fall short of ideal connections to the truth in order to be rational. In fact, full perspectivalism predicts it.

In short, the considerations that Christensen raises for adopting a bracketing picture that falls short of full perspectivalism give us no reason to resist the latter view. Instead, they highlight many of the considerations that augur well on behalf of a move from more restricted admissions of the perspectival character of rationality to a fully perspectival approach to it. Rationality is related in important ways to ideal arguments that are either truth-preserving or probability-preserving, but is not controlled by it, precisely for the reason of the rational significance of reflective ascent. The bracketing of arguments and evidence that Christensen rightly notes is, to change the metaphor, full perspectivalism that has not yet come out of the closet.

4.6 Conclusion

A fully perspectival approach of the sort initially developed in the last two chapters thus has much to recommend it. It can avoid procrustean approaches to the rational significance of disagreement, and it opens a path on which one can find a unity in one's theory that is immune from the demand for a distinction between primary and secondary propriety or between acceptability and excusability. By acknowledging the epistemic significance of reflective ascent, we can preserve the perspectival character of justification in a way that avoids these common discontents in the theory of epistemic rationality or justification. There remains, of course, the large and difficult task of saying precisely when and to what extent these meta-level features affect object-level epistemic status, but even in the absence of a full investigation of these issues, the benefits noted can be sustained by the mere recognition of an appropriate recognition of what is involved in a total perspective, relative to which rationality or justification is understood. Before turning to this final task, however, we can see a further implication of the outline of a theory developed to this point regarding the issue of the scope and possibility of epistemic obligations.

5

Perspectivalism and Optionalism

5.1 Introduction

The issue for this chapter is the question of whether there are obligations to believe, and the answer I will press is "No." The primary argument for a negative conclusion arises from the implications of the Quine–Duhem thesis concerning the underdetermination of theory by evidence. But before developing that argument, I want to begin by addressing the perplexity that a denial of obligations for belief engenders. A similar claim about the realm of action would strike us as deeply counter-intuitive: who would claim that though there are permissions regarding actions and things forbidden in the realm of action, there are no obligations to act? Such a view would be strange fruit of any philosophical tree. So I begin with this issue, arguing that there is an obvious difference between belief and action that explains why a denial of obligations for belief is an expected outcome once we gain a proper appreciation of the way in which we have obligations to act.

5.2 The Rational Difference Between Belief and Action

Begin by assuming the obvious: obligations regarding what to do are commonplace and ubiquitous. Since epistemic normativity is either a specific instance of general normativity, or an analog of it, shouldn't we expect the same to be true of belief? That is, if beliefs are the sorts of things that are subject to the categories of obligation theory (forbiddings, permissions, etc.), shouldn't we expect obligations regarding what to believe to be just as commonplace and ubiquitous as obligations regarding what to do? Since I will be defending a negative answer to this question, I want to rebut this initial objection before working constructively on an argument in favor of a negative answer.

The answer to this concern, I believe, is found in the generic nature of obligations to act. At a quite general level, we are obligated to be good parents, to obey the law, to pay our taxes, to do our homework, to keep our promises, etc.

But how we go about satisfying these general obligations typically leaves open a variety of options. For example, I can have an obligation to repay a debt to you, but that obligation leaves open whether I write you a check, use paper currency, or give you coins instead. Moreover, however I repay the debt, I will perform some maximally specific action to do so, even though the obligation will be more generic than that. Each of the specific actions counts as an act of keeping a promise, and so there is always, or nearly always, an underlying optionality involved in the normativity of action, even though obligations regarding that domain are commonplace. In short, the underlying optionality with respect to action is compatible with obligations to act because of the general tendency of obligations to be generic.

My point isn't that one can't have more specific obligations than something so generic as repaying a debt. Repaying one's debts is an obligation, but so is repaying a specific debt to, say, a particular mortgage company. So when an action that fulfills an obligation is performed, there will be a range of things one does, from the maximally specific, fine-grained action that details every aspect of the token behavior in question, all the way up to the generic description of having done something rather than nothing. In this hierarchy of things done, as we move from the more general to the more specific, it is to be expected that obligations tend to disappear: we are required to do something rather than nothing, we are required to pay our debts, some are required to pay our mortgage by the 5th of every month to Bank of America, but those under this last obligation are not required to fulfill that obligation by paying by check. Of course, one could easily imagine a situation in which paying one's mortgage by check was also required, but in that case one wouldn't be required to pay by check where the check had the particular background image it has. Nor would one be required to print the name of the bank on the check rather than write it in cursive. In short, as we move from the more general descriptions of actions to more specific ones, we typically pass from the region of obligation to the region of optionality. The region of obligation is a significant conceptual distance from very specific descriptions of the variety of actions that satisfy the obligation.

Belief, however, is automatically a very fine-grained item from the start. Beliefs are individuated in terms of their semantic contents, so to have an obligation to believe a given proposition is analogous to actions that are nearly maximally specific. If beliefs were individuated solely in terms of their propositional content, the appropriate analog would be maximally specific actions, and we have already seen that it is rare at best for there to be obligations regarding such maximally specific actions. It is plausible, however, to think of beliefs as being individuated by mode of presentation as well as by propositional content.[1] So it would be a mistake to say that any obligation to believe would be an obligation toward something maximally specific.

The force of the analogy, however, remains in spite of this fact. For when we look at a particular hierarchy of actions performed in any case of satisfying an obligation, we typically find that the level at which obligations occur is quite a distance away from the maximally specific token action which satisfies the obligation. As specificity increases, so does optionality. So if we are talking about a domain in which the claimed items of obligation are but one small step from maximal specification, we shouldn't expect the analogy with obligations to act to give us much reason, if any at all, to expect there to be obligations of that sort. In short, while there are generic action types that are the usual objects of obligation, belief types are hardly generic at all. They are so close to being maximally specific that a best rendering of the analogy with action predicts that we won't generally have obligations to believe. So it shouldn't surprise that there are few if any obligations regarding belief whereas obligations in the realm of action are ubiquitous.

5.3   Optionalism and Restrictivism

We may begin to develop a positive argument for this conclusion—the conclusion that there are few if any obligations regarding belief—by clarifying the extreme options available in this debate. At the far right of the spectrum are views that insist that there is precisely one attitude[2] that one may take toward any proposition. At the other end of the spectrum are views that claim there is always more than one option available. In between are positions that modify each of these extremes in one way or another. Let us refer to the first position as "Restrictivism" and to the other extreme as "Optionalism."

It is easy to see that the most extreme version of Restrictivism is implausible. It maintains that no matter what one's background system of information or totality of experience, precisely the same attitude is required for any given

---

[1] The notion of a mode of presentation is Fregean, helping to explain how some identity statements can be informative even if we have a purely referential theory of names that makes $a = a$ express the same proposition as $a = b$ when both claims are true. For discussion and defense, see Salmon (1989).

[2] I will assume here, for purposes of simplicity, that the attitudes in question are believings, withholdings, and disbelievings. We could think instead in terms of degrees of belief, and perhaps as well in terms of confidence intervals (on this issue, see Sturgeon (2008)). The complexities here are, however, a diversion from the main issue I'm investigating, so I will opt for the simple account for present purposes.

proposition. We saw just such a position in the discussion of disagreement, where the view was that no two people can ever disagree rationally about anything. The only possible underlying rationale for such a bizarre view here derives from the idea that one ought to believe the truth, and that one is irrational in a purely intellectual way whenever one fails to fulfill one's purely cognitive obligations. As argued before, such a view does violence to the perspectival character of a notion designed to address the egocentric predicament of what to do and what to think, confusing the evaluative dimension with the normative. So, if Restrictivism is going to be plausible at all, it will have to be in a less extreme form.

I have described each position as a group of views, since as each view is delimited further, the views move closer to each other. There is another reason as well for thinking of each position as involving a group of views, for each view comes in both synchronic and diachronic versions. Diachronic views focus on what types of changes are required or allowed in the face of new learning. Synchronic views focus on what can correctly be said of any particular attitude regarding any particular content at a given time. We thus have four fundamental extreme positions to begin with, and a first pass at making our descriptions of these positions more precise is as follows:

Synchronic Restrictivism: Where S is in state of information I and p a proposition, there is exactly one cognitive attitude permitted for S regarding p by I.

Diachronic Restrictivism: Where S is in state of information I at time t and S acquires some new information between t and $t*$, there is exactly one total change in attitude permitted for S between t and $t*$ in response to this new learning.

Synchronic Optionalism: Where S is in state of information I and p a proposition, there is always more than one cognitive attitude permitted for S regarding p by I.

Diachronic Optionalism: Where S is in state of information I at time t and S acquires some new information between t and $t*$, there is always more than one total change in attitude permitted for S between t and $t*$ in response to this new learning.

One might think of this distinction in slightly different terms. The primary arguments on behalf of Optionalism, and against Restrictivism, focus on the implications of underdetermination of theory by evidence, or what comes to the same thing, underdetermination of viewpoint by available information. One sort of underdetermination is holistic in nature, pointing out that any testing of a particular theory arises in a context that leaves open whether the theory in question has been undermined by a negative test result or whether some of the auxiliary assumptions involved in setting up the test are responsible for the failure. Another sort of underdetermination is contrastive, claiming that any given body of evidence or information never contrastively confirms any particular theory or viewpoint against all possible competing theories or viewpoints, leaving open the option of rationally embracing an alternative to any particular viewpoint one is rationally permitted to take in light of that evidence or information. Holistic underdetermination, so described, suggests Diachronic Optionalism and contrastive underdetermination suggests Synchronic Optionalism.[3]

We turn, then, to the question of turning these suggestions into arguments that inform us of the proper response to the debate between Restrictivists and Optionalists. Fair warning, however, before proceeding: much of the discussion to follow is an effort at refining the characterizations of the four theses in question, attempting with each round of precisification to take more and more logical territory away from Restrictivists. The ultimate goal is to get us to see what Last Hope Restrictivism looks like, which turns out to be better named "Lost Hope Restrictivism". In short, we shall Chisholm away at Restrictivist positions to the conclusion that no version of the view is defensible.

It is important to set parameters at the outset regarding what kinds of retreat by Restrictivists are allowable. If S and S' differ in their rational beliefs, we should expect some explanation as to why they differ. The initial proposals under consideration already involve one such restriction, since fully general Restrictivism would claim that no differences of opinion on any subject matter are ever permitted: not by anyone anywhere anytime. That is an absurd view, and the earlier accounts involve a retreat from it, restricting permissible disagreements (from the Restrictivists' point of view) to cases where the states of information for the two who disagree must be different. Optionalists still think that such a view is mistaken, and this way of viewing where the earlier characterizations come from yields a strategy for Restrictivists to follow when faced with any objection or counterexample that their latest proposal cannot handle. Such theoretical difficulties will chastise a Restrictivist proposal for being too prohibitory, and any such difficulty will at least hint at an explanation of what has been overlooked by the latest Restrictivist retreat. The hint might then be thought to point the way to an adequate Restrictivist retreat: it will point to a factor that Restrictivists need to control for. And, once the control is in place, Restrictivists can view the retreat as yielding a more precise version of the correct approach.

There must be a limit, however, on what kinds of retreats are legitimate. To see why, note that if we allow any and all retreats, all the way to holding fixed the entire state of the universe and all other normative features of it, we should expect no normative optionality to remain save any that would constitute further counterexamples to the Principle of Sufficient Reason. For the arguments

---

[3] See Stanford (2009) for this distinction and further discussion.

against Restrictivism to be interesting in epistemology, the objections raised by Optionalists must be explicable objections, ones that can cite why it is that the latest Restrictivist retreat doesn't yield the prohibitions the view requires. But if the objections are explicable, not just any and every retreat is acceptable, and the answer to what kinds of retreats are allowable is found in the subject matter under discussion. The subject matter is a purely intellectual, purely theoretical one: it is, we might say, an *alethically* oriented subject matter, not one oriented practically or aesthetically or politically or in any way other than one involving an orientation concerning truth and what it is to be cognitively successful in terms of the fit between mind and world. In light of the subject matter in question, the kinds of factors that Restrictivists can use in refining their position are those involving *purely intellectual* factors, factors such as the nature of the evidence for and against the truth of a proposition, factors such as the kinds of abilities we have or can develop for getting to the truth and avoiding error. Restrictivism, if it is intended to be a substantive epistemological thesis, must be limited to the idea that once all alethic, truth-related, factors have been filled in, only one attitude is permitted.

So, to give a perfectly ridiculous example, suppose there is a plausible objection to Synchronic Restrictivism as characterized earlier, that hints that the rate of digestion accounts for why two people can take different attitudes toward some proposition even though in the same total state of information. Such a scenario is wildly implausible, but if we suppose it has occurred, it would not be appropriate for Restrictivists to thank the objector for revealing a further factor to control for in giving a more refined version of Restrictivism. Rate of digestion is simply not a purely intellectual factor, so if it explains why Synchronic Restrictivism as characterized earlier, is false, it refutes Restrictivism, rather than showing Restrictivists how their theory needs to be refined to avoid difficulties.

These points are essential for setting proper parameters on the debate, and each time we see the temptation for Restrictivists to retreat further, we should consider whether the envisioned retreat is one that is philosophically acceptable, which in the present context requires, as I will put it, that the retreat involves a purely intellectual factor, one that arises from the alethic orientation of the subject matter under discussion.

I have put this point in the perspective of a theory that makes getting to the truth and avoiding error the defining goal for the domain of epistemology. That assumption, however, is not central to our discussion. The language I'm using here is better thought of as code for making the cited factors relevant to whatever epistemic teleology one prefers. If the epistemic goal is knowledge, then the factors have to be related to knowledge; if understanding, the factors have to be related to it. So the point is that the factors that make for Restrictivism or Optionalism have to be articulated relative to the (or an) epistemic goal, rather than to some more general metaphysical perspective seeking to explain why the world, both normative and descriptive, is one way rather than another. So, we can think of Restrictivism as the view that eliminates optionality regarding epistemically rational belief relative to the factors identifiably related to the epistemic goal, whatever that might be. In discussing this issue, I'll assume the truth goal, however, since it is the most common view concerning the epistemic goal, and will thus serve to focus our discussion in a helpful way.

5.4 The Quine–Duhem Thesis and Diachronicity

In the early part of the twentieth century, Pierre Duhem formulated in a quite clear way various problems of underdetermination for the confirmation of theories in physics (Duhem, 1914), and by the middle of the century, W. V. O. Quine had argued that the same problems arise for confirmation in general and not just for confirmation in the sciences (Quine, 1953). The problem for confirmation in science is that no hypothesis has empirical implications all on its own, and hence any testing of any given hypothesis involves that hypothesis together with auxiliary hypotheses and background assumptions. The result is that when a test disconfirms, it is an open question whether it is the hypothesis being tested that is at fault or whether something else. Since disconfirmation is the flip-side of confirmation, we should expect something similar when the test is positive: exactly how to dispense the confirmatory power of a positive test in terms of change of attitude is not fixed by the test situation itself, since it involves more than just the hypothesis being tested.

The first, and immediate, implication of such holistic underdetermination is one within the sphere of practical rationality. For the scientist and the scientific community, when testing generates disconfirmation, there is an immediate optionality implied regarding how to proceed in terms of future actions. If the test doesn't tell one which hypothesis or assumption is at fault, one can be fully rational in proceeding in any of a number of different ways. One way is to abandon the research program that involves the hypothesis, but there are far less dramatic routes to take. One might, for example, look for flaws in the experimental design.

The implications here are not merely practical, however. If an entire research program is abandoned, one would expect the explanation to involve lost faith or belief by the scientist in the theory in question. Some might wish to counsel scientists never to form beliefs about the truth or falsity of their theories, and treat all research as a matter of practical rationality only, but such advice would be poor advice. Cognitive attitudes guide organisms with regard to how to behave, so we should expect that there will be changes in doxastic attitudes involved in any practical decision about how to proceed in light of the experimental result. And presumably, we will find different changes when an entire research program is abandoned than when the adequacy of the test situation itself is blamed.

Once we find such changes in doxastic attitude, the question we need to ask is whether these changes themselves are rational. The argument that they are is straightforward: if they weren't rational, we wouldn't be able to defend the view that the practical decisions they lead to are themselves rational. So, if there is rational optionality in terms of different practical paths to take upon learning of the experimental results, we should expect to find a similar optionality in the cognitive changes that underlie the practical behavior.

This is the fundamental argument from holistic underdetermination to Diachronic Optionalism, and there is but one way to resist it (other than arguing against the holistic premise itself, which would be the truly heroic route, and will thus be ignored here). To resist it, the Diachronic Restrictivist must insist on separating practical responses to an experimental result from cognitive ones, insisting on neutrality at the cognitive level even when some practical response is demanded. Even though the scientist must choose, for example, between trying to figure out what went wrong with the experimental design and abandoning the research project entirely, such a choice must not be based on any difference in cognitive attitudes between those who would rationally take the first route and those who would rationally take the second route. The scientist is in what we might call a cognitive Buridan's Ass Situation: there is no allowable cognitive difference between a scientist who chooses to abandon the theory and one who chooses to question the experimental design of the test. Since the test is not decisive enough, no commitment beyond withholding judgment is allowed.

In this way, the Diachronic Restrictivist faces the same challenge faced by Pyrrhonian Skeptics: it is the problem of paralysis. If we are advised not to form cognitive attitudes in response to changes in our experience, on pain of irrationality, the question is how such an approach allows for reasonable choices among the various practical options available. The criticism of Pyrrhonism was simple: if I have a headache and want rid of it, what am I to do? The answer is obvious: my choice of action will be guided by my cognitive attitudes, and will be a rational response to the situation to the extent that these motivating cognitive attitudes are rational. But what if I'm told that I should have no cognitive attitudes stronger than withholding judgment about how to get rid of my headache? Then I'm a rudderless ship at sea, being tossed to and fro, with no guidance at all. The result is either paralysis or random behavior, attached to hope: bang the head on the wall, count to three million, read a novel, etc. One could legitimately hope that something on such a random list would get rid of the headache, but such a miserly perspective on how to cope with life signals a poor philosophy.

Just so, if the Diachronic Restrictivist advises the scientist to make no changes in cognitive attitude because there is no such unique cognitive change demanded by the experimental results, such a Restrictivism will encounter the problem of paralysis. Cognition guides behavior, and if two behavioral paths are equally rational while no change in cognitive attitudes has occurred, the only available story for explaining the rational optionality in the practical sphere is to appeal to something wholly non-cognitive such as utilities or preference orderings. For, given the Quinean extension of the holistic point, there never was a time where an experiential input yielded a non-optional requirement regarding cognition.

Perhaps the Quinean extension overreaches, however. Perhaps Descartes was right that there is no rational option to believing that I am a thinking thing and that thus I exist and that I am here now. Think of this category as the category of the contingent a priori. Perhaps as well some of the Rationalists were right, that there are uniquely rational attitudes toward some things that are necessary a priori: claims such as *Everything is what it is and not another thing.* Even if we grant both points, however, the earlier point remains, the point that all the work in explaining the rationality of different choices will need to be explained by non-cognitive elements, since, we may assume, individuals who diverge on what to do in the face of a negative experimental result do not diverge in their attitudes toward these rare contents where Restrictivism gains a foothold.

What might these non-cognitive elements be? Well, individual scientists like to keep their funding, so would prefer that over an approach that eliminates it. But that is too cynical an approach to generalize: if all one can cite are things like self-interest and individual preference orderings, the story of the rational optionality in the practical sphere is simply too impoverished. A more convincing story is one that involves the joint scientific enterprise, and expected utility judgments about which direction of future research shows the most promise. But one can't adopt this story without either allowing rationally unacceptable cognitive attitudes in the judgments or facing the problem of paralysis all over again.

The only alternative to this conclusion is to think of such practical decisions as rationally optional precisely because they all involve a cognitive Buridan's Ass Situation (BAS). When a donkey faces a choice between two equally attractive haystacks, and somehow resolves the situation to eat from one of them rather than starve, there is no rational cognitive explanation available for why the left stack was chosen rather than the right stack. So, a BAS is a situation in which the choice between two or more options is simply *rationally inexplicable*: anything said that counts in favor of one option counts equally in favor of the other. But that is a poor account of the choices we face when responding to new input from experience: when scientists are asked why they decided to look for a flaw in the experimental setup rather than abandon a research program entirely, they do not throw up their hands and say "It's just a toin-coss decision." Sometimes they do, and sometimes they don't, and only when they do are they granting that they have no rational basis for preferring one option to other options. In the more normal case, they make a judgment about which practical course to follow, while at the same time granting that the choice isn't uniquely rational. That is, they can make such a choice while finding it understandable and rational to make the opposite judgment.

The Restrictivist will complain, however, that our discussion here is not paying sufficient attention to the precise beliefs being envisioned. The Restrictivist might say that it is fine to take some cognitive attitude or other in response to new learning, but only those attitudes regarding which no optionality is present. One shouldn't identify one of the auxiliary hypotheses as the one at fault in a disconfirming experiment, but one might identify that hypothesis as the one *likely*, or *most likely* to be at fault. So, the complaint goes, the earlier response overreaches, accusing the Restrictivist of barring changes in cognition when that is simply false.

This Restrictivist response is correct that we must be careful to control for propositional content when discussing which cognitive attitudes are involved in any case of underdetermination. But there is no safe haven here for Restrictivism. For, if we move away from the claim that a particular auxiliary hypothesis is at fault in a given case to the claim that it is *most likely* at fault, what story can the Restrictivist tell about why, exactly, that attitude is demanded by the experimental result plus background information? There is no more plausibility to the suggestion that the test results uniquely confirm such an attitude than there is that the test results uniquely confirm that one particular claim is false.

It is important to note here the central role that sense-making plays in the argument in favor of at least a limited version of Diachronic Optionalism. When faced with new input from experience, the rational challenge is to make sense of the new information. Central to such sense-making are judgments about how to proceed, and these judgments are not themselves uniquely constrained by the new input or by background information already in place before the judgment is made. One simply finds oneself in a position where things look more promising in one direction than another, and there is no escape from this aspect of the cognitive dimension of our egocentric predicament. Martin Luther might have been right to declare, "Here I stand; I can do no other," but if he's stating the truth, that says something more about his particular psychological makeup than about the force of the reasons presented to him. Underlying our rational choices are judgments, presuppositions, and assumptions which are rarely dictated by the content of our experience together with background information already in place. It is certainly true that there are strong conservative forces at work in explaining the particular attitudinal changes to be expected, but such conservative tendencies aren't uniquely rational and never were, even though they are clearly rational in ordinary circumstances.

In short, the Diachronic Restrictivism at every turn faces the "Turtles All the Way Down" Problem: challenged to explain the uniquely rational underpinnings of the optionality of practical rationality, such a Restrictivism begins by appealing to some cognitive attitudes to avoid the problem of paralysis, and then has to explain the unique rationality of these attitudes in terms of background information already in place prior to the decision point together with the new experiential input that must be made sense of. But whichever contents of cognitive attitudes are proposed, the same problem re-appears: those contents are not uniquely rational either.

An important point to notice here makes things even worse for the Restrictivist. For any argument for Restrictivism is going to have to take for granted that the epistemic principles governing rational belief must remain constant across the new learning. Nothing in the earlier argument relied on denying this point, but once it is denied, there is an independent argument against Restrictivism. The sketch of the Perspectivalism defended here makes a denial of such constancy a central feature of the view. The central point in the arguments for this view is that when reflection occurs, there is no guarantee that the principles in place prior to the reflection are the same principles in place after reflection has occurred, and without fixity of principles, there is no basis whatsoever for thinking that there is some uniqueness to be found among the attitudes permissible in light of new learning.

Thus, there seem to be multiple good arguments against Diachronic Restrictivism. These arguments, however, fall short of establishing Diachronic Optionalism. As noted earlier, there may be isolated pockets where rational opinion is constrained to a single viewpoint. The examples there involved the a priori, including contingent examples and some instances of necessary truths. The reservations expressed there, however, left open a version of Optionalism not quite as dramatic as that characterized earlier, one we might call A Posteriori Diachronic Optionalism:

A Posteriori **Diachronic Optionalism:** Where S is in state of information I at time t and S acquires some new information between t and $t*$, there is always more than one total change in attitude permitted for S between t and $t*$ in response to this new learning for any *a posteriori* claim.

This diachronic version surely underreaches, since there are vast regions within the category of the a priori where all the points that apply to scientific confirmation and disconfirmation apply as well. To use one simple example, the set theoretic paradoxes for Naive Set Theory underdetermine what cognitive response to take to the problem. So the reach of optionalism is much larger than is encoded in *A Posteriori* Diachronic Optionalism. But for purposes of resisting Restrictivist alternatives to Optionalism, it is intrusion enough.

5.5 Synchronicity

It would be nice if the Quine–Duhem considerations cited earlier settled the issues of synchronicity as well, but unfortunately they do not. To see why, we must first be more careful about distinguishing exactly what the synchronic options are. For, as characterized earlier, it is both too easy and too hard to avoid Restrictivist implications.

First, it is too easy because for any finite individual, there are many propositions that are beyond comprehension. In such a case, any theory of rationality that requires that some attitude or other be taken toward such a proposition is clearly too strong. So if Restrictivism is characterized as it was earlier, it fails much too easily. To address this problem, some restriction is needed on the class of propositions to which the categories of epistemic deontology apply. At a minimum, only those propositions one has the power to grasp should be included, but it is plausible to think that further restrictions will be needed as well: just think of all the propositions there are that you have the power to comprehend but no reason to ever consider (the number of carbon atoms in your little finger, for example). How cluttered would the mind become if attitudes had to be taken toward everything one is capable of taking an attitude toward? Such a Restrictivism is surely too demanding, but we shouldn't view this difficulty as revealing the implausibility of Restrictivism as such, but only of those versions of it that fail to be adequately judicious about the class of propositions governed by the categories of epistemic deontology.

It would take us too far afield to try to find a precise characterization of this class of propositions, so I propose simply to note the issue and grant that it would be an exaggeration to think of this issue as providing a refutation of Restrictivism.

Equally true, however, is that the earlier characterizations lead to a much-too-simple objection to Optionalism. Consider the entire collection of propositions toward which S can take an attitude, and assume that S takes some attitude or other toward each of these propositions. Included, then, in the state of information I for S is this information, since among the things we are capable of is reflecting on our attitudes and taking an attitude toward what attitude we take. Perhaps there is some limit of complexity here beyond which we cannot go, but all we need here is the first level of reflection, chronicling all of S's believings, disbelievings, and withholdings. But relative to such states of information, no Optionalism can leave open the possibility of some different (object-level) belief or disbelief, for it is never rational to believe a claim while believing its negation.[4] So, given this entire state of information, no other attitude toward each of these claims will be permitted, since to do so would require of some proposition that one takes two incompatible attitudes toward it. First, it may not be possible to take two different cognitive attitudes toward the same proposition, but even if it is possible, a theory of rationality shouldn't recommend it. It is obvious, however, that any objection to Optionalism arising from the wisdom of never counseling contradictory beliefs shows a fault with our characterization of the competing views.

At a minimum, to avoid this problem, we will need a distinction between two parts of a system of information. The most common path here is to distinguish one's evidence from what it is evidence for. This is a global approach to such a distinction, viewing the part of the system on which we test the categories of epistemic deontology as being the same part of the system of information for any claim whatsoever. We can characterize the extreme positions, under this approach, as follows:

Global Synchronic Restrictivism: Where p is a proposition and I the state of information S is in that counts as S's evidence, there is exactly one cognitive attitude permitted for S regarding p by I.

Global Synchronic Optionalism: Where p is a proposition and I the state of information S is in that counts as S's evidence, there is always more than one cognitive attitude permitted for S regarding p by I.

---

[4] There is a complication that I will note here, but ignore in the text. On Fregean theories of mental content, a mental state involves three places, one for the attitude, a second for the propositional content, and a third for the mode of presentation of that content. If we don't hold fixed the mode of presentation, the remark in the text is mistaken, since under different modes of presentation, one can rationally believe and disbelieve the same propositional content: Lois Lane believes that one particular person is both a hero and not a hero, under the two guises of Superman and Clark Kent. I will avoid this complication in the text, noting here that I intend my remarks about what a theory of rationality allows or disallows to involve contexts in which we hold fixed all other features of mental content other than attitude and propositional content.

There is, however, a different approach, one that takes a state of information and substracts elements from it, relative to a given proposition under consideration, to see whether the proposition in question survives scrutiny relative to the remainder of the system. Whereas global approaches use the same part of the system of information to determine the status of every proposition, this atomistic approach may use different subparts of the system of information for each different proposition. Such an atomistic approach can be characterized as follows:

Atomistic Synchronic Restrictivism: Where p is a proposition and I the state of information S is in that is alethically relevant to p (but not including p)[5], there is exactly one cognitive attitude permitted for S regarding p by I.

Atomistic Synchronic Optionalism: Where p is a proposition and I the state of information S is in that is alethically relevant to p (but not including p), there is always more than one cognitive attitude permitted for S regarding p by I.

I am not sure which of these ways of refining Restrictivism is best, and point out the difference merely to highlight the idea that the version I'll focus on isn't the only possible one. I'll focus on the atomistic version, since I find it the most promising, but the arguments I'll rely on can easily be seen to threaten both global and atomistic versions of the view. I view the differences between the two as more of an in-house squabble between various Restrictivist positions, and thus not central to the arguments I want to bring against the view. So in what follows, I'll focus on the atomistic versions of each view, leaving it to the reader to see how to adjust the discussion if more global approaches are thought preferable.

Further refinement of Restrictivism is going to be required because of the argument from the rational significance of reflective ascent, and it is worth rehearsing again a brief summary, to show how it undermines synchronic versions of Restrictivism. In slogan form, the cash value of reflective ascent is to allow a distinction between the evidence itself and what we make of it. That is, the epistemic principles that connect this evidence with what the evidence supports will vary in ways that are a function of the kind of reflection a person engages in, reflection that leaves, or can leave, untouched the total collection of basic evidence. The consequence of this fact is obvious: as the epistemic principles change,

---

[5] The parenthetical restriction here needs further emendation, but I won't take the space to do that, since the issues don't affect the prospects for Restrictivism or Optionalism. One problem is that I may not only include p, but also other information that trivially entails p (for example, the conjunction of p with some other piece of evidence) but is "downstream," epistemically from p. Another problem is what to do with self-justifying beliefs, since the system won't contain any information that explains such justification once the belief itself is removed. How precisely to develop the atomistic view here isn't clear, but we can ignore the issue in the present context.

the basic evidence is fully compatible with different cognitive attitudes by the same person at the time in question toward the same proposition.

Working out the details of such Perspectivalism requires an account of the structure of epistemic principles that includes a placeholder for level of reflective ascent, and explaining how a particular group of such principles comes to govern a situation of rational assessment. What is crucial in our present context, however, is not the details of the project but the motivation for it. The motivation is the one developed earlier, that we need a fully general fallibilism that doesn't pretend that we have infallible access to anything: not to the evidence, and not to what to make of it once we acquire some. In the process of intellectual maturation, we learn about the world and our place in it at the same time and in roughly the same way as we learn what to make of our experience and any other new information we glean in the process of discovery. Such a fully general fallibilism honors the perspectivality platitude about rationality in a way that other approaches cannot, the platitude that what is rational for you is a function of your total perspective, both in terms of differences in informational content and in terms of the significance of that information, not a function of what is true or what someone more or differently informed would think.

Once we appreciate the motivation for such a version of perspectivalism, it becomes obvious that no Restrictivism that relies only on holding fixed the evidence, or the total information in one's system of information that is unrelated to the target proposition, can succeed. But it also shows the Restrictivist a way to retreat that might still preserve the view: just hold more things fixed. That is, instead of only holding fixed one's total evidence, one should also hold fixed the epistemic principles linking this evidence with the rest of a belief system.

Atomistic Synchronic Restrictivism II: Where p is a proposition and I the state of information S is in that is alethically relevant to p (including the governing set of epistemic principles but not including p), there is exactly one cognitive attitude permitted for S regarding p by I.

Atomistic Synchronic Optionalism II: Where p is a proposition and I the state of information S is in that is alethically relevant to p (including the governing set of epistemic principles but not including p), there is always more than one cognitive attitude permitted for S regarding p by I.

The change from the earlier characterization of the two atomistic versions is the inclusion of the phrase "including the governing set of epistemic principles." This alteration allows these versions of Restrictivism to avoid the last objection, since it allows the Restrictivism to honor the point that there is both the evidence and what we make of it.

There is, however, one further argument against Restrictivism that this latest refinement doesn't handle. The objection is due to Thomas Kelly:

> Suppose that the evidence available to me is just barely sufficient to justify my belief that it will rain tomorrow: if the evidence was even slightly weaker than it is, then I would be unjustified in thinking that it will rain. Suppose further that you have the same evidence but are slightly more cautious than I am, and so do not yet believe that it will rain tomorrow. It is not that you are dogmatically averse to concluding that it will rain; indeed, we can suppose that if the evidence for rain gets even slightly stronger, then you too will take up the relevant belief. Is there some guarantee, given what has been said so far, that you are being less reasonable than I am?—I doubt it. (Kelly, 2010, p. 121, n. 10)

We can call this objection "the risk tolerance objection." Some people find it easier to risk being wrong than others, while others reveal a deeper horror at the thought of making a mistake. At the extremes, each of these character traits can lead to irrational attitudes, but in between, Kelly suggests, is an area where a tolerance of differences should be shown by our theories of rationality.

This objection calls for one further emendation to the official Restrictivist position,[6] one that puts in place controls for how the competing goals of finding the truth and avoiding error are weighted:

Atomistic Synchronic Restrictivism–Final Version: Where p is a proposition and I the state of information S is in that is alethically relevant to p, including the governing set of epistemic principles but not including p and including the weighting for S of the competing goals of getting to the truth and avoiding error, there is exactly one cognitive attitude permitted for S regarding p by I.

5.6 Full Rejection of Restrictivism

The earlier discussion can be accurately characterized as an argument that puts Restrictivism into retreat, forcing the view to give up more and more territory to Optionalism. What this discussion does not attempt to show, however, is that there is no safe haven of any sort for the Restrictivist.

I want to pursue a deeper argument against Restrictivism, but even given the limited results achieved to this point, the discussion has probative value, since it

---

[6] It also calls for an additional gloss on the sketch of the epistemic principles for the beastly dimension. We can accommodate the role played by such a default range of acceptable variation in risk tolerance in one of two ways. The first is by adding to the account of undercutting diminishers and defeaters that the maximum level of epistemic support provided for a target by a conferrer can be diminished or defeated by lower risk tolerance. The other way is to restrict the maximum level of support that a conferrer provides for a target so that this maximum is itself relative to the subjective attitude in question.

shows that the most common versions of Restrictivism are inadequate. Consider, for example, the Uniqueness Thesis defended in Feldman (2007):

Uniqueness: For a given body of evidence and a given proposition, there is some one level of confidence that it is uniquely rational to have in that proposition given that evidence.[7]

The forced-retreat argument given earlier undermines Uniqueness, forcing Restrictivists into a much smaller territory than Uniqueness versions of the view wish to claim. It also undermines the slightly weaker, conditional version of Uniqueness that Jeremy Fantl and Matthew McGrath endorse, according to which you are justified in believing a claim if and only if, of the three attitudes of believing, disbelieving, and withholding, belief is the one you should have (Fantl and McGrath, 2009, p. 131, n. 6), which they identify as roughly the same as what Earl Conee and Richard Feldman label "Evidentialism":

Evidentialism: "if S has any doxastic attitude at all toward p at t and S's evidence at t supports p, then S epistemically ought to have the attitude toward p supported by S's evidence at t." (Feldman and Conee, 2004, p. 178)

For both Fantl–McGrath and Conee–Feldman, Uniqueness is qualified conditionally, allowing that one take no attitude at all toward some propositions. But even given this conditional qualification, the position is undermined by the forced-retreat argument against Restrictivism given earlier. In short, even though the forced-retreat argument isn't a conclusive argument for Optionalism, its reach is nonetheless significant.

Still, it would be nice to have an argument that there is no safe haven of any sort for any substantive Restrictivism. As we have seen, any version of Restrictivism that has a hope of being successful is going to have to hold much more fixed than just the body of evidence a person possesses. The Final Version of Atomistic Synchronic Restrictivism shows exactly how extensive those controls have to be for Restrictivism to avoid arguments in favor of optionality.

The question that such a view must face is not the question of whether further refinements are needed, but rather the question raised initially about whether the controls in place are legitimate controls in the context of this debate. When I first introduced this question, I used the example of rate of digestion as a kind of control that couldn't be legitimately controlled for. In saying why, I pointed out that it lacks the kind of alethic orientation appropriate to the debate in question, and so if rate of digestion constituted a difficulty for Restrictivism, it would be an

---

[7] For the best defense of Uniqueness, without endorsement of the position, see White (2005).

objection that demanded surrender rather than one that leaves open the option of further retreat.

Of course, rate of digestion isn't such a feature—it is irrelevant to the question of whether a belief is rational. But it raises an important concern for any retreat that those inclined toward Restrictivism might take. It isn't enough to refine the position by imposing a further control on the things that one cites that yield the required prohibitions on optionality. The controls must also be legitimate controls.

One way for the controls to be illegitimate is for them to come from an improper domain—that is what the rate-of-digestion example shows. But there is another way for the controls to be improper, even when they come from within the proper domain. That is the kind of argument I want to develop here against the retreat positions Restrictivists have been forced to take.

The argument, at a vague level, is that even controls that fall within the alethic orientation of our subject matter can be illegitimate if those controls themselves involve logical dependence on non-alethic factors. To continue using a ridiculous example, suppose rate of digestion explains why the early formulations of Restrictivism are false, but it does so in the following way: rate of digestion is logically sufficient for a particular weighting of the epistemic goal. In such a case, the latest version of Restrictivism would be controlling for rate of digestion by controlling for weighting of the epistemic goal: any change in the weighting in question would require a different rate of digestion. In such a case, the restriction would be illegitimate, just as much as if rate of digestion were controlled for directly.

It is important here that the controls in question are logically connected to the items that wouldn't be legitimate to control for, and not ones that are causally or nomically connected. If rate of digestion caused one person to have different evidence than another, that wouldn't imply that it was illegitimate to control for sameness of evidence when formulating a new version of Restrictivism.

It is for this reason that defenses of Restrictivism in the literature take the controls needed to defend Restrictivism to be invariant except for the total evidence requirement. The version of Restrictivism that fails to control for total evidence is obviously mistaken: it says that no variety of opinion on any subject matter is ever rationally available. So the first thing to control for is total evidence or total information: if we hold this feature fixed, we can allow rationality to come apart from truth without having to abandon Restrictivism.

This control seems perfectly appropriate, since it is a control, unlike rate of digestion, that falls within the alethic orientation of the debate. But appearances here can be deceiving. We assume the restriction is licit because the body of evidence or state of information in question is assumed to be within the mind of the person in question, and to have arisen in the usual sorts of ways in which information gets into heads. In particular, we assume that there are no logically sufficient conditions for variability of total information that would be problematic. If, for example, the Restrictivist were to note that one's rate of digestion logically determines which state of information is relevant for a given person, then the control would no longer be a legitimate one. The lesson is that the control itself can look perfectly innocuous and yet be illegitimate because of logical connections to non-alethic domains.

Of course, the restriction in terms of total evidence both looks legitimate and is legitimate: the Restrictivist doesn't grant, and doesn't need to grant, some cock-eyed story about what determines total evidence of the sort imagined in the last paragraph. So the move from uncontrolled Restrictivism to the usual views in the literature—Uniqueness and Evidentialism—is certainly a permissible move in the debate. What is more interesting, however, is that none of the succeeding refinements of Restrictivism enjoy a similar status.

To see why, consider a different cockeyed story about what counts as a person's total evidence. Suppose the Restrictivist controls for total evidence while holding that it is a logical truth that something is part of your evidence if and only if you want it to be and choose to include it within what you are willing to count as being relevant to the question of what to believe. Then the control in question is, in logical effect, a control arising from outside the alethic orientation of the issue in question: it is subjective, falling on the affective side of one's being, and something logically dependent on the optionality involved in making choices. It is also true that the restriction would be quite implausible. But the more basic point I want to press is that even if the resulting view were not subject to any counterexample or other objection, it wouldn't be a suitable reply to the challenge of Optionalism, since it wouldn't be a restriction on uncontrolled Restrictivism that honored the requirement that Restrictivism contrast with Optionalism. So, even if the resulting view were completely adequate in specifying a set of controls which yield a loss of optionality, it would be a version of Restrictivism in name only.

These examples of illicit controls provide the basis for an argument against Restrictivism. For among the long list of controls that we find in the Final Version of Atomistic Synchronic Restrictivism are controls that the Restrictivist admits are a function of what one wants or chooses to use in assessing the matter of what to believe. To grant the rational significance of reflective ascent is to grant just such a point, and to grant that rational opinion depends crucially on the weighting of the epistemic goal is also to grant such a point. Restrictivists thus grant that the surface appearance of Restrictivism in the Final Version is just a superficial veneer that covers a vast and robust engine of optionality driving the rational machine. And the right conclusion to draw from this fact is that the restrictions are not ones that are legitimate in defending and defining a version of Restrictivism that is the sort of position meant to oppose the Optionalisms arising from the underdetermination arguments.

There is work to be done in filling out the details of this theory, in particular concerning the mechanism governing when rational reflection changes the operative epistemic principles and when it does not, but what is important here is simply the account in slogan form: rationality is a function both of one's information and what one makes of it, and what one makes of it is where optionality reigns. Once decisions have been made about what to make of the evidence, lots of epistemic elements end up being fixed as a result. And these elements then become temptations to include in a further Restrictivist retreat. But here the Optionalist is right: it is forbidden fruit in the current context. Whatever general personality characteristics are involved in the fixing of these items, the Restrictivist has granted that the items are fixed by such things, and that is in the same conceptual neighborhood as granting that they are fixed by rate of digestion. In neither case is the control suitable for use in the attempt to defend Restrictivism against Optionalist challenges.

In a way, this point serves as a vindication of the debate found in the literature. It is instructive to note that the versions of Restrictivism found in the literature—those defending Uniqueness or some variant of it (e.g., in White (2005), Feldman and Conee (2004), Feldman (2007), and Fantl and McGrath (2009))—never control for the factors just being discussed here, but rather control only for total evidence. If our methodological constraints are sound, that is as it should be: the truth or falsity of Restrictivism really is a matter of whether, once total evidence is controlled for, optionality is eliminated.

5.7 Between Restrictivism and Optionalism

Even if we reject Restrictivism, however, Optionalism doesn't win, since the two approaches are not exhaustive of all the options. Between the two are positions that say that with respect to certain claims in certain contexts, no optionality can be found, while in other contexts or for other propositions, optionality reigns.

The view I want to propose and argue for here is that optionality can be eliminated only when the rationality of opinion in the context in question is infallible in a Cartesian-like way. First, it is obvious that optionality can't be eliminated short of infallible evidence for the claim in question. For if the evidence leaves open the possibility of error, there are a number of ways in which rationality can dissipate for an individual in possession of such evidence. A person might view the possibility of error as serious, or a person might adopt different weighting for truth over error in the particular domain of the claim in question, leaving the claim in question as not supported sufficiently in the context of such weighting. Such possibilities cannot arise for infallible evidence, but short of infallible evidence, optionality is king.

This result is expected, once we see that the arguments against Restrictivism arise from facts about underdetermination of theory by evidence. Seen in this light, we should expect Restrictivism to win out when infallible evidence is available, and to lose out when it isn't.

Suppose, though, that one has infallible evidence. Even so, the infallibility in question might be cheap, as I have termed it, and then it requires no loss of optionality. Cheap infallibilism arises in various forms of Disjunctivism, in which one's evidence isn't the same in non-skeptical scenarios as it is in skeptical scenarios. In the context of such theories, a rational false belief will be based on different evidence than a rational true one, generating a kind of cheap infallibilism that maintains that one's evidence in non-skeptical scenarios entails the truth of the beliefs supported by that evidence. Cheap infallibilism will not escape the intrusions of optionality characterized earlier, since it won't be clear precisely what the content of one's evidence is. In such a case, reflective individuals can reasonably adopt attitudes toward their evidence and situation that make irrational believing what is supported by this evidence. So cheap infallibilism is not infallibilism enough to provide any limit on optionality.

Consider, however, the kind of metaphysical certainty which Descartes famously required for all knowledge. Such certainty is most plausibly claimed for the fundamental claims of Cartesian epistemology: the claim that I am a thinking thing and that I exist. Regarding such claims, it is impossible in the strongest epistemic sense for one's evidence to fail to confirm them decisively. If there is any area to which optionality has no title, it would seem to be here.

To conclude that Unrestricted Optionalism fails because of the possibility of metaphysical certainty, however, we need more than the assurances provided in the last paragraph. For underlying our rejection of Restrictivism is the idea that, in slogan form, there is both the evidence and what we make of it. And a defender of Unrestricted Optionalism may try to insist that even if the evidence is fully conclusive in the strongest possible way, one might view it as not conclusive.

But this response misses the central feature of the earlier characterization of metaphysical certainty. That characterization quantified over possible bodies of evidence, and noted that every such possible body of evidence will be conclusive in this way. So even if reflection occurs regarding a particular body of evidence, replacing it with another and governed by different epistemic principles, the new epistemic context will still involve a total epistemic situation that still provides the most conclusive case for the claims in question. So even though the imagined defense of Unrestricted Optionalism is correct that for any given body of evidence, it can come to be viewed as less than adequate for the claims in question, any such reflective conclusion about a given body of evidence will not generate a new context in which the claims in question are anything but fully rational to believe. So the conclusion stands that regarding that which one is metaphysically certain of, optionality disappears.

The most promising arena for a similar limitation on optionality concerns the contents of one's present experience, which Empiricists have often held to partake of the same epistemic status as the Cartesian starting points. If they are right, then there is a further domain in which optionality cannot be found, though the case for such certainty is, perhaps, harder to sustain than the one for Descartes' Foundationalism. Externalist approaches to mental content make it plausible to think that one could easily mistake a particular mental state, individuated by the particular content in question, for a different mental state. And Lehrer's pain/itch example casts doubt on the idea that we have infallible access to the nature of our sensation states (see Lehrer (2000, especially chapter 3) for explanation and argument). But we need not pursue these arguments here, for our intent has not been to reveal the precise range in which optionality holds sway, but to indicate how extensive it is in spite of not being unrestricted.

5.8 Conclusion

The conclusion to draw, then, is that optionality should be embraced in the theory of rationality. Not the fully general optionality that requires optionality always and everywhere in one's intellectual life, for there are special cases where optionality is not present. Even with this admission, however, the broad-stroked painting is still clear: the landscape of rationality is one in which optionality is predominant and nearly ubiquitous.

6

From Schema to Theory: The Role of Autonomy in the Theory of Rationality

6.1 Introduction

To this point, we have seen the role that reflection plays in the story of rationality, a role that allows us to avoid the extreme of overintellectualizing the theory of rationality while at the same time avoiding the other extreme of reducing all of rationality to the beastly dimension. Our discussion has argued for a picture of rationality on which the fundamental principles of rationality can give way to other principles as reflection begins and rational ascent occurs.

In order to preserve a fully general fallibilist element in our theory, we have not presupposed that the principles that govern rationality at any level of reflective ascent are themselves transparent to the reflector. Nor have we assumed that doing one's best to get to the truth and avoid error is any guarantee that one's beliefs will be rational. These two points are opposite sides of the same coin. They allow our value-driven inquiry to result in a theory that gives full credence to the perspectivality platitude without sacrificing one of the central lessons of the history of epistemology, the lesson that there is no safe haven, intellectually speaking, but there is always some element of cognitive risk when engaging in the sense-making project that addresses the fundamental human concern about what to do and what to think.

This refusal to embrace elements of infallibilism, however, forces us to confront the question of the conditions under which reflection leads to replacement of particular epistemic principles with other principles, and what particular reflective contents get encoded in the new governing principles. One way to think about this question is to think of reflection in terms of developing a background epistemic theory relative to which given conferrers function to make certain attitudes the attitudes to adopt in a given context. The task of the present chapter is to investigate the methods and mechanisms that detail how and when reflection affects background theory in a way that allows such reflection to play the role schematically indicated in previous chapters.

Of course, the language of a background epistemic theory is merely honorific. It presents an ideal that hardly any actually achieve. Instead, our efforts are more like piecemeal efforts to make sense of what we've experienced and learned. For the use of the language of theory to be appropriate, the effort would have to generate something much more systematic and organized. Such development is possible, but rare. Nothing in the language of background theory should be taken to imply that the changes in perspective that result from reflection have no status until something truly deserving of the name is achieved.

The point of view that I will defend here is that properly motivated reflection generates an expression of autonomy that changes the governing principles. Improperly motivated reflection causes rational stultification. We begin the defense of these claims by considering the central place of autonomy in intellectual life.

6.2 The Role of Autonomy in the Story of Rationality

In order to address this issue, it is important to notice the options we cannot take. We cannot make reflection answerable to external data, such as whether the added background theory puts one in a position to do a better job of getting to the truth and avoiding error. Such proposals fail to honor the perspectivality platitude adequately, and exhibit a failure of fit with the first feature of the double double-aspect view developed earlier, the feature according to which the theory of epistemic value should be kept quite distinct from the theory of epistemic normativity. More generally, one might hope for some objective indicator to signal when such a change occurs, but such proposals will serve us no better here than they did initially. The initial use of appeals to objectivity led to theories of rationality that were not sufficiently responsive to changes in total perspective, and the same point will hold here as well. For, when a person reflects about their current cognitive condition, the choices made in such a process will generate a change in total perspective that simply cannot be ignored by an adequate account of rationality: one that honors the perspectival character of the notion.

Once we grant the point that it confuses the theory of evaluation with the theory of normativity to insist on such objectivity, we are in a position to determine what it takes, from the subject's own point of view, to resolve appropriately the predicament regarding what to do and what to think. What is valuable about purely cognitive rationality is something that allows it to address our egocentric predicament concerning what to do and what to think, and once we look inward to find the source of this value, the answer is that it is constituted as an expression of our autonomy as cognitive beings (in search of the truth or other purely intellectual interests). Autonomy here has nothing to do with libertarian freedom, but is instead the Kantian notion involving the following of rules that one gives to oneself as a rational agent, rather than following rules that are imposed by some external authority or the realm of objectivity itself. Once we appreciate the need for a perspectival solution to the predicament in question, together with a proper acknowledgement of the normative significance of reflective ascent, it is easy to see that the proper constraints on the kind of reflection that generates such significance is reflection involving rules that one adopts out of one's own perspective relative to the goals of getting to the truth and avoiding error, of making sense of reality and one's place in it.

The argument on behalf of this source in autonomy derives from the nature of the predicament toward which the theory in question is addressed. It is a predicament that is intensely personal, and not one the responsibility for which can be passed off to another. Each individual must address the predicament individually, beginning from what is common to all cognitive beings (the beastly dimension) and instituting changes to the beastly story in virtue of a quality of reflection that informs one about what to make of the evidence one has. What makes reflection have the appropriate quality for generating the changes in question is a matter of giving rules to oneself for addressing the predicament in question that are properly motivated. One's reflection on purely intellectual matters can be adequate or inadequate, and given the intensely personal character of the predicament in question, the only relevant standards for adequacy here have to be intensely personal as well. We thus must look inward to find the difference between adequate and inadequate reflection from a purely intellectual point of view, and the point of view in question identifies clearly what kind of answer is defensible here. When we reflect from a purely intellectual point of view, we are interested in developing, we aim at, a perspective on the world that conduces toward getting to the truth and avoiding error, toward a perspective that generates knowledge and understanding of various aspects of reality, and the rules that are appropriate for such interests are rules that we endorse for this purpose. The endorsement of the rules must itself answer to the interest in question, and thus must be motivated by the purely intellectual point of view, uncorrupted by what we want or hope or wish were true. When the reflection and endorsement are pure and undefiled in this way, the rules so formulated are an expression of our autonomy as rational agents, an expression of our desire or interest or motivation to make sense of things uncorrupted by other interests or needs or purposes.

This approach leaves the cognitive agent with two possibilities when reflection occurs. Once one determines what to make of the evidence one has (as well as once one determines what the evidence is that one has), the results of reflection might be either corrupted or uncorrupted. When they are uncorrupted, the governing principles change to conform to the new perspective adopted, and the story of rationality proceeds in terms of the new principles. When reflection is corrupted, however, something more sinister occurs. Instead of the governing principles changing, they do not change, and the reflection in question introduces subjective diminishers and defeaters into the story of rationality so that the reflection in question causes the mechanism of rationality to be self-stultifying. The perspective taken on what to make of the evidence one has is corrupted, and as such, not controlling with respect to the rationality of belief. But the old perspective isn't controlling either, since it no longer exists. Instead, what happens is that a new perspective comes into being, one that remains under the control of the old epistemic principles, with the new elements of the perspective elements that threaten to undermine rationality in virtue of being subjective undercutters of the conferring relationship between possessed evidence and target proposition.

Why does mere such reflection threaten to introduce undercutting defeaters? Consider an example. You've had a long history with your lawn, trying to achieve something up to neighborhood standards. In doing so, you've taken certain looks of the grass as signs for certain tasks: yellowing means add iron, browning means water more, etc. All of this, we imagine, is happening at the purely beastly level. Try as you might, however, your lawn is an embarrassment to the neighborhood, so you begin to reflect on how to proceed. You assess your own skills at diagnosing lawn problems, and you assess your own knowledge base concerning what kind of grass you are growing and how such grasses flourish or languish. You decide your knowledge base is inadequate to the task, and choose Wikipedia as a source of information to redress this grievance your lawn has against you. Why do you choose Wikipedia? Well, it showed up first in your Google search, for one thing. But, we imagine, you don't choose it out of obliviousness to the flaws of this source, nor out of respect for the quality of information in that source. You choose it because you had a date last night, with a person you are deeply attracted to, who showed admiration for the source. You want to create a connection, in hopes the relationship will develop further. Yes, you are a total idiot. But that's not the point. The point is found in asking what happens next? So you internalize the article from Wikipedia, which says that people are confused in thinking that lawns that are browning and yellowing are not flourishing. It says that this is the natural state for healthy grass to be in, and people who fertilize and water are harming their grass. In each case, you believe the article in hopes that you'll remember the information to be able to pass along on your next date in order to further the relationship. Even more idiotic, but such is the case. You've now developed a more sophisticated(!), reflective perspective on your lawn, one in which yellowing and browning means that one should rejoice at how good a lawn-care expert one is. But you still retain your old belief that yellowing and browning is a source of embarrassment.

What are we to say about the rational status of this opinion? The obvious answer is that it is now irrational: it is clearly unsatisfactory from your own perspective. The explanation of irrationality has to be in terms of something within your total perspective, and the obvious answer is that your new perspective on what evidence you have and what to make of it undercuts the presumed and former rationality of your belief in some way. The only candidates for such undercutting are the new beliefs you've acquired, ones that have nothing going for them intellectually. You have corrupted your perspective in such a way that, from that very perspective itself, your old belief is inappropriate. But notice that if you gave it up, or adopted the new belief that fits with the information you acquired, such changes of opinion would not be rational either. No matter what you do intellectually at this point, you will be doing something wrong by your own lights.

In such a case, what was rational before reflection ceases to be (or has a diminished level of rational support) after such corrupted reflection, because of the presence of undercutters. But the reach of self-stultification does not encompass the entire belief system in question, but only the parts that fall within the scope of the reflection in question. This is one way in which the present version of Perspectivalism has much to recommend it over the standard version of Perspectivalism, which is holistic Coherentism. A Coherentism of this sort that refuses to discriminate within the belief system is threatened with the result that any incoherence anywhere in the system of beliefs undermines the rationality of the entire belief system. This result is deeply mistaken, and the present approach, one that we might characterize in terms of achieving a limited type of incoherence in a system of belief on the basis of corrupted reflection, is superior precisely because the implication for failure of rationality is limited by the range of evidence and the principles of rational support within the purview of the reflection in question.

6.3 Perspectivalism and Bayesianism

This central role for autonomy explains how the governing principles of rationality change upon reflection, in a way that supports the fundamental tenets of Optionalism. The best-known example of a theory that can preserve a role for autonomy in this way is a version of Bayesianism, where updating by condition-alization explains how changes in attitude in response to new information are rational: one's new attitude toward p should match one's prior conditional at-titude toward p given the new information learned. This view is interesting to Perspectivalists in two ways. First, the theory of evidence—what confirms what and to what degree—is subjectively encoded in one's conditional attitudes at any given time. The significance of information is itself a function of one's attitudes, rather than some objective truth found in Plato's Normative Heaven. Second, the Perspectivalist will insist on several possibilities that standard Bayesian con-ditionalization ignores. A first possibility is that the set of conditional attitudes need not be complete, and another is that conditional attitudes can change over time. This point about incompleteness shows that the theory of evidence can't be elicited entirely from within a subject's own attitudes, but the point of auton-omy is that revision to the theory of evidence is always possible in virtue of some level of reflective ascent. Finally, Perspectivalists recognize the possibility that the conditional attitudes that exist might be corrupted from a purely intellectual point of view, contrary to fully subjective versions of Bayesianism that place no constraints at all on which conditional attitudes govern change of opinion.

Even given these differences, however, the similarities with Bayesianism allow a clearer picture of how the story of rationality evolves for the Perspectivalist. The two central features of Bayesian epistemology are (i) the use of the laws of probability in providing a synchronic coherence constraint on rational degrees of belief and (ii) the use of conditionalization as a diachronic constraint on changes in rational degrees of belief. Most instructive for present purposes here is the second item, though seeing how requires a bit of explanation concerning where Perspectivalism demurs concerning standard Bayesianism.

First, Perspectivalism holds no brief on the metaphysics of cognition, neither endorsing nor rejecting the idea that there are precise degrees of belief. In an im-portant sense, Perspectivalism is not even built on top of a metaphysics of belief. What matters here is whatever is the cognitive condition involved in having a perspective on the world or some aspect of it. Our current, best vocabulary for talking about such invokes the notion of belief as well as degree and strength of belief, but if advances in our understanding of cognition lead to replacement notions, Perspectivalists have no particular reason for balking at the changes. So when standard Bayesians insist on precise degrees of belief for the underlying metaphysics of cognition, they make commitments that extend well beyond what is needed for Perspectivalist purposes.

This point remains intact when standard Bayesianism is supplemented met-aphysically by positing coarse-grained confidence intervals in addition to, or in place of, fine-grained degrees of belief (credences). A fine-grained degree of belief can be identified with some number between 0 and 1 inclusive, and (at first pass) a level of confidence is some interval in the same numerical region.[1] Here Perspectivalism need take no stance. Moreover, when Bayesians attempt to be more realistic in their assessment of the nature of cognitive attitudes, introducing the possibility of vague borders for either credences or confidence levels, the Perspectivalist once again can remain neutral. Perspectivalism as developed here remains unperturbed by whatever relevant scientific and metaphysical inquiry might reveal about cognition.

Second, Perspectivalism is developed intentionally to be less holistic than Bayesianism. Given a synchronic probabilistic coherence requirement, a system of belief becomes completely irrational when probabilistic incoherence is present in any part of that system. The Perspectivalism developed here refuses any such coherence requirement on rationality, insisting on a more piecemeal story regarding synchronic rationality, one involving a multiplicity of epistemic principles under the umbrella of the general theory of rationality rather than some überprinciple that governs the rationality of everything in the entire system of belief.

Third, Perspectivalism as developed here does not imagine the story of rationality to be driven by anything immediately and directly connected with the idea of a conditional probability. What matters for the Perspectivalist is the epistemic conditionals that govern the story of rationality, conditionals derived from the epistemic norms that constitute the theory of rationality. Perspectivalists grant that one's attitude toward any claim can be stronger or weaker, so there is a possibility of connecting the Perspectivalist's use of epistemic conditionals with the Bayesian reliance on conditional probabilities, if an attitude of strength S toward a conditional $p \rightarrow q$ could be identified with a conditional attitude of strength S toward p given q, i.e., $(A_s(p|q)$ obtains$) \Leftrightarrow (A_s(p \rightarrow q)$ obtains$)$. The prospects for such an identification are not good, however, for as David Lewis has argued, a conditional probability is not the probability of a conditional.[2]

We can gain insight into the nature of Perspectivalism by keeping these differences in mind while seeing how conditionalization works in standard Bayesianism. A simple conditional principle begins from the assumption that any given rational agent has in place a system of unconditional attitudes toward every proposition. Once this assumption is in place, together with the standard account of conditional probability in terms of unconditional probability (i.e.,

---

[1] For discussion of these issues, see Sturgeon (2008).　　[2] See Lewis (1976).

$P(p|q = P(p\&q)/P(q)$, where $P(q) \neq 0$), we can state a simple conditionalization principle:

Conditionalization: For any probability P_i at time t for p, if one learns e (and only e) at a later time $t*$ (i.e., at $t*$, $P_f(e) = 1$), then $P_f(p) = P_i(p|e)$.

Changes in attitude, on this idea, involve two stages. The first stage involves learning a new piece of information e, understood to involve a change in unconditional attitude toward e to certainty from whatever it was prior to becoming certain of it. The second stage involves changing one's attitude toward any proposition affected by this new learning, so that, for any p, if $P_i(p) \neq P_i(p|e)$, then $P_f(p)$ will be different from $P_i(p)$. What is the difference? Exactly the difference between $P_i(p)$ and $P_i(p|e)$.

There are various ways in which Bayesians have adjusted this framework in the face of perceived difficulties with the simple picture. Some follow Richard Jeffreys in looking for a diachronic principle that accommodates the possibility of new learning that doesn't require certainty for the new information learned.[3] Given the underlying full fallibilism being assumed here, this alternative to the simple picture provides a much more enlightening analogy with Perspectivalism, for there is a natural affinity between fallibilists and those who counsel the wisdom of avoiding attitudes of certainty toward anything but especially toward anything contingent.

Of special interest in the present context, however, are Bayesian approaches that place restrictions on either Conditionalization or Jeffrey Conditionalization. One of the primary arguments for Perspectivalism is the way in which the governing epistemic conditionals can change for a person over time, and in the Bayesian context, the analog of this phenomenon is when, in response to new experience, the relevant conditional probabilities rationally change. Neither Conditionalization nor Jeffrey Conditionalization accommodates this possibility, and a standard approach here is to restrict these principles to cases in which the relevant conditional probabilities remain unchanged. Such restrictions fit well with the Perspectivalist slogan "There is both the evidence and what we make of it," since such restrictions acknowledge the importance of the second conjunct. It is instructive to note, however, that such approaches have nothing to say in the face

---

[3] See Jeffrey (1984). The principle defended there is:

Jeffrey Conditionalization: $P_f(p) = (P_i(p|e) \times P_f(e)) + (P_i(p|{\sim}e) \times P_f({\sim}e))$

What is crucial on this picture is not that learning involves coming to be certain of something that one was uncertain of before, but that learning involves a non-inferential change of opinion with respect to the evidence.

of changes to what we make of the evidence—they merely comment on rational status when no such changes occur. In this respect, one can view Perspectivalism as providing a friendly amendment to such restricted Bayesianisms, giving an explanation of how rational status is affected by such changes, albeit not a formal one of the sort Bayesians seek.

It doesn't work in the other direction, however: Perspectivalists need not endorse any principle of conditionalization, even a restricted one, since those principles universally suffer from the problem of logical omniscience and completeness in cognitive attitudes. On the second point, standard Bayesianism adopts the pretense of supposing that every rational individual has a complete set of attitudes, both conditional and unconditional. So, for all propositions p and q, the supposition is that the agent assigns some credence or confidence level to p as well as to $p|q$. Once this assumption is in place, an agent's attitudes cannot satisfy the probability calculus without being certain of all logical truths, thus raising the problem of logical omniscience. Perspectivalism makes no such assumptions, refusing to assume that a set of attitudes is complete and refusing to endorse the requirement of probabilistic coherence among the attitudes that in fact exist.

The primary difference, however, between Bayesians and Perspectivalists is found in the difference between epistemic conditionals and conditional attitudes (or probabilities). The theory of evidence governing the rationality of attitudes is encoded in one's conditional probabilities, for Bayesians, and in epistemic conditionals for Perspectivalists. For the beastly dimension, the epistemic conditionals are generated from epistemic principles by dropping the enabling clause and the epistemic operator from the consequent. For the reflective dimension, we generate the relevant epistemic principles by starting with the epistemic conditionals. When reflection occurs uncorrupted by non-cognitive interests, needs, and purposes, an epistemic conditional comes to be rational to accept (with a given strength), and the relevant epistemic principle places an operator on the consequent of this conditional (one that specifies a rational status at least as high as is needed to make the given strength of attitude rational), adding an enabling clause to the antecedent as well as a clause specifying the level of reflective ascent achieved and the background information generated by the reflection in question. This epistemic principle will be necessarily true if and only if the epistemic conditional is itself acceptable in the given circumstances for the individual in question, given the way in which the principle is generated from the related epistemic conditional. We thus generate the complete story of rationality in terms of necessarily true epistemic principles and the epistemic conditionals that govern changes in attitude, either implicitly in non-inferential changes or explicitly in the kind of changes involved at the reflective level and in inferential changes at the beastly level.

This difference provides an important advantage for the Perspectivalist over the Bayesian. When Bayesians limit their theoretical resources to conditional attitudes or probabilities, the available story they have for inferential rationality has difficulty preserving the story of proper basing. Cognitive rationality requires both the presence of adequate evidence to support the attitude in question, but also properly basing that attitude on the evidence in question. In fully explicit, inferential cases, people do not usually or often engage in explicit probabilistic reasoning. The reasoning that is typical is done in the logic of conditionals. In order to represent such reasoning in a probabilistic framework, Bayesians need a formal principle connecting the acceptability of a conditional statement with a conditional probability. An obvious suggestion is to identify the probability of a conditional with a conditional probability:

Conditionals Link: $P(p \to q) = P(q|p)$.

The difficulty for Bayesians is that Conditionals Link is known to be false, as argued by Lewis (1976). Yet, if Conditionals Link is false, some alternative linking principle is required. For suppose you learn q, coming to change your attitude toward p to conform to your earlier conditional attitude toward $p|q$. There are two quite different ways for this to happen, both involving a causal link between learning q and the changed attitude toward p. In one case, you change your attitude toward p because you infer p from q, seeing that the latter shows the former to be true. In the other case, you learn q and this causes you to change your attitude toward p, but you don't infer the latter from the former. Perhaps, for example, learning q triggers deep emotional trauma, and one expression of a heightened sense of anxiety is your changed attitude toward p. In such a case, even though the content of your attitude is rational in light of the evidence you have, your attitude toward it is not rational because it is not properly based on the evidence for it.

A theory of rationality that involves appeals to epistemic conditionals has no difficulty explaining the difference, since explicit inference in the logic of conditionals can be included in an account of proper basing as one way in which proper basing can be achieved. Bayesians can include attitudes toward conditionals in the story of rationality, but when it comes to characterizing changes in attitude, the only theoretical resources they have involve making changes that conform to the conditional attitudes that are in place. Of course, such an approach can be supplemented with an account of proper basing that appeals to features that go beyond the standard Bayesian theoretical resources, but then the beauty and simplicity of the Bayesian story becomes corrupted by theoretical inelegance. And once such a hybrid theory is developed, the argument will be in place for accepting Perspectivalism instead, and thinking of the Bayesian story as perhaps an appropriate subplot for certain parts of the story of rationality (in particular, perhaps for that subplot involving explicit probabilistic reasoning).

6.4 Autonomy and Pathologies

Perspectivalism can be summarized as the view that the theory of rationality is partly constituted by non-autonomous epistemic norms concerning the beastly dimension and autonomous epistemic norms concerning the reflective dimension. When reflection occurs with the required autonomous motivation, epistemic conditionals can come to be acceptable for the person in question, and when an epistemic conditional is acceptable for a person on the basis of autonomous reflection, there is a recipe for discerning the underlying epistemic principle. Epistemic principles, which are necessarily true if true at all, are constructed from such conditionals by adding an enabling clause, an epistemic operator, and a level of reflective ascent. Recall from Chapter 2 the general form of epistemic principles:

If

- S's senses report that p,
  _{conferrer}
- under level of reflection n linking p and q,
  _{ascent level}
  where n is the highest level of reflection achieved, and
  _{ascent limit}
- no defeater exists for the connection of this report to q,
  _{enabler}

then

- it is rational for S to believe that q.
  _{operator}   _{target}

The fundamental role for autonomous reflection is to provide a link between conferrer and target. Such a link provides prima facie rationality for the target proposition, since there is no guarantee that the link provided is not defeated by other information available to the person who is reflecting. Moreover, the link between conferrer and target is a link that is dependent on the level of reflective ascent achieved and the information generated by that reflection. We can thus think of the level of reflective ascent as providing background information I, and a fuller articulation of the form of an epistemic principle would then be:

If

- S's senses report that p,

  conferrer
- under level of reflection n linking p and q *via* background information I,

  ascent level
  where n is the highest level of reflection achieved, and

  ascent limit
- no defeater exists for the connection of this report to q,

  enabler

then

- it is rational for S to believe that q.

  operator   target

The intuitive idea of Perspectivalism can thus be put as well in terms of the nature of the relation that confers prima facie rationality on a target proposition. At the reflective level, the relation of rational support is a three-place relation, involving a target, a conferrer, and some background information generated by reflection. This feature of Perspectivalism is compatible with the position that at the beastly level, the relation of rational support is a two-place relation only. Some versions of the view will want to insist, however, that background information is essential at the beastly level as well, even if that background information is not generated by reflection. For our purposes it is not necessary to arbitrate this dispute, since the focus here is more on the general structure of a theory of rationality answering to the value-driven motivation of characterizing what a theory will look like that answers to the egocentric predicament regarding what to do and what to think.

Even given the conclusion that autonomy must play the central role here posited, important questions remain. One important issue arises from the fact that motivations come in degrees, and a given endorsement of a rule on the basis of reflection might be more or less motivated in the way described earlier. This point raises the question of whether the motivation must be pure and uncorrupted, or whether some degree of latitude is allowed in determining when governing principles change and when they do not.

Equally important is what we might call "the objection from pathologies." This objection notes the subjective character of Perspectivalism and complains that it treats pathological beliefs, such as those held by individuals suffering from schizophrenia, the same as non-pathological beliefs. The objector may grant the barest possibility of pathological beliefs surviving epistemic scrutiny, but insists that there must be some flaw noted for such beliefs. The nature of the flaw may be hard to characterize precisely, but the rough idea is clear: in some sense, we don't want pathological practices and attitudes, nor ones in debunked disciplines such as astrology or phrenology, to count as being just as good, from an epistemic point of view, as our best scientific practices and most careful inferences.

This problem is a more general version of the problem of the priors that bothers Bayesians. When prior probabilities are uncontrolled, critics claim that Bayesianism allows for no distinction between scientific practices and less respectable practices. In response, some Bayesians impose objective constraints on the priors (e.g., Rosenkrantz (1981)), while others place their hope in various convergence results that show that wide variance in priors gets washed out in the long run (e.g., Gaifman and Snir (1982)).

It should be granted that there may be purposes for which such revisions to a subjective theory are needed, but in the present context the objection from pathologies should be resisted. Recall that we are developing a theory to answer to the predicament of what to do and what to think, and this predicament needs a solution both for fully functioning and healthy human beings as well as for those suffering from various pathologies. For those who find problematic this failure to discriminate between these classes of individuals, I recommend pursuing their own value-driven inquiry, stating clearly what the needs, interests, and purposes are for which a different normative theory is needed, and then developing such a theory to answer to this motivation.

So the first point in response to the objection from pathology is that it is ill-motivated in the present context but may be well motivated in other contexts. I wish to press a second point as well, a point that makes it much harder to find any context in which the objection is well motivated. Philosophers often have a predilection for blanket terminology to describe that which is objectionable, to the point where the term becomes so abstract and vapid as to be cognitively uninformative, serving only to express distaste or contempt.[4] Such predilections mirror the behavior we acquired early on in having catch-all terminology when our vocabularies fail us. Consider, for example, the variety of uses of "cool," "gay," and for those of my own ethnicity and geographic home, "uff da." Such expressions can mean, pretty much, whatever you want them to mean, though the first two are much inferior to the latter in that they can only mean things positive or negative, respectively. For those in need of greater flexibility, I recommend something of more Nordic heritage.

---

[4] The *locus classicus* of this complaint regarding moral theory is Anscombe (1958).

In any case, perhaps "irrational" functions in this way in epistemology, and it certainly functions in this way in much of ordinary language. When behavior and belief are significantly unlike ours, ordinary people look for a catch-all term to describe, and commonly land on "irrational." An anecdote in point: in giving advice on how to respond to the Iran hostage crisis in 1979, radio commentator Paul Harvey said something like this—"We must first understand that these people are irrational, and so the best response would be to spray pig oil over the entire country." The moral and religious insensitivity on display here should not go unrecognized, but what interests me more is the need to classify behavior and belief in negative terms, and the quite natural use of "irrationality" to so characterize.

Any philosophical methodology that is guided by ordinary language will have to take such uses into account, for they involve no misuse of language. But for value-driven approaches, especially one of the sort pursued here, such uses should be seen as mysterious. There is certainly no impetus from the egocentric predicament that would help us explain or understand such uses—from that perspective, the remark seems simply mistaken. One is thus left wondering what other need or purpose or interest might lead to a normative theory that would sustain such a remark.

Moreover, a value-driven approach of the sort pursued here insists on a clear distinction between normative theory and the theory of value, noting the ease with which ordinary thought and talk conflate the two. When a person engages in a course of action that turns out badly, it is quite natural to describe the situation as one in which the person took the wrong course of action. A more careful theory, however, one that recognizes that purely teleological theories of normativity will fail, insists on more information before deriving the wrongness of an action from its disvalue. The same point holds in the realm of belief. When practices of belief formation and inquiry are viewed as being insufficiently truth-conducive, as is surely the case with pathological beliefs, it is natural to describe such practices and the beliefs that result from them as irrational. More careful theory, however, requires a different response. Failure of truth-conductivity is a feature relevant to the theory of epistemic value, not the theory of epistemic normativity.

This last remark overreaches slightly, since nothing argued here shows that there cannot be purposes, interests, and needs relative to which a purely teleological normative theory answers. I know of no such purposes, interests, or needs, and what is clear is that the interest in a theory that answers to the egocentric predicament regarding what to do and think is not such an interest.

"But what of the fundamental intellectual interest in getting to the truth and avoiding error?" That is a very good question, since it is as obvious as anything can be that we do have an interest in getting to the truth and avoiding error. But if that is the sole interest for which we are constructing a normative theory, the obvious normative theory to construct is one that requires the formation of true beliefs and proscribes the formation of false beliefs. Once this point is appreciated, however, the motivation for using normative terminology here disappears. We have other needs, interests, and purposes regarding which we can motivate the use of normative terminology; the interest in getting to the truth and avoiding error is addressed fully by the theory of epistemic value itself.

One might show hesitance in accepting this point because of the recognition that truth and falsity are often opaque to fallible beings such as we are. That concern is well taken, but it provides no comfort to truth-conducive approaches to epistemic normativity. Every epistemic theory of rationality arises in the context of recognizing the opacity of truth and the predicament it generates for fallible cognizers. That predicament is precisely the predicament to which the present approach answers, so purely truth-conducive approaches to rationality can't be defended at this point by appeal to an interest in truth *sub specie* opacity, where that interest is somehow different from the interest or need or purpose involved in the egocentric predicament regarding what to do or think. For that concern is precisely the concern being addressed by the present theory.

In response, those wishing for a more objective, truth-conducive theory of rationality might press: "So what exactly is the connection between rationality and truth on the Perspectivalist theory?" The challenge is important, and arises because of the intuitive link between belief and truth. Beliefs differ from desires in terms of their direction of fit with the world. Whereas the direction of fit for desires goes from mind to world, the direction of fit for beliefs and other cognitive states goes from world to mind. With respect to desires, the point of the mental attitude is to demand or request that the world conform to the state; with respect to belief, the aim or point is for the mental state to conform to the world. So, simply in virtue of taking a cognitive attitude, one has established some link to truth, and the challenge of the truth connection is to say what additional connection to the truth we get when we compare a rational belief to a non-rational one.

The approach I favor goes as follows. We can say that when a total body of evidence makes epistemically rational believing a given claim, that body of evidence also makes rational believing the claim that the belief in question is the appropriate belief to hold in the interests of getting to the truth and avoiding error. Put in shorthand, the total body of evidence not only makes rational believing the claim in question, but also makes rational believing that the belief is epistemically rational. This point is sufficient for distinguishing epistemic rationality from other kinds of rationality, such as practical or moral. It also ties epistemic rationality to truth in a way different from, and in addition to, the way in which belief itself is tied to truth.

A couple of remarks about what this approach does not say will help us appreciate what it does say. It doesn't require that the rationality in question is all-things-considered rationality—the only requirement is that the connection obtains for prima facie rationality. Second, it doesn't say that the very same evidence must justify both claims—only that if a total body of information justifies one of the claims, it justifies the other as well. Finally, it doesn't require that to rationally believe a claim, one must also believe that believing that claim is rational. The claim is, rather, that any body of information that makes a claim rational also makes the claim that believing the first claim is rational as well—and both of these facts can obtain without any beliefs being present.

Even if we accept these responses to the objection from pathologies, there remains the other difficulty concerning mixed motivations. To this problem we turn in the next section.

6.5 Motivational Purity and Delicate Rationality

Perhaps it is endemic to the human condition that we are always subject to mixed motivations, but even if the phenomenon is more limited, the theory as developed to this point says nothing about the rational status of beliefs arrived at by merely partially autonomous reflection on how to get to the truth and avoid error. The simplest and most demanding approach to the problem of mixed motivations would be to say that any admixture of non-autonomy prevents one's beliefs from providing a suitable response to the predicament regarding what to do and what to think. An alternative approach counsels considering various counterfactuals about what conclusions one would come to if one's motives were purified.[5]

The demanding approach might be objected to because it makes rationality so delicate that it is rarely present. Such an objection is overstated, of course, since the motivational purity issue arises only for reflective levels of rationality. But the concern that such an approach is overly demanding is still present. If we side with the critic here that the first approach is too demanding, the alternative,

---

[5] For such approaches, see Foley (1986); Lehrer (1974), and Lehrer (2000).

however, is not to explore the domain of counterfactuals, imagining what would be true if the motives were purer. We seek an account that speaks to the actual situation of reflective beings, and counterfactual approaches to this issue provide no guarantee of that.[6]

If we do so, what is needed is an additional dimension of evaluation in our theory. This dimension also involves the idea of a degree to which a given belief is rational, but it is relative to a different scale than that notion of degree of rationality that is reflected in the epistemic operators of our epistemic principles. In order to distinguish this scale from the more ordinary one, I will refer to it in terms of degree of taintedness for reflective rationality. We measure the degree of taintedness in terms of the degree to which the reflection involved is autonomous (when the reflection in question is suitably positive with respect to that belief). We then understand the overall degree of rationality of a belief in terms of the degree'd notion involved in the epistemic operators in question as well as the degree of taintedness, allowing the taint to diminish overall rationality and perhaps rise to the level of defeating it as well (more on such defeat in a moment). We thus need a threshold, where anything above the threshold is rational to believe, anything short of it is not.

With respect to the first function, we can think of it in roughly the same way we think of the interaction between conferrers and enablers in the epistemic principles that characterize the beastly dimension. Conferrers set an upper limit on the degree to which a beastly belief is rational, and difficulties with respect to the enabling clause either diminish or defeat this level of rationality. Just so, the reflective perspective achieved, together with the available conferrers, sets an upper limit on the level of rationality which can be diminished or defeated by difficulties with respect to the enabling clause and with respect to the ideal of full autonomy in reflection.

The hard problem here is the hard problem for every theory of rationality of any type: where is the threshold that distinguishes diminution of rationality from defeat of it? On that topic I will have little to say here, noting only that it is a general concern for every theory of rationality, whether epistemic or non-epistemic. The generic nature of this problem leaves some hope that any decent answer to

---

[6] It is worth noting that Foley (1986) speaks in two different ways on this score. Foley seeks an account that adverts to one's deepest standards for getting to the truth and avoiding error, but also speaks of what principles one would endorse after unlimited reflection, free of merely medical limitations. The former description speaks to the actual situation, but the latter need not. I suspect that the latter, counterfactual formulation is just a way of operationalizing the former notion. As we've learned, however, counterfactual accounts don't work well, and so the better approach would be to refuse to try to operationalize in the first place.

this issue for any theory can be incorporated into the present approach without loss of plausibility.

This characterization of the taintedness of reflection is an initial characterization only, since the issue of purity of motivation can itself become incorporated into a higher level of reflective ascent. At such a level, some cognizers will impose the very strong requirement of purity of motivation as the appropriate standard for rationality. Others will counsel dispersing a bit more epistemic grace, allowing mixed motives so long as the love of truth is primary. Still others may be even more lax, allowing that even the slightest efforts toward the truth are enough. When such a higher-level reflective standpoint is achieved, it has the capacity to control the story of rationality for that individual. Of course, as before, merely thinking it doesn't make it so: the reflective conclusions achieved must themselves, at a minimum, reflect the level of motivational purity encoded in the reflective conclusions.

We thus have no set standard here for all cognizers in all circumstances, in much the same way that we have no set standard to impose regarding the weighting of the competing goals of getting to the truth and avoiding error. For each such topic, whatever default setting is in place at lower levels of reflection or at the beastly level itself, these settings can be changed as higher-level reflection occurs.

This picture of reflective rationality raises two issues, both originating in a concern that this theory, as developed, has become overly permissive. The first issue where this concern can arise is in the earlier claim, that the level of motivational purity needed can be changed by reflection, but only when that reflection itself rises to the level of motivational purity embraced in the reflection. The worry here is that if this is all the theory has to say, the smart thing to do, for those desiring to be rational, is to "game the theory," that is, to adopt very low standards for motivational purity and very risky standards in terms of valuing truth over the costs of error.

The second issue generalizes on the first, wondering how hard it can be, on this theory, for reflective cognizers to end up with irrational opinions. Doesn't the present approach imply that all that is needed for full epistemic rationality is to adopt standards that one knows are satisfied? And doesn't that make rationality way too easy to achieve?

To the contrary, I believe the account here makes it very difficult to have reflectively rational beliefs, so difficult, that reflective rationality is a rare and delicate flower indeed. Let me explain.

Regarding the first issue, it is important to note that, as formulated, the requirement—that one's reflection concerning purity be at least as pure as the standard one adopts in the process of reflecting—is only a necessary condition. The interesting cases are ones where the level of motivational purity one displays when one is trying as best one can to get to the truth and avoid error is much higher than the conclusion one comes to about what level of motivational purity is needed. In such cases, two points are important. First, the reflection must be fully general: it is reflection on the issue of motivational purity for all rational creatures. So, if the reflection endorses a position for the purpose of being kind to one's lessers, nothing is changed from the default setting for motivational purity, whatever that level is. Second, even though it is possible for one to be exceptional regarding motivational purity, it is a suspicious situation to be in, where one typically does more than one thinks needs to be done. The suspicion is that one is engaged in a bit of self-deception, in this case, in service of an attitude of exceptionalism toward oneself. In such a case, there is rational incoherence in one's cognitive attitudes, of just the self-stultifying sort we have discussed before.

One way to determine whether the reflective attitude toward purity is one that is constructed in service of an attitude of exceptionalism is to see what happens when the people in question notice the failure of fit between their practices and the judgment they come to about the appropriate level of motivational purity. We inquire, not of the public face of such, where expressions of humility dominate even for those most plagued by attitudes of exceptionalism, but rather about the private experience of such. We should predict that those plagued by attitudes of exceptionalism will experience some smugness here, while those not so plagued will experience perplexity at the difference in question.

This point leads directly to the second issue, for the explanation of how hard it is to be reflectively rational on the theory in question—how delicate such rationality is—arises once we begin to plumb the depths of the human psyche. When we reflect from a purely epistemic point of view, the results we embrace are general results, applying to all rational creatures (of the type specified in the reflection) in a given set of circumstances (of the type specified in the reflection). Moreover, these types are rarely so precisely circumscribed so as to be completely specific. As one's reflective capacities increase and are exercised, the potential for incoherence between various reflective episodes increases, and it is precisely the kind of incoherence that is rational incoherence, resulting in stultification with respect to one's prospects for achieving a perspective that legitimately informs one about what to think. Such incoherence is endemic to the human condition. It surfaces in formal educational experiences, but also in therapeutic settings. A good therapist helps one to uncover such incoherencies in attitude, and a good professor, at least a good philosophy professor(!), helps one to see that what one says or thinks about one context often has unacceptable implications for other contexts.

The reason that our reflections are rarely completely specific is that we are motivated not only to get to the truth and avoid error, but to do so in a way that generates a simple and powerful theoretical approach to how to think. This emphasis on simplicity and power is an important practical limitation on reflection, guiding our reflective thinking to greater levels of generality. But the more general, the greater is the risk for conflict between various reflective episodes.

Finally, each of us, no matter how exceptional we take ourselves to be, have experienced the chagrin that accompanies heretofore unnoticed rational incoherencies in our thinking. We have certainly noticed it about our past selves, and we have a compelling pessimistic induction concerning our current and future selves as well. The proper conclusion to draw here, then, is that the greater and more systematic one's alethic reflections, the better one might become at getting to the truth, but the greater the likelihood that the delicate flower of epistemic rationality will be lost in the process.

So, our theory does not predict that it will be an easy matter to achieve reflective rationality. Instead, when combined with an appropriate understanding of the human condition and its fallen character, intellectually and otherwise, the prediction is that rationality becomes more difficult to achieve as reflection increases.

6.6 Conclusion

The goal of the present chapter has been to reveal the central place of autonomy in filling out the final details in the Perspectivalist story about rationality. In the process of explaining this role, several objections to the Perspectivalist story arose, primarily respecting the subjective character of the theory, but also concerning the possibility of mixed motivations. In each case, we have seen some of the resources for defending Perspectivalism. Whether the responses are adequate, I now submit to the reader to judge.

7

Conclusion

The central focus of this work has been on providing an epistemic theory supported by a defensible, value-driven meta-theory. The particular value-driven feature of this approach has been to try to solve the problem for the egocentric predicament regarding what to do and what to think while avoiding one of two extremes. The first extreme fails to accommodate the role that reflection can plan in changing the epistemic standards that are in place at any given time. The second extreme fails to accommodate the fact that an appropriate response to the issue of what to think does not require reflection. Finding a middle path between these two extremes leads to the kind of theory presented here.

Once these parameters are in place for a theory capable of defense, the central issue to be faced at the level of theory construction is how to determine which particular changes to the standards that are in place are legitimate ones, and the story presented here is in terms of a Kantian-inspired appeal to autonomy. The central idea of such an approach is that reflection can change the governing standards when it counts as an example of reason giving rules to itself, in terms of the epistemic value of getting to the truth and avoiding error. When, and only when, the reflective perspective involves such an autonomous expression of the intellectual self does the new epistemic perspective replace the default one. It is this mechanism that gives content to the slogan for this approach, the slogan that the evidence is one thing, and what we make of it another.

Those enamored with taxonomy and its history will want to know whether the resulting theory is a version of Foundationalism or Coherentism, Internalism or Externalism (and if the former, whether a version of Access Internalism or not), Subjectivism or Objectivism. My preferred terminology at the level of meta-theory is that it is a version of Perspectivalism. Perspectivalism is a generalization of Coherentism, and thus one might be inclined to think of the view presented here as more akin to Coherentism than Foundationalism. Even so, this version of Perspectivalism includes a default set of epistemic principles and norms that involve evidence of an apparently basic sort, leading to the possibility that this version of Perspectivalism is better thought of as a version of Foundationalism.

Since I view epistemological meta-theory as better done apart from the clearly metaphorical taxonomy deriving from the structure of buildings and either ships at sea or spiders' webs,[1] I will leave it to those more impressed with such a taxonomy to worry about the details here. As for the question of whether it is a version of Internalism or Externalism, the first clear point is that it is not a version of Access Internalism:[2] there is nothing in this version of Perspectivalism that says that what makes a belief rational is something that is accessible to the individual in question on the basis of reflection. Moreover, it is also not a version of Mentalism,[3] given the role of proper motivation in an expression of autonomy. If it is a version of Internalism, it is in a category of its own. Perhaps, though, the role of proper motivation in the story of rationality told by the theory implies that it isn't a version of Internalism at all, but rather a version of Externalism. Again, since my primary concern here is not with taxonomy, there is no pressing need to settle this issue, and so I leave it to those more interested in such to determine the correct answer.

A primary virtue of this form of Perspectivalism, apart from the features mentioned earlier, is that it constitutes an approach to rationality that speaks with a single voice. It does not take back a positive appraisal using one normative notion that it offers with a different normative notion. When a total theory of normativity is presented, there will obviously be more than one normative notion involved: in addition to epistemic normativity, there is also practical, aesthetic, and moral normativity, not to mention religious normativity. One can hope that one of these types will be fundamental and the others explained in terms of it, but no defense of that hope has occurred here. Moreover, no defense of the claim that the entire domain of epistemic normativity can be addressed with the notion characterized in this version of Perspectivalism. Instead, I have wished to argue that multiplicity is to be avoided where possible, and that the value-driven source of the present theory can be accommodated by a theory that speaks with a single voice. So, at least, within this particular value-driven arena, no multiplicity is needed. This result, then, can be seen as a challenge to the multipliers: find another value-driven concern with the proper domain of epistemology and show that a different theory is needed to accommodate it. Just don't pretend that for every value-driven motivation for a theory, multiplicity is inevitable. As this version of Perspectivalism shows, it isn't.

---

[1] See, e.g., Kvanvig (1984, 1986), and Kvanvig and Riggs (1992).

[2] For concerns about the precise nature of different forms of Internalism, see Fumerton (1988).

[3] Mentalism is the name chosen for the view that rationality is a function of (and only of) the mental states that one is in; see Feldman and Conee (2004).

Appendix A

Reducing Personal to Doxastic Justification

Chapter 1 included a discussion of the variety of locutions involving any given epistemically normative term, and defended an account of epistemic justification which explained doxastic uses in terms of propositional uses. In the process, the question of the relationship between locutions attributing a complex justificatory property to persons, as in 'S is justified in believing p', was postponed to this appendix. Our concern is thus to consider whether personal justification involves a distinct form of epistemic appraisal from that involved in doxastic justification (in the next appendix, we'll consider the issue of whether doxastic justification can be used to explain propositional justification).

The motivation for the idea that personal justification is distinct from the other two typically runs something like this: it is one thing for a belief to be justified, but another for a person to be judged adequate from an epistemic perspective in holding a belief. The latter, it might be thought, carries with it the scent of epistemic virtue or excellence, so that the person's character is being assessed rather than merely the particular expression of that character in a given instance of believing. Thus, it might seem, there is a difference between a *person* being justified in holding a given belief and that belief itself being justified.

Kent Bach has used this idea to provide an original defense of reliabilism against certain counterexamples to it. He says,

I propose that we distinguish between a person being justified in holding a belief and the belief itself being justified. What makes a person justified in holding a belief resides in the quality of his epistemic action. There is much that this can involve, including asking fruitful questions, considering plausible alternatives, and properly evaluating evidence. Without trying to spell out precisely what good epistemic action involves, let's just say that a *person* is justified in believing something to the extent that he holds the belief rationally and responsibly. However, a *belief* can be justified even in the absence of any action on the part of the believer, as in the case of beliefs formed automatically or routinely, without any deliberate consideration. (Bach, 1985, p. 251)

Bach claims that there is a distinction between personal justification and the sort of justification which attaches to a belief. Personal justification is a kind of justification which attaches to, or is predicated of, persons and not of propositions or beliefs; doxastic justification is predicated of beliefs and not persons. Of course, it does not follow from the fact that Bach draws this distinction that he also holds, or should hold, that the kinds in question are irreducibly distinct. However, if Bach thought the two kinds of justification were not distinct, it would be crucial for the force of his argument that he noted the way the two kinds were related in order to defend his claim that the distinction between the two is as he sees it. In particular, he would need to argue that the way the two kinds were related definitionally implies that only doxastic justification can obtain in the purported counterexamples to reliabilism. Since Bach engages in no such discussion, it is reasonable to conclude that he intends to be drawing a distinction between two distinct kinds of justification. And, if Bach is right, we have good reason for thinking that personal justification is not equivalent to doxastic justification and perhaps not to propositional justification either.

Bach claims that S is justified in holding a belief (i.e., S is the locus of personal justification in the situation of holding the belief in question) roughly if and only if that person's epistemic action, which resulted in the belief, is of sufficiently high quality. Since basic beliefs are not products of action at all, it follows (and Bach agrees that it follows) that no person can be justified in holding a basic belief. This claim is belied by ordinary parlance. For instance, Descartes can be justified in believing that he thinks even though he performs no epistemic action in arriving at that belief. Further, it is worth noting that the appeal to ordinary parlance is appropriate for the task before us, for the question of the reducibility of personal justification concerns the relationship between the syntactic formulations of ordinary English which employ the word 'justified' and variants on it. Thus, even if there is a sense of 'justification' on which basic beliefs all fail to be justified, this fact would not show the irreducibility of personal justification to other kinds of justification. One way to put this point is this: the reducibility claim is a different claim than an ambiguity claim about justification, and at best, Bach's arguments give us a reason for claiming ambiguity. The reason this ambiguity claim seems important in our context is that Bach couples the ambiguity claim with a claim at least apparently relating that ambiguity to the locutions we have identified as distinctive of personal and doxastic justification. This latter claim is false: if there is an ambiguity in the notion of justification, it is not reflected in ordinary locutions distinctive of personal and doxastic justification. Hence, even if Bach should have found a defense of reliabilism against certain counterexamples to it, his defense fails to provide any definitive argument for the irreducibility of personal justification to propositional and doxastic justification.

Clayton Littlejohn urges a similar conclusion, that personal justification is an Internalist notion and doxastic an Externalist one.[1] Littlejohn cites Catherine Lowy (1978) as being the first to recognize the distinction between personal and doxastic justification, and the same idea has been pursued in Engel (1992) to attempt to explain away at least some of the controversy between Internalists and Externalists.

As a claim about how ordinary language or philosophical discourse about epistemic normativity actually functions, however, these claims are suspect. Consider John Locke's remark, for example:

> He that believes, without having any reason for believing, maybe in in love with his own fancies; but neither seeks truth as he ought, nor pays the obedience due his maker, who would have him use these discerning faculties he has given him, to keep him out of mistake and error. He that does not this to the best of his power, however he sometimes lights on truth, is in the right but by chance; and I know not whether the luckiness of the accident will excuse the irregularity of his proceeding. This at least is certain, that he must be accountable for whatever mistakes he runs into: whereas he that makes use of the light and faculties God has given him, and seeks sincerely to discover truth, by those helps and abilities he has, may have this satisfaction in doing his duty as a rational creature .... For he governs his assent right, and places it as he should, who in any case or matter whatsoever, believes or disbelieves, according as reason directs him. (Locke, 1698, IV.xvii.24)

Locke does not use the language of justification in this passage, but does engage in epistemic appraisal using the language of reasonability. Note that he begins with a situation involving no reasons for *belief*, and characterizes such a situation in deeply personal terms: such a person is accountable, is without excuse (at least when in error), has not done his duty. In contrast, those who have reasonable beliefs are those who make use of the faculties God has given them, believing or disbelieving as reason directs. It is clear that Locke's position on epistemic appraisal here makes no distinction between the reasonability of a belief and the reasonability of the person holding the belief.

The same is true in W. K. Clifford's famous article "The Ethics of Belief." Clifford switches easily and without syntactic or semantic awkwardness between constructions involving doxastic and personal justification:

> Shall we steal and tell lies because we have had no personal experience wide enough *to justify the belief* that it is wrong to do so? (Clifford, 1877[1999], p. 347, emphasis mine)

---

[1] See Littlejohn (2012, pp. 5–8) and the earlier Littlejohn (2009).

But are we not trusting our spectroscope too much? Surely, having found it to be trust-worthy for terrestrial substances, where its statements can be verified by man, *we are justified in accepting* its testimony in other like cases; but not when it gives us information about things in the sun, where its testimony cannot be directly verified by man?

Certainly, we want to know a little more before *this inference can be justi-fied* ... (Clifford, 1877[1999], p. 363, emphasis mine)

No evidence, therefore, can *justify us in believing* the truth of a statement which is contrary to, or outside of, the uniformity of nature. (Clifford, 1877[1999], p. 361, emphasis mine)

Note that Clifford, in these passages, switches with ease between locutions attributing justification to persons, beliefs, and inferences. It would be surpris-ing indeed if these remarks by Locke and Clifford revealed some failure to grasp appropriate syntax or semantics of ordinary language, even though such an hy-pothesis is of course compatible with the data. Moreover, any modestly careful perusal of the history of epistemology and its language of justification shows that this language simply doesn't fall into the categories posited by those who wish to distinguish personal from doxastic justification, nor is there any evidence from ordinary language outside of philosophy to sustain their conclusions.

But we need not go so far as to accuse these authors and other speakers of nat-ural language of such mistakes in order to make sense of the positions of Lowy, Bach, Littlejohn, and Engel. To put the point bluntly, anyone can be mistaken, even about matters epistemic, without that mistake being traceable to syntactic, semantic, or logico-metaphysical confusion. It is worth seeing how that point plays out in the context of theorists who wish to distinguish between personal and doxastic justification.

To make sense of their position, we need only note that their discussions in-clude something like what we see in the Bach quote: we begin with the drawing of a distinction, to the effect that we can evaluate persons or we can evaluate their beliefs, and the two might in some way be independent of each other. Perhaps, for example, the person might have done all that can reasonably be expected in search of the truth, while the belief is simply not shown to be true by the evi-dence available. Then, after drawing a distinction, the syntactic constructions in question are put to use to encode the distinction in question.

There is, of course, nothing wrong with distinction-drawing, and there is also nothing wrong with using a distinction together with existing syntactic construc-tions to make a philosophical point. This is, after all, how terms of art develop, and a clear sign of when a syntactic construction is being turned into a term of art is when its interpretation involves a gloss on the intended sense to be attached to the construction. And to be clear here, I have no objection whatsoever to the project of finding multiple normative notions appropriate in epistemology, nor to the using of various syntactic constructions to signal important distinctions that might be overlooked in various debates in epistemology.

These points raise the issue of exactly what is at stake in our discussion and what isn't. We are interested in the question of what kinds of things are fundamentally the objects of epistemic appraisal and we want to know whether we can find a unifying philosophical account of this diversity. If we can find such a unified explanation, it will help undergird the fundamental motivation for the theory proposed here, one which is capable of speaking with a single voice to the predicament of what to do and what to think. Success in this project leaves open the possibility that ambiguity must be posited on other grounds, so the goal is not that of arriving at results that prohibit epistemologists from engaging in distinction-drawing and then introducing various parts of language as terms of art to characterize the distinctions drawn. The goal is, rather, to see if the territory in which the substance of epistemology is addressed and developed is characterized, or can profitably be characterized, by an underlying unity at the more formal level at which logic, philosophy of logic, and metaphysics intersect.

We begin, then, with a direct examination and evaluation of the relation between personal and doxastic justification. Some formal machinery will aid us in this task. We will assume a first-order language with variables 's' ranging over persons, 'p' and 'q' ranging over propositions, and 'x' ranging over all objects. This language also contains complex expressions of the form $\ulcorner [\lambda x_1 \ldots x_n \psi] \urcorner$,[2] where '$\lambda$' here is an abstraction operator and ψ any formula.[3] λ-expressions will be considered to be both terms and predicates so they can occur both in subject and predicate position in atomic formulas. Intuitively $\ulcorner [\lambda x_1 \ldots x_n \psi] \urcorner$ denotes the n-place relation that holds between objects $a_1, \ldots, a_n$ just in case $\psi(x_i/a_i)$.[4] Where $n = 0$, $\ulcorner [\lambda \psi] \urcorner$ denotes the proposition that ψ. Thus, where L is the loving relation, '$[\lambda L j m]$' can be read as "(the proposition) that John loves Mary," and '$[\lambda x L x m]$' as "(the property of) being an x such that x loves Mary."[5]

---

[2] In the formal details of this language, not every formula can be legitimately substituted for ψ in '$[\lambda x_1 \ldots x_n \psi]$'. Nonetheless, all formulas relevant to our project can function in such expressions, so the additional complexities required by the language and logic we are assuming will not be introduced here. For more on the assumed logic and language, see Menzel (1986).

[3] There are certain restrictions which must be placed on ψ in a rigorous presentation of the logic underlying our discussion. We will not state these restrictions overtly, but we note that our use of the logic here follows them.

[4] Where $\psi(x_i/a_i)$ is the result of evaluating ψ with a_i as the value of x_i.

[5] Here as elsewhere I am assuming that formulas are implicitly time-indexed, so to say that John loves Mary is to say that John loves Mary at a particular time.

Doxastic justification has an agent's belief as the subject of predication, to which a property is attributed. What is not clear, however, is whether the belief in question is a belief-type or a belief-token. To get at the distinction, suppose Sid stops every day at the same stop sign, and does so justifiably. When we assert on one such occasion that he stops justifiably, are we attributing justification to that particular token of his stopping, or to that type which is common to all such stoppings?

Decisions regarding cases of this sort may not seem that pressing, for it may seem that not much hinges on one answer as opposed to another in this case. However, there are other cases in which the type/token distinction is critical because there is no token of the type in question of which to predicate anything. For example, suppose Joe is driving from Dallas to Houston at a rate of 45 miles per hour. Given that the speed limit is 55, we might say that Joe's driving 55, or his driving 10 miles per hour faster than he is driving, is justified, even though he is not in fact driving that fast. Analogously, when we say that a person's believing a proposition is justified, we may mean to imply that the person has the belief in question, but we may not mean to imply this either. Hence, doxastic justification locutions are ambiguous.

To capture the ambiguity, we need a notation which will allow us to distinguish between types and tokens. To this end, terms for token states of affairs will be indicated by braces rather than square brackets. We then get two readings of the nature of doxastic justification:

(1) $J[\lambda Bsp]$

and

(1a) $J\{\lambda Bsp\}$.

(1a) implies that an actual belief of S's is justified; (1) does not imply that there is any actual belief, but rather claims that an abstract state of affairs of S's believing p is justified. Note that in representing this difference, I am assuming that it is the same normative property involved in both type and token cases. We might assume that the properties are different, but there is no special reason to do so at this point. Recall that the goal is not to try to find ambiguity but to avoid it, so there would need to be a special reason to think the properties are different in the two cases to justify representing the properties differently. It is surely false that different objects, or even different types of objects cannot instance the same property, so there is no good reason at this point to represent the properties differently. What is different is the object that has the property in question, not the property itself.

Note also that in representing the type-level reading of the claim, I am assuming an identification of states of affairs and propositions. Should the reader find this identification objectionable, we could introduce a further propositional operator which takes one from a proposition to the correlative abstract state of affairs. I see no reason for such an operator for a couple of reasons. First, the identification of propositions and states of affairs is common in the metaphysical literature on abstract entities,[6] and even if we really need two distinct types of abstracta here, there will be a necessary equivalence available, to the effect that a proposition's truth is necessarily equivalent to the obtaining of a state of affairs. Given the latter point, we won't have a good reason to think ambiguity of any sort that yields different truth-values could arise for epistemic appraisal merely on the basis of a difference between states of affairs and propositions. If ambiguity of the significant sort (e.g., the kind that yields differences in truth-values for doxastic vs. personal appraisals) is going to arise, it will have to be on some other basis than some reticence on the metaphysical issue of identifying propositions and states of affairs.

Personal justification occurs in claims of the form *S is justified in believing p.* This claim is ambiguous as well, and its ambiguity is the same sort of ambiguity that infects attributions of doxastic justification. Consider again the case of Joe's driving 45 when the speed limit is 55. We might say, in such a case, that Joe is justified in driving 10 miles per hour faster than he is; or we might just say that Joe is justified in driving 55. In either case, we have an attribution of a property to Joe which involves only an act-type and not an act-token. In the belief case, the matter is similar. When we say that *S* is justified in believing *p*, one reading of this ambiguous claim involves *S*'s believing *p* and one does not.

It may be objected here that the two different readings are better understood by taking one of the readings to involve conversational rather than semantic implicature. If that idea is true, however, the task of avoiding ambiguity is easier: we just need to focus on one of the two readings. If the goal is to show that there is no logico-metaphysical barrier to eliminating ambiguity, it would be best not to appeal to the difference between semantic and conversational implicature without a decisive argument for such in the present context.[7] Since I have no such argument, I'll assume for present purposes that the ambiguity is semantic.

The issue, then, is how to represent the two readings of "*S* is justified in believing *p.*" If we are to give the fairest hearing to those who believe that personal

---

[6] See, for example, Chisholm (1976).

[7] The distinction between semantic and conversational implicature traces to Paul Grice's seminal (1968).

justification is irreducible to doxastic justification, we should perhaps heed their intuitions regarding personal justification. It will be recalled that, for Bach, personal justification involves attributing a property to a person. If that is so, then personal justification involves the attribution of a property, being justified in believing p, to a person S. This property, however, is complex and should be represented as such. One way to understand its complexity is as follows: it involves the attribution of some form of justification to S's (token or type) believing of p. Since we are here assuming the identity of abstract states of affairs and propositions, the abstract state of affairs S's *believing* p is just the proposition that S believes p. Further, the representation of the same claim read as an attribution of justification to a token state of affairs should have the same logical form as that of an attribution to the correlative abstract state of affairs, with the exception that the abstract state is replaced by a corresponding token state. So, in the abstract case, the complex property in question can be understood as involving the attribution of some form of justification to the proposition that S believes p. We then get the following for the abstract case:

(2) $[\lambda x][\lambda Bxp]]s.$

And for the token case we have by the earlier reasoning:

(2a) $[\lambda x]\{\lambda Bxp\}]s.$

(2) reads as follows: S has the property of being an x such that x's believing p (a type, rather than token, state of affairs) is justified. (2a) reads as follows: S has the property of being an x such that a token believing of x's that p is true is justified. In both cases, these representations capture the intuitive points noted earlier, for they attribute a complex property—the property of being an x such that x believes that p is true is justified—of S.

Given the representations in (2) and (2a), we are in a position to see that personal justification is easily explainable in terms of the two readings of doxastic justification. For by λ-conversion,[8] (2) and (2a) are equivalent to:

---

[8] The general form of λ-conversion is

$$[(\lambda x_1 \ldots x_n)\psi]y_1 \ldots y_n \leftrightarrow \psi(x_1 \ldots x_n/y_1 \ldots y_n)$$

where $\psi(x_1 \ldots x_n/y_1 \ldots y_n)$ is the result of simultaneously replacing each x_i with y_i in ψ.

This general form does not hold in the assumed logic, but the inference from (2) to (2') and from (2a) to (2a') licensed by λ-conversion does hold in that logic nonetheless. The same is true of all other such inferences in this chapter. For more on the assumed logic, see Menzel (1986).

(2') $J[\lambda Bsp]$

and

(2a') $J\{\lambda Bsp\}$.

Consider, then, the following claims of logical equivalence between personal and doxastic justification:

Personal–Doxastic Type-Equivalence(PD[E]): $[\lambda x J_4[\lambda Bxp]]s \Leftrightarrow J_2[\lambda Bsp]$

and

Personal–Doxastic Token-Equivalence(PD{E}): $[\lambda x J_5\{\lambda Bxp\}]s \Leftrightarrow J_3\{\lambda Bsp\}$

Given the adequacy of PD[E] and PD{E}, personal justification obtains if and only if doxastic justification obtains as well. Given these results, a simple theory can be developed that adopts Chisholm's view about the priority of epistemic appraisal applying to doxastic states without fear of counterexample from locutions attributing personal justification.

One might choose to resist Chisholm's view in a couple of ways. First, one might resist outright, claiming that the earlier formalisms misrepresent what they intend to capture. For, it might be claimed, if we pay closer attention to the syntactic structure involved, there are two importantly different ways to parse those sentences other than the one underlying the representations on which we have focused. First we have

S is (justified in believing) p,

and on the other hand we have

S is (justified in) believing p.

In either case, it might seem that personal justification should be understood as a relation. If read in the first way, the objection would be that we should analyze personal justification as involving the relation *being justified in believing* which holds between a person and a proposition. If read in the second way, the objection would be that it should be analyzed as involving the relation *being justified in* which holds between a person and a believing of p. As before, both readings would still be subject to the type/token ambiguity; the heart of the objection, however, is that by ignoring the relational character of personal justification, our conclusion about the logical equivalence of personal and doxastic justification is too easily achieved.

A quick response focuses on a point we have already made: those who believe that personal justification is not explicable in terms of doxastic justification are more likely to think of personal justification in terms of a property residing in a person. If personal justification is treated as a relation between a person and some other thing, perhaps a belief state, this point is lost.

But there is a more substantive response. Nothing said previously implies that there are no relations which obtain in virtue of the obtaining of personal justification as represented earlier. The relation *being justified in believing* obtains between S and p; the relation *being justified in* obtains between S and the belief-state of believing p. In each case, these relations will be at the very least logically equivalent to, and perhaps definable in terms of, those representations we have used in (2) and (2a) to represent the nature of personal justification. For, if they are not, there must be some more direct objection to these representations, an objection showing that our representations of personal justification somehow get it wrong. So the objection we are considering has no force against our conclusion unless it is bolstered by an as yet unformulated objection. Hence this objection does not undermine the basic thrust of our discussion: namely, that personal justification locutions are logically equivalent to attributions of doxastic justification.

Appendix B

Reducing Doxastic to Propositional Justification

The issue in this appendix concerns the direction of reduction DJ implies between propositional and doxastic justification:

DJ: A token of S's believing of p is justified $=_{df.}$ (i) that token believing is based on something not epistemically posterior to p for S, which justifies p for S, or (ii) p is justified for S, but not by anything other than itself and S believes p.

Even if the right side of DJ provides necessary and sufficient conditions for doxastic justification as defended in Chapter 1, it does not follow that the direction of reduction should be from doxastic justification to propositional justification, as DJ claims. It might well be that the two notions are interdefinable, so that if we take doxastic justification as primitive, propositional justification can be defined in terms of it as well. As a further defense of the Propositionalism endorsed in Chapter 1, I'll argue here that no such account of propositional justification in terms of doxastic justification is possible.[1]

It is interesting to note that most epistemologists have, without argument, sided with Chisholm on the issue of the basic items of epistemic appraisal. For example, Plantinga writes,

According to the central and paradigmatic core of our notion of warrant (so I say) a belief B has warrant for you if and only if (1) the cognitive faculties involved in the production of B are functioning properly … (2) your cognitive environment is sufficiently similar to the one for which your cognitive faculties are designed; (3) … the design plan governing the production of the belief in question involves, as purpose or function, the production

---

[1] Some may be puzzled by this form of argument, for it may seem that if one can define one notion in terms of another, one should also be able to define the first notion in terms of the second. This viewpoint is mistaken, for when one notion can be defined in terms of another with the aid of auxiliary concepts, it is often the case that the second concept cannot be defined in terms of the first. A simple example out of number theory is this. The relation less than or equal to can easily be defined in terms of addition: $x \leq y$ just in case $\exists z(x + z = y)$. There is, however, no way to define addition in terms of the relation less than or equal to.

of true beliefs ... ; and (4) the design plan is a good one: that is, there is a high statistical
or objective probability that a belief produced in accordance with the relevant segment of
the design plan in that sort of environment is true. (Plantinga, 1993, p. 194)

The crucial element in this quote is right up front: according to Plantinga, the
"central and paradigmatic core" of warrant is where "a belief B has warrant for
you." Talk of beliefs here is not some causal language that could be replaced with
talk of the content of a hypothetical belief, i.e., a proposition, for clause (1) of the
account in question makes clear that B is an actual belief of yours. Plantinga thus
endorses Doxasticism with regard to the concept of warrant, just as Chisholm
did with respect to a different term of epistemic appraisal.

Plantinga and Chisholm are far from alone here in recent epistemology. John
Greco's agent reliabilism claims that "a belief p has positive epistemic status for
a person S just in case S's believing p results from stable and reliable dispositions
that make up S's cognitive character" (Greco, 2000, p. 177). Ernest Sosa under-
stands aptness in such a way that a belief is apt when it is the result of the use of an
intellectual virtue, i.e., a faculty or power to produce true beliefs in a certain field
of propositions (Sosa, 1991a, esp. chapters 13–16). And Linda Zagzebski's agent-
centered version of virtue epistemology is defined this way: "A justified belief is
what a person who is motivated by intellectual virtue, and who has the understanding of his cognitive situation a virtuous person would have, might believe
in like circumstances" (Zagzebski, 1996, p. 241).

It is unsurprising to find reliabilists such as Alvin Goldman in agreement.
Goldman (1979) claims that the primary type of justification attaches to beliefs
in virtue of having been produced by a reliable belief-producing mechanism,
but his work is rare in this regard for taking up the question of the relationship between propositional and doxastic justification. Other Doxasticists, from
Chisholm on, have simply ignored the question entirely. Goldman considers
the question explicitly, defending the idea of defining propositional in terms of
doxastic justification. He says,

The account I have offered is a theory of when an *actual* belief is justified. It is a theory of
what I call ... *ex post* justification. But [there is also a sense of 'justification' which] deals
with being justified in believing a proposition which one does not actually believe. The
idea is that it is a proposition one would (or could) be justified in believing, given one's
present cognitive state, although one does not in fact believe it. This is what I call *ex ante*
justification. (Goldman, 1986, p. 112)

Goldman holds that doxastic justification is primary and that propositional justification is to be defined in terms of it. According to Goldman, the definition

is in the form of a counterfactual. If we let '□→' be the symbol for counterfactual implication, the most straightforward counterfactual approach to reducing propositional justification to doxastic (P-to-D) is:

P-to-D1: $J_1ps =_{df} Bsp$ □→ $J_2\{\lambda Bsp\}$.[2]

P-to-D1 claims that propositional justification can be defined in terms of the claim that if S were to believe p, S's believing of p would be justified. This definition is, however, inadequate. Suppose superstitious Sam has sufficient evidence for the claim that he will have a bad day today, but believes it instead because a black cat crossed his path. We can then say both that the proposition in question is justified for Sam, but also that his believing is not justified. If this is so, however, the counterfactual in P-to-D1 will be false, for its antecedent is true in virtue of the fact that Sam believes he will have a bad day today, but his believing is not justified. Hence, the definition in question does not give us a sufficient condition for propositional justification.

It does not provide a necessary condition either. Suppose Joe does not believe that it is raining and would not believe that it is raining unless he had good evidence for that claim. Further, if he had good evidence for the claim, he would accept that claim because of his evidence for it. At present, though, he lacks any evidence that it is raining and hence that claim has no justification for Joe at present. Yet, if Joe were to believe that claim at present, he would have doxastic justification for it, for he would not believe it unless he had good evidence for it and if he had good evidence for it, he would accept the claim because of the good evidence for it.

These counterexamples to P-to-D1 show that two different restrictions are needed on the right side of P-to-D1 if the Doxasticist is to succeed in offering an account of propositional justification. The first point is that the epistemic support for the content of the belief which is held in the counterfactual situation must be the same as in the actual situation; in brief, when moving to the counterfactual situation, sameness of epistemic situation for p must be preserved. Second, it must be specified that in adding the belief p, S comes to believe p on the basis of that which epistemically supports it.

The problem for Doxasticism is that both of these restrictions are put in a form acceptable only to the Propositionalist, for both restrictions appeal as stated to the notion of propositional justification. I'll first say why there is an implicit

---

[2] To make this definition work properly here, we need a principle which correlates true propositions about beliefs with appropriate token states of affairs. The following seems to capture what we need: $\Box(Bsp \leftrightarrow \exists x(x = \{\lambda Bsp\}))$, i.e., necessarily, a person S believes p (at t) if and only if the token state which is S's believing p (at t) exists.

appeal to that notion, and then argue that the prospects are not good for finding a Doxasticist way of satisfying these requirements without employing the notion of propositional justification.

The proposal in question attempts to explicate propositional justification in terms of the following counterfactual: were S's total epistemic situation to remain the same and were S's belief p properly based on that which epistemically supports it, S's believing of p would be justified. The appeal to the notion of propositional justification in this definition is, however, thinly veiled at best. First, the notion of a total epistemic situation regarding p must preserve the identity of epistemic support relations regarding p, where the notion of an epistemic support relation regarding p is quite obviously to be explicated in terms of propositional justification for p.[3] Second, the appeal to proper basing of belief on that which epistemically supports it is equally an appeal to the notion of propositional justification. For consider the case of superstitious Sam again. Sam has a belief which is propositionally, though not doxastically, justified. The explanation of why the belief is propositionally though not doxastically justified involves two parts. The first part denies that the possession of the evidence justifies the belief state; instead, it only justifies the content of the belief. Once the possibility is opened up in this way for a belief state to obtain and yet fail to be justified even though the person who has the belief has sufficient evidence for it, the basing relation is brought into the picture in order to bridge the gap between merely having evidence for a belief and that belief being doxastically justified. The first part of this explanation is the crucial part. For it simply cannot be granted that the evidence possessed by Sam justifies his believing, for otherwise there would be no room to maintain that he fails to believe justifiably. Hence it must be maintained that the epistemic support relation between the evidence and his belief is properly thought of only as a relation between the evidence and the propositional content of his belief. Without this view of the epistemic support relation, there could be no room for thinking that the basing relation makes up the gap between justified content and justified belief state. Hence any reference to an epistemic support relation will vitiate Doxasticists' attempt to explain propositional justification.

---

[3] It may be that the notion of an epistemic support relation is to be clarified in terms of the notion of evidence, and it may also be that a proper account of propositional justification is to be clarified in terms of the notion of evidence. In claiming that the restrictions needed on P-to-D1 appeal to the notion of propositional justification, I do not claim that the notions of epistemic support and evidence are to be defined in terms of propositional justification. Instead, all I mean to claim is that all these notions are in the same region of conceptual space, a region distinct from that of doxastic justification. No assumptions are made about the structuring of this region; in particular, it would be amenable to the claims here if the notion of propositional justification were to be in need of a clarification in terms of the notion of evidence.

The task facing the Doxasticist is, then, the task of finding a way to restrict the antecedent of the counterfactual on the right side of P-to-D1 to meet the earlier requirements without appealing to the notion of propositional justification. We can begin to see how a Doxasticist might try to do this by returning to the Goldman quote earlier. For in formulating and objecting to P-to-D1, we do not find a principle that Goldman endorses in the passage quoted. Instead, his claim was that propositional justification should be understood in terms of what one would justifiably believe, given one's present cognitive state. So Goldman shows no interest in defending P-to-D1, for no such qualifier is to be found on the right side of P-to-D1. Let us, then, consider whether Goldman's approach to restricting the counterfactual in P-to-D1 is adequate.

The most obvious point to note is that Goldman's restriction is at best a way of dealing with the first problem, the problem put earlier in terms of requiring sameness of epistemic situation regarding p. As to the problem of proper basing, Goldman has nothing to say. However, his restriction concerning sameness of epistemic situation regarding p is instructive, for it is an attempt to include that restriction without appeal to any notion of propositional justification. The problem for his proposal is not that it appeals to the very notion he is attempting to define, but rather that his proposal is just woefully inadequate. In particular, it is both too strong and too weak. It is too strong in that the addition of any belief engenders difference of cognitive state, so there is no possibility of a counterfactual situation in which sameness of cognitive state is found and a belief is added. And, as already noted, it is too weak in that it fails to address the problem of improper basing. This failure is due to Goldman's starting point, for in the quoted passage, he explicitly claims that the kind of justification he is going to explain is that kind which "deals with being justified in believing a proposition which one does not actually believe." As we have seen, however, the problems facing the Doxasticist include cases of both kinds: cases where the proposition is not believed, but also cases where it is believed but for the wrong reasons.

So Goldman's attempt is not successful in solving the problems we saw for P-to-D1. Goldman, however, does give us insight into how the Doxasticist might attempt to solve the first problem, the problem of securing sameness of epistemic situation regarding p in the counterfactual situation in question. Goldman's suggestion is to attempt to avoid employing the notion of sameness of epistemic situation by employing the notion of sameness of cognitive state instead. As we have seen, this approach will not work as it stands, but perhaps we can substitute the notion of similarity of cognitive state and solve the first problem. The trick is to specify the kind of similarity negatively. One might claim, for example, that two total cognitive states are sufficiently similar with respect to p just in case the second cognitive state involves no changes other than the addition of belief p and those changes entailed by the proper basing of that belief.

This proposal puts the weight of the solution to the first problem on the possibility of a solution to the second problem, the problem of specifying what proper basing comes to without employing the notion of an epistemic support relation. Contemporary approaches to the basing relation fall into two categories: psychological accounts and causal accounts.[4] On a psychological account, to base one's belief p on e is to believe p, to believe or be aware of e, and also to believe or be aware of the force of evidence e, i.e., to believe or be aware that e is sufficient evidence for p, that e shows that p is true, that e confirms p, or some such formulation in this general ballpark. Clearly, no such psychological account of the basing relation can be employed by the Doxasticist, for to be aware of the force of one's evidence is just to be aware of what that evidence propositionally justifies. Hence, employing a psychological construal of the basing relation would result in a proposed account of propositional justification which appealed to that very notion. Thus the most convenient move here is for the Doxasticist to employ a causal account of the basing relation. We can conjoin these responses to the two problems facing P-to-D1 to obtain:

P-to-D2: p is justified for $S =_{df.}$ there is some proposition q which S believes or of which S is aware which is such that were (i) S to believe p, (ii) S's belief p caused by S's belief or awareness q, and (iii) S's cognitive state to remain the same except for the addition of the belief p, entailments from the addition of the belief p, and changes required in S's cognitive state by S's being a cause of the belief p; S would justifiably believe p.

P-to-D2 avoids the problems facing P-to-D1, and does so without obviously employing the notion of propositional justification. Thus, at the very least, it is an instructive attempt at reformulating P-to-D1 in the face of the counterexamples to it.

P-to-D2, however, is not adequate. In Propositionalist language, the problem is that it fails to claim that q is evidence for p. Because of this lack, it is subject to the following alteration of the case of Joe. We already know that Joe has no evidence for believing that it is raining. But suppose he does believe that it is sunny outside, and further suppose that this belief that it is sunny outside could cause the belief that it is raining, and that it would so cause it in the following way. If Joe were to have his present belief that it is sunny outside cause a belief that it is raining, it would be because sunny times and rainy times, though rarely conjoined in this world, are so consistently conjoined that at least one rational view to hold is that

---

[4] For a defense of a causal basing requirement, see Audi (1983). For a defense of a psychological awareness requirement, and objections to a causal requirement, see Lehrer (1974, esp. pp. 124–5).

there is an explanatory connection between sun and rain (this explanation fits in with the fact that Joe is assumed to have an unusually high degree of cognitive admirability). In P-to-D2, then, let q = it is sunny outside, and let p = it is raining outside. The right side of P-to-D2 is satisfied in the case as described, and yet, by hypothesis, p is not justified for Joe.

There are two ways to avoid this problem. The first is to insert the claim that q must be evidence for p in P-to-D2, evidence adequate to justify p. Clearly, however, this move will not be attractive to Doxasticists, for it obviously appeals to the notion of propositional justification. The other way is to make the connection between q and p a more intimate one: instead of saying that believing p would be justified if caused by q, the Doxasticist can say that believing p would necessarily be justified if caused by q. More exactly, the Doxasticist might replace P-to-D2 with:

P-to-D3: p is justified for $S =_{df.}$ there is some proposition q which S believes or of which S is aware which is necessarily such that were (i) S to believe p, (ii) S's belief that p caused by S's belief or awareness that q, and (iii) S's cognitive state to remain the same except for the addition of the belief that p, entailments from the addition of the belief that p, and changes required in S's cognitive state by q's being a cause of the belief that p; S would justifiably believe that p.

P-to-D3 avoids the earlier problem with P-to-D2, for there is nothing in the case as described which suggests that Joe is essentially such that he would only come to believe that it is raining if he had adequate evidence for the claim. Instead, all that was claimed earlier was that he would only come to believe that it is raining if he had adequate evidence for the claim.

Concerns remain, however, about the possibility of understanding propositional justification in terms of doxastic justification. Some of these difficulties are quite esoteric, but others are more mundane. Since I will put more stock in the mundane concerns, I will leave those for last.

The esoteric objections to P-to-D3 claim that its right side is too strong for its left side. The first way affects only those Doxasticist theories which, like many versions of reliabilism, include a claim to the effect that justification involves the propensity for a belief to be true (perhaps by being produced by a mechanism which is likely, or which has the propensity, to produce true belief). It is well known that the propensity towards truth is a world-bound property, i.e., it is not a property which applies to the same beliefs or belief-producing mechanisms in all possible worlds. If so, however, no propensity theorist can be happy with P-to-D3, for it requires that the justification-producing power of q obtain in all possible worlds. So, if P-to-D3 were adequate on other grounds and were the best the Doxasticist could do, such propensity theorists would still be in deep trouble. For if P-to-D3 were adequate, it would follow quite straightforwardly that justification does not involve any propensity for a belief to be true.

The second way in which P-to-D3 is too strong is relevant to all forms of Doxasticism and not just to propensity versions of it. The difficulty here is a version of the problem of deviant causal chains. Causal theories of the basing relation must specify when a causal relation between beliefs or awarenesses is appropriate for the production of justified belief, for not every case in which an awareness of evidence, even sufficient evidence, causes belief is a case in which the belief state itself is justified. The burden on P-to-D3 is even greater than the usual burden on causal theories, for P-to-D3 requires that it be a necessary truth that a justified believing of p result when a belief or awareness with content q causes the belief p in the context of S's being in a particular total cognitive state. This modal enhancement of the causal theory makes it suspect, to say the least; on the face of it, it is wholly implausible to think that any and all possible causal connections between believing q and believing p would result in justified believing of p, even given the kind of cognitive state specified. The general point is that causal routes from one belief to another can be either relatively normal or wildly exotic, and until some way of ruling out the wildly exotic routes is forthcoming, there should be a great deal of suspicion about the prospects for a successful Doxasticist account of propositional justification.

If this problem weren't deep enough already, there is a way to show that it is even more severe than what one might think given only the content of the last paragraph. For the problems facing causal theories of the basing relation regarding deviant causal chains ordinarily count as evidence in favor of a psychological account of the basing relation. The general strategy in inferential cases of belief, for example, is to describe a causal route from awareness of evidence to belief which obtains even though the person in question has no idea what the force of the evidence is. It might seem that such cases are the downfall of the causal theory, for it would seem to be a paradigm example of a case where the content of belief may be justified and yet the belief state itself, or the believing itself, is not justified when there is a causal route from evidence to belief and yet the person has no idea how the evidence is connected to the belief.

We need not draw that conclusion here immediately, however, for there is a response available to the causal theorist to solve this difficulty. In particular, at least some causal theorists can exploit psychological connections in describing which causal routes are the appropriate ones. Such theorists can claim that a causal route in inferential cases from evidence to belief is appropriate only when it proceeds through a psychological awareness of the force of the evidence.

Note, however, that the Doxasticist cannot resurrect the causal theory in this way, for as we have seen, appealing to notions such as an awareness of the force of the evidence clearly reintroduces the notion of propositional justification into the discussion. So the most attractive strategy for salvaging the causal theory from one kind of objection concerning deviant causal chains cannot be employed by the Doxasticist.

We can put our second objection concerning how P-to-D3 is too strong, then, as follows. The problem is a problem of deviant causal chains, but it is not just any ordinary deviant causal chain problem. For causal theories of the basing relation have an inviting path to take in avoiding objections intended to support psychological construals of the basing relation, but it is a path on which the Doxasticist cannot travel. Some causal theories can exploit the view of their opponents by insisting that the appropriate causal route is through the very psychological connection the opposition is intent on emphasizing. The plight of the Doxasticist in this regard is severe. For Doxasticists must delineate the appropriate kinds of causal routes from awareness of evidence to belief without employing any notions of evidence or of psychological awareness of the force of evidence. And, even worse, they must solve this problem not just for this world, but for all possible worlds. One reasonable conclusion to draw is that the task is hopeless.

There are two other problems, problems that I label "mundane," that cause deeper problems. The first is the Problem of Essential Cognitive Admirability. Theists typically hold that God is essentially cognitively admirable about every proposition: if the proposition is true, he can't fail to believe it, and if it is false, he can't fail to believe that it is false. We humans are not like that, but anti-skeptical epistemologists have tried for centuries to find some limited range of propositions regarding which we display this image of God. For some, it was propositions about our own existence or the fact that we are thinking beings; for others, it was propositions characterizing the nature of immediate experience, or the contents of our minds, or our own ideas. Such epistemologists may be right that there is a range of propositions regarding which we are essentially cognitively admirable, and then again, they may not. Any such possibility shows, however, that the definition in question cannot be adequate, for it implies justification for all propositions within the range of essential cognitive admirability (because it is impossible to believe such propositions and be wrong). This result is mistaken; to see that it is, just note that it implies that both a proposition and its negation could be justified for a person at one time in one set of circumstances.

The other problem that is insoluble results from a special way in which evidence and belief can interact. It is well known that belief by itself can create evidence. For example, if you believe you will be successful, that can offer additional evidence that you will be successful; and if you believe you'll fail, that can give additional confirmation that you will fail. These facts raise the possibility that your evidence barely falls short of confirming that you'll fail, and that adding the belief that you'll fail gives just enough additional confirmation so that your belief that you'll fail is justified. But absent the belief, the proposition itself was not justified, contrary to the implications of the proposal under consideration.

There are starker examples. Suppose you are just learning about physics and are reflective enough to have kept track of your sparse experience with it. You know, for example, that you have only considered the Newtonian understanding of force, defined as mass times acceleration. Then let p = I have never considered the proposition that force equals mass divided by acceleration. In such a situation, you have evidence for p: you know something that entails it, and seeing the entailment would take no complicated reasoning on your part—merely considering the propositions would make it intuitively obvious to you that only having considered that mass equals force times acceleration entails that you have not considered that mass equals force divided by acceleration. It is possible, therefore, for the proposition *I have never considered the proposition that force equals mass divided by acceleration* to be justified for you by information you presently know. But coming to believe this proposition not only would create some evidence against it, it would completely destroy the evidence for it. It is a proposition which can be propositionally justified but cannot be doxastically justified.

In summary, then, Doxasticists face two severe problems. One arises from the Problem of Essential Cognitive Admirability and the other from the recognition that believing itself can both create and destroy justificatory status. These problems, combined with the other, more esoteric issues concerning deviant causal chains, make clear that the direction of reduction posited in DJ is the correct one. This definition allows the possibility of a unified explanation of the fundamental items to which epistemic appraisal applies that is a version of Propositionalism.

Bibliography

Alston, William. 1981. "Level-Confusions in Epistemology." *Midwest Studies in Philosophy* 5: 135–50.

Alston, William. 2005. *Beyond Justification: Dimensions of Epistemic Evaluation*. Ithaca: Cornell University Press.

Anscombe, G. E. M. 1958. "Modern Moral Philosophy." *Philosophy* 33: 1–19.

Audi, Robert. 1983. "The Causal Structure of Indirect Justification." *Journal of Philosophy* 80: 398–415.

Austin, John Langshaw. 1961. "A Plea for Excuses." In *Philosophical Papers*, edited by J. O. Urmson and G. J. Warnock. 175–205. Oxford: Oxford University Press.

Bach, Kent. 1985. "A Rationale for Reliabilism." *The Monist* 68.2: 246–65.

Beilby, James, ed. 2002. *Naturalism Defeated?: Essays on Plantinga's Evolutionary Argument Against Naturalism*. Ithaca: Cornell University Press.

Bergmann, Michael. 2005. "Defeaters and Higher-Level Requirements." *The Philosophical Quarterly* 55 (220): 419–36.

Blackburn, Simon. 2005. *Truth: A Guide*. New York: Oxford University Press.

Boghossian, Paul. 2006. *Fear of Knowledge: Against Relativism and Constructivism*. Oxford: Oxford University Press.

Brown, Jessica. 2008. "Subject-Sensitive Invariantism and the Knowledge Norm for Practical Reasoning." *Noûs* 42.2: 167–89.

Byrne, Alex and Heather Logue, eds. 2009. *Disjunctivism: Contemporary Readings*. Cambridge, Mass.: MIT Press.

Chalmers, David J. 2012. *Constructing the World*. Oxford: Oxford University Press.

Chisholm, Roderick. 1976. *Person and Object*. LaSalle: Open Court.

Chisholm, Roderick. 1977. *Theory of Knowledge*. Englewood Cliffs: Prentice-Hall. 2nd edn.

Chisholm, Roderick. 1991. *Theory of Knowledge*. Englewood Cliffs: Prentice-Hall. 3rd edn.

Christensen, David. 2007. "Epistemology of Disagreement: The Good News." *The Philosophical Review* 116: 187–217.

Christensen, David. 2010. "Higher-Order Evidence." *Philosophy and Phenomenological Research* 81.1: 185–215.

Clifford, W. K. 1877[1999]. "The Ethics of Belief." In *The Ethics of Belief and Other Essays*. 70–97. Amherst, New York: Prometheus Books.

Cohen, Stewart. 2002. "Basic Knowledge and the Problem of Easy Knowledge." *Philosophy and Phenomenological Research* 65: 309–29.

Cohen, Stewart and Keith Lehrer. 1983. "Justification, Truth, and Knowledge." *Synthese* 55: 191–207.

Darwall, Stephen. 2009. *The Second-Person Standpoint: Morality, Respect, and Accountability*. Cambridge, Mass.: Harvard University Press.

DeRose, Keith. 1991. "Epistemic Possibility." *Philosophical Review* 100: 581–605.

DeRose, Keith. 2002. "Assertion, Knowledge, and Context." *The Philosophical Review* 111: 167–203.

Duhem, Pierre. 1914. *La Théorie Physique: Son Objet et sa Structure*. Paris: Marcel Riviera & Cie.

Dutant, Julien. 2007. "The Case for Infallibilism." In *Proceedings of the 4th Latin Meeting in Analytic Philosophy*, edited by C. Penco, M. Vignolo, V. Ottonelli, and C. Amoretti. 59–84. Genoa: University of Genoa.

Elga, Adam. 2007. "Reflection and Disagreement." *Noûs* 41.3: 478–502.

Elga, Adam. 2010. "How to Disagree about How to Disagree." In *Disagreement*, edited by Richard Feldman and Ted A. Warfield. New York: Oxford University Press.

Engel, Mylan. 1992. "Personal and Doxastic Justification in Epistemology." *Philosophical Studies* 67: 133–50.

Fantl, Jeremy and Matthew McGrath. 2009. *Knowledge in an Uncertain World*. Oxford: Oxford University Press.

Feldman, Richard. 2006. "Epistemological Puzzles About Disagreement." In *Epistemology Futures*, edited by Stephen Hetherington. 216–36. Oxford: Oxford University Press.

Feldman, Richard. 2007. "Reasonable Religious Disagreements." In *Philosophers without Gods: Meditations on Atheism and the Secular Life*, edited by Louise Antony. 194–214. Oxford: Oxford University Press.

Feldman, Richard. 2009. "Evidentialism, Higher-Order Evidence, and Disagreement." *Epistemic* 6.3: 294–313.

Feldman, R. and E. Conee. 2004. *Evidentialism*. Oxford: Oxford University Press.

Firth, Roderick. 1959. "Chisholm and the Ethics of Belief." *The Philosophical Review* 68.4: 493–506.

Firth, Roderick. 1978. "Are Epistemic Concepts Reducible to Ethical Concepts?" In *Values and Morals: Essays in Honor of William Frankena, Charles Stevenson, and Richard Brandt*, edited by Alvin Goldman and Jaegwon Kim. 215–29. Dordrecht: Kluwer.

Foley, Richard. 1986. *The Theory of Epistemic Rationality*. Cambridge, Mass.: Harvard University Press.

Foley, Richard F. 2001. "The Foundational Role of Epistemology in a General Theory of Rationality." In *Virtue Epistemology: Essays in Epistemic Virtue and Responsibility*, edited by Linda Zagzebski and Abrol Fairweather. 214–31. Oxford: Oxford University Press.

Fumerton, Richard. 1988. "The Internalism/Externalism Controversy." *Philosophical Perspectives* 2: 443–59.

Fumerton, Richard. 2004. "Epistemic Probability." *Philosophical Issues* 14: 149–64.

Gaifman, Haim and Marc Snir. 1982. "Probabilities Over Rich Languages, Testing and Randomness." *Journal of Symbolic Logic* 47.3: 495–548.

Goldman, Alvin. 1979. "What is Justified Belief?" In *Justification and Knowledge*, edited by George Pappas. 1–25. Boston: D. Reidel.

Goldman, Alvin. 1986. *Epistemology and Cognition*. Cambridge, Mass.: Harvard University Press.

Goldman, Alvin. 1988. "Strong and Weak Justification." In *Philosophical Perspectives*, edited by James E. Tomberlin. Vol. II, 51–71. Atascadero, Calif.: Ridgeview Publishing Co.

Greco, John. 2000. *Putting Skeptics in Their Place*. Cambridge: Cambridge University Press.

Grice, Paul. 1968. "Logic and Conversation." In *Studies in the Way of Words*. Cambridge: Cambridge University Press.

Hawthorne, John. 2004. *Knowledge and Lotteries*. Oxford: Oxford University Press.

Hawthorne, John. 2005. "The Case for Closure." In *Contemporary Debates in Epistemology*. 26–42. Malden, Mass: Blackwell.

Hawthorne, John and Jason Stanley. 2008. "Knowledge and Action." *Journal of Philosophy* 105.10: 571–90.

James, William. 1897. "The Will to Believe." In *The Will to Believe and Other Essays in Popular Philosophy*. 1–15. New York: Longmans, Green, and Co.

Jeffrey, Richard. 1984. "Bayesianism with a Human Face." In *Testing Scientific Theories*, edited by John Earman. Vol. 10 of *Minnesota Studies in the Philosophy of Science*, 133–56. Minneapolis: University of Minnesota Press.

Kelly, Thomas. 2005. "The Epistemic Significance of Disagreement." In *Oxford Studies in Epistemology*, edited by John Hawthorne and Tamar Gendler. Vol. I, 167–96. Oxford: Oxford University Press.

Kelly, Thomas. 2010. "Peer Disagreement and Higher-Order Evidence." In *Disagreement*, edited by Richard Feldman and Ted A. Warfield. 111–75. Oxford: Oxford University Press.

Klein, Peter. 2004. "Closure Matters: Skepticism and Easy Knowledge." *Philosophical Issues* 14: 165–84.

Kriegel, Uriah. 2003. "Consciousness as Intransitive Self-Consciousness." *Canadian Journal of Philosophy* 33: 103–32.

Kriegel, Uriah. 2006. "The Same-Order Monitoring Theory of Consciousness." In *Self-Representational Approaches to Consciousness*, edited by Uriah Kriegel and Kenneth Williford. 143–70. Cambridge, Mass.: MIT Press.

Kvanvig, Jonathan L. 1984. "What is Wrong with Minimal Foundationalism?" *Erkenntnis* 21: 175–84.

Kvanvig, Jonathan L. 1986. "The Confusion Over Foundationalism." *Philosophia* 16.3-4: 345–55.

Kvanvig, Jonathan L. 1996. "Plantinga's Proper Function Theory of Warrant." In *Warrant and Contemporary Epistemology*, edited by Jonathan L. Kvanvig. 281–306. Savage, Maryland: Rowman and Littlefield.

Kvanvig, Jonathan L. 2003. "Propositionalism and the Perspectival Character of Justification." *American Philosophical Quarterly* 40.1: 3–18.

Kvanvig, Jonathan L. 2008. "Pointless Truth." *Midwest Studies in Philosophy* 32: 199–212.

Kvanvig, Jonathan L. 2009. "Knowledge, Assertion, and Lotteries." In *Williamson on Knowledge*, edited by Duncan Pritchard and Patrick Greenough. 140–60. Oxford: Oxford University Press.

Kvanvig, Jonathan L. 2010. "Norms of Assertion." In *Assertion*, edited by Jessica Brown and Herman Cappellan. Oxford: Oxford University Press.

Kvanvig, Jonathan L. 2011. "The Rational Significance of Reflective Ascent." In *Evidentialism and Its Critics*, edited by Trent Dougherty. 34–54. Oxford: Oxford University Press.

Kvanvig, Jonathan L. 2013. "Curiosity and a Response-Dependent Account of the Value of Understanding." In *Knowledge, Virtue, and Action*, edited by Timothy Henning and David Schweikard. London: Routledge.

Kvanvig, Jonathan L. and Christopher P. Menzel. 1990. "The Basic Notion of Justification." *Philosophical Studies* 59: 235–61.

Kvanvig, Jonathan L. and Wayne D. Riggs. 1992. "Can a Coherence Theory Appeal to Appearance States?" *Philosophical Studies* 67: 197–217.

Lackey, Jennifer. 2008. *Learning from Words: Testimony as a Source of Knowledge*. Oxford: Oxford University Press.

Lehrer, Keith. 1974. *Knowledge*. New York: Oxford University Press.

Lehrer, Keith. 2000. *Theory of Knowledge*. Boulder: Westview Press. 2nd edn.

Lewis, David. 1973. *Counterfactuals*. Oxford: Blackwell.

Lewis, David. 1976. "Probabilities of Conditionals and Conditional Probabilities." *Philosophical Review* 85: 297–315.

Lewis, David. 1996. "Elusive Knowledge." *Australasian Journal of Philosophy* 74.4: 549–67.

Littlejohn, Clayton. 2009. "The Externalist's Demon." *Canadian Journal of Philosophy* 39: 399–435.

Littlejohn, Clayton. 2012. *Justification and the Truth-Connection*. Cambridge: Cambridge University Press.

Locke, John. 1698. *Essay Concerning Human Understanding*. London: William Tegg.

Lowy, C. 1978. "Gettier's Notion of Justification." *Mind* 87: 105–8.

Lynch, Michael. 2004. *True to Life: Why Truth Matters*. Cambridge, Mass.: MIT Press.

Markie, Peter. 2005. "Easy Knowledge." *Philosophy and Phenomenological Research* 70: 406–16.

Menzel, Christopher P. 1986. "A Complete, Type-free "Second-order" Logic and Its Philosophical Foundations." Tech. Rep. CSLI-86-40, Center for the Study of Language and Information, Stanford University.

Moffett, Marc. 2007. "Reasonable Disagreement and Rational Group Inquiry." *Episteme* 4.3: 352–67.

Neta, Ram. 2005. "A Contextualist Solution to the Problem of Easy Knowledge." *Grazer Philosophische Studien* 69: 183–206.

Nozick, Robert. 1981. *Philosophical Explanations*. Cambridge, Mass.: Harvard University Press.

Pappas, George. 1979. "Basing Relations." In *Justification and Knowledge*, edited by George Pappas. 51–65. Boston: D. Reidel.

Pascal, Blaise. 1966[1669]. *Pensées*. Baltimore: Penguin Books.

Plantinga, Alvin. 1991. "An Evolutionary Argument Against Naturalism." *Logos* 12: 27–48.

Plantinga, Alvin. 1993. *Warrant and Proper Function*. Oxford: Oxford University Press.

Plantinga, Alvin. 1999. "Pluralism: A Defense of Religious Exclusivism." In *The Philosophical Challenge of Religious Diversity*, edited by Kevin Meeker and Philip Quinn. 172–92. New York: Oxford University Press.

Plantinga, Alvin. 2000. *Warranted Christian Belief*. Oxford: Oxford University Press.

Plantinga, Alvin. 2011. *Where the Conflict Really Lies: Science, Religion, & Naturalism*. New York: Oxford University Press.

Plantinga, Alvin and Michael Tooley. 2008. *Knowledge of God*. Oxford: Blackwell Publishers.

Pollock, John. 1974. *Knowledge and Justification*. Ithaca: Cornell University Press.

Pollock, John. 1986. *Contemporary Theories of Knowledge*. Totowa, New Jersey: Rowman and Littlefield.

Pollock, John and Anthony Gillies. 2000. "Belief Revision and Epistemology." *Synthese* 122: 69–92.

Quine, Willard V. O. 1953. "Two Dogmas of Empiricism." In *From a Logical Point of View*, edited by Willard van Orman Quine. 2–46. New York: Harper Torchbooks.

Rorty, Richard. 1989. *Contingency, Irony, and Solidarity*. Cambridge: Cambridge University Press.

Rosenkrantz, Roger D. 1981. *Foundations and Applications of Inductive Probability*. Atascadero, Calif.: Ridgeview Publishing Co.

Salmon, Nathan. 1989. *Frege's Puzzle*. Oxford: Oxford University Press.

Sellars, Wilfred. 1956. "Empiricism and the Philosophy of Mind." In *Minnesota Studies in the Philosophy of Science*, edited by H. Feigl and M. Scriven. Vol. 1, 253–329. Minneapolis: University of Minnesota Press.

Sher, George. 2009. *Who Knew? Responsibility Without Awareness*. Oxford: Oxford University Press.

Shope, Robert. 1978. "The Conditional Fallacy in Contemporary Philosophy." *Journal of Philosophy* 75: 397–413.

Sosa, Ernest. 1991a. *Knowledge in Perspective: Selected Essays in Epistemology*. London: Cambridge University Press.

Sosa, Ernest. 1991b. *Virtue in Perspective*. Cambridge: Cambridge University Press.

Sosa, Ernest. 2003. "The Place of Truth in Epistemology." In *Intellectual Virtue: Perspectives from Ethics and Epistemology*, edited by Linda Zagzebski and Michael DePaul. 155–80. New York: Oxford University Press.

Sosa, Ernest. 2007. *A Virtue Epistemology*. Oxford: Oxford University Press.

Stalnaker, Robert. 1984. *Inquiry*. Cambridge, Mass.: MIT Press.

Stanford, Kyle. 2009. "Underdetermination of Scientific Theory." Stanford Encyclopedia of Philosophy. <http://plato.stanford.edu/entries/scientific-underdetermination/>.

Stanley, Jason. 2005. *Knowledge and Practical Interests*. Oxford: Oxford University Press.

Sturgeon, Scott. 2008. "Reason and the Grain of Belief." *Noûs* 42.1: 139–65.

Swain, Marshall. 1980. *Reasons and Knowledge*. Ithaca: Cornell University Press.

Thomson, Judith Jarvis. 2008. *Normativity*. Chicago: Open Court.

Turri, John. 2010. "On the Relationship Between Propositional and Doxastic Justification." *Philosophy and Phenomenological Research* 80.2: 312–26.

van Fraassen, Bas. 1980. *The Scientific Image*. Oxford: Oxford University Press.

van Inwagen, Peter. 1996. "Is it Wrong Everywhere, Always, and for Anyone to Believe Anything on Insufficient Evidence?" In *Faith, Freedom and Rationality*, edited by Jeff Jordan and Daniel Howard-Snyder. 137–54. Savage, Maryland: Rowman and Littlefield.

Vogel, Jonathan. 2000. "Reliabilism Leveled." *Journal of Philosophy* 97: 602–23.

Wedgwood, Ralph. 2007. *The Nature of Normativity*. New York: Oxford University Press.

Weiner, Matt. 2005. "Must we Know What we Say?" *The Philosophical Review* 114.2: 227–51.

White, Roger. 2005. "Epistemic Permissiveness." *Philosophical Perspectives* 19: 445–59.

Williams, Bernard. 2002. *Truth and Truthfulness: An Essay in Genealogy*. Princeton, New Jersey: Princeton University Press.

Williamson, Timothy. 1996. "Knowing and Asserting." *The Philosophical Review* 105: 489–523.

Williamson, Timothy. 2000. *Knowledge and Its Limits*. Oxford: Oxford University Press.

Williamson, Timothy and Igor Douven. 2006. "Generalizing the Lottery Paradox." *The British Journal for the Philosophy of Science* 57.4: 755–79.

Zagzebski, Linda. 1996. *Virtues of the Mind: An Inquiry into the Nature of Virtue and the Ethical Foundations of Knowledge*. Cambridge: Cambridge University Press.

Author Index

Subject Index

Made in the USA
Las Vegas, NV
07 October 2022

56742851R00116